"If you have the gift, this book will show you how to use it."
—Victoria Wisdom, Literary Agent, Becsey, Wisdom & Kalajian

"Contains chapter and verse on all aspects of screenwriting, and addresses every key and fundamental principle from how far to indent dialogue to how to speak to the agent's assistant."
—Script

"Offers all the essential information in one neat, script-sized volume. . . . New screenwriters will find The Screenwriter's Bible *invaluable; experienced screenwriters will find it an excellent addition to their reference shelf."*
—Hollywood Scriptwriter

"Delivers more in 386 pages than can be found in several screenwriting books. A true gem that measures up to its title."
—Writer's Connection

"The best screenwriting book available, and the book to buy if you're buying just one."
—Dov S-S Simens, Founder, Hollywood Film Institute

". . . easy to read and surprisingly broad in its coverage."
—New York Screenwriter

"The formatter alone is worth the price of the book."
—Melissa Jones, Hollywood Story Analyst

"Good, common sense. Sets up practical guidelines without encroaching on the writer's creativity. Easy to follow—feels like a workbook that will be used and not just read. The author is encouraging, but reminds the writer of the realities of the business."
—Candace Monteiro, Partner, Monteiro Rose Dravis Agency

"Just what the script doctor ordered . . . a 'must have' reference tool for new and experienced screenwriters. Straightforward, to the point, and accurate."
—Wisconsin Screenwriter's Forum

The Bible provides clear answers to crucial questions:

- How do I find an agent in today's difficult marketplace?
- How do I sell my script if I don't have an agent?
- How do I break into Hollywood when I live in Peoria?
- How do I summon my Muse and increase my creative energy?
- What is the Character/Action Grid and what makes it so fast and effective in evaluating and revising my work?
- What common formatting mistakes turn off agents and readers?
- What are the tricks to effective scene construction and transition?
- How do I write a query letter that will get my script read?
- How do I build a winning, compelling pitch? What are the unwritten rules?
- Where is Hollywood's *back door* and how do I get through it?
- How do I break into television and the cable markets?
- What are the ten keys to creating captivating characters?
- What basic plot paradigms do virtually all stories conform to?
- What writing opportunities are often overlooked by screenwriters?
- What is *high concept* and how can I use it to sell my screenplay?
- Where can I find a clear writing process that will motivate me to finish my script?
- How can I add dimension, depth, and emotion to virtually any story?
- What are the ten tools every writer needs (and few have) before approaching the market?
- Where can I find a list of contests, software, help lines, and other resources?
- What is the single most important key to writing great dialogue?
- Where can a new writer find an inexpensive critique of his or her script?
- How does Hollywood really work?
- How do you write a spec script?

It's all in *The Bible*

Here's what the fourth edition contains:

- The latest in proper screenplay format. This section has been completely updated and expanded by "Dr. Format" himself with additional examples of virtually every conceivable formatting situation. Shows correct format plus how to apply it.

- Timely new advice on writing query letters and pitching, including additional sample query letters.

- An expanded marketing section that has been reorganized into a user-friendly, step-by-step process that you can use to sell your screenplay.

- More than 50 pages of sample scenes written in proper format and a complete analysis of each.

- Plenty of worksheets with detailed instructions that will guide you in creating a laser-sharp strategic marketing plan.

- 70 pages of new information that will make a difference in your writing and selling efforts.

- Includes over a half-dozen writing and revising exercises with suggested revisions to help you excel in your writing craft.

- More on character development and dialogue writing that will help make your characters compelling and clear.

- Two new sample treatments, a Hollywood coverage, and a sample release form.

- Hundreds of writing tips, examples, and illustrations that you can apply right now to your own writing or script marketing project.

- A formatting index and an expanded general index.

Completely up-to-date and completely reliable

EVERTHING YOU NEED UNDER ONE COVER

The Screenwriter's Bible—your authoritative source

THE SCREENWRITER'S bible

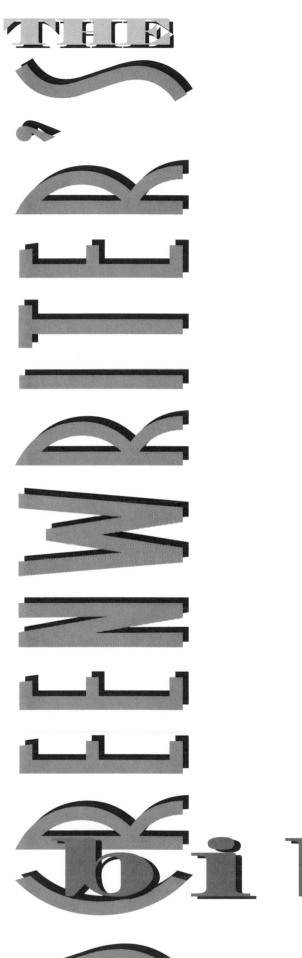

THE SCREENWRITER'S BIBLE

A COMPLETE GUIDE TO WRITING, FORMATTING, AND SELLING YOUR SCRIPT

4TH EDITION EXPANDED & UPDATED

BY DAVID TROTTIER

SILMAN-JAMES PRESS
Los Angeles

Tom Basham, Excerpt from *Boundaries*, © 2005 Tom Basham

Ryan Tremblay, Excerpt from *Vicious Cycle*, © 2005 Ryan Tremblay

Lori Liddy and Sue Holzinger, Excerpt from *Getting What We Want*, © 2005 Lori Liddy and Sue Holzinger

Denise Ann Wood, Excerpt from *Quality of Life*, © 2005 Denise Ann Wood

Barbara Reitz, Excerpts from *The Blue Lobster*, © 2004 Barbara Reitz

David S. Freeman, "The 'It' Girl," © David S. Freeman

Excerpts from *Dr. Format* column, reprinted courtesy of *Scr(i)pt* magazine, © David R. Trottier

Conversation with Taylor Russo ("A Dynamite Experience") used with permission

Martin Carbonella, Excerpt from *Knife in My Heart*, © 1998 Martin Carbonella

Debi Tuccio, Excerpt from *Oh What a Night*, © 1998 Debi Tuccio. Reprinted courtesy of *Scr(i)pt* magazine, 5638 Sweet Air Road, Baldwin, MD 21013.

Leslie Paonessa, coverage of *The Secret of Question Mark Cave*, © 1996 Leslie Paonessa, All Rights Reserved. Reprinted courtesy of Leslie Paonessa.

Daniel Stuenzi, Excerpt from *The Helpers*, © 1998 Daniel Stuenzi

Jose Barranca, *A Cuban Cigar* query letter, © 1997 Jose Barranca

Kerry Cox, *Bed of Lies* query letter, © 1993 The Hollywood Scriptwriter, All Rights Reserved. Reprinted courtesy *The Hollywood Scriptwriter*.

Joni Sensel, Excerpts from "More Queries From Hell" and *The Wizard of Oz* query letter, © 1993 Northwest Screenwriter, All Rights Reserved. Reprinted courtesy Joni Sensel and Northwest Screenwriter.

Karen Mitura, *Heart of Silence* query letter, © 1993 Forum Publishing. Reprinted courtesy Karen Mitura and the *Screenwriter's Forum*.

Jeff Warshaw, *The Silk Maze* query letter, © Jeff Warshaw.

10 9 8 7 6 5 4 3 2

Library of Congress Cataloging-in-Publication Data

Trottier, David.
The screenwriter's bible : a complete guide to writing, formatting, and selling your script / by David Trottier.-- 4th ed., expanded & updated.
p. cm.
Includes bibliographical references and index.
1. Motion picture authorship. 2. Television authorship. I. Title.
PN1996.T76 2005   808.2'3--dc22   2005054119

ISBN 1-879505-84-3 (alk. paper)

Cover design by Heidi Frieder

Printed in the United States of America.

Silman-James Press
1181 Angelo Drive
Beverly Hills, CA 90210

*Dedicated to the developing screenwriter
and to students and clients
who have inspired me with their dedication and creative vision.*

*A special thanks to three writers
who years ago encouraged me to write:
Greg Alt, Don Moriarty, and Stephen J. Stirling*

Contents

How to use the fourth edition of *The Bible*

I have spent more than a decade working with aspiring writers in Southern California and around the world. Throughout this period, I have realized that there are core principles and techniques that help writers get off to a fast start. In this volume, I help you begin the journey and guide you along the way. Not that you won't need help and encouragement from others—you will—but every aspect of screenwriting is covered in this work. That's why I call it *The Screenwriter's Bible*.

There are six guidebooks or sections in *The Bible*. Each book is self-contained and can be read independently of the others. In addition, each can be used as a handy reference. You will find yourself turning to *The Bible* again and again. Most writers, regardless of experience, will benefit from a thorough reading of all six books. Here's a helpful insight into each book or section.

- *Book I: How to Write a Screenplay* is based on my award-winning cassette series and national seminar. My hope is that you'll find it a concise and clear presentation of screenwriting essentials. Use it as a textbook, or as a refresher when you're stuck. Books I and II can be used concurrently as you write your script. In fact, Book I will occasionally refer you to Book II (actually a *work*book) at appropriate junctures.

- *Book II: 7 Steps to a Stunning Script* is a workbook that takes you step by step through the writing process. The first step deals with creativity, "summoning your Muse," and overcoming blocks. The other six steps include the pre-writing, writing, and revision phases.

- *Book III: Correct Format for Screenplays & TV Scripts* not only provides the crucial formatting standards by which your script will be judged, but teaches something of screenwriting itself. Even if you have a complete knowledge of formatting, reading this book will improve your writing style. In addition to a complete formatting index at the end (pages 195-197), this useful book is cross-referenced throughout.

- *Book IV: Writing Your Breakthrough Spec Script* is an annotated guide to spec writing. Since samples of spec scripts are so rare, this section will prove valuable to you because you must write a spec script to break into the business. Try your hand at revising the poorly written sample scenes and then compare your version with mine. Also review the first ten pages of an actual spec script with my line-by-line analysis.

- *Book V: How to Sell Your Script* presents a detailed marketing plan with useful worksheets that takes the mystery out of selling to Hollywood and to the many other screenwriting markets. The plan is comprehensive as well as specific. With it, you'll be able to target your market with effective sales strategies.

- Finally, *Book VI: Resources and Index* lists more than 100 screenwriting resources that you can use from the moment your idea is born to the consummation of a deal. The expanded general index at the end will help you find the topics you want in an instant.

The Screenwriter's Bible is sold with the understanding that neither the publisher nor the author are engaged in rendering legal advice. If legal assistance is required, the services of an entertainment attorney or other professional should be sought.

I invite you to share with me your reactions to *The Bible* and hope it becomes a help and a guide to your personal writing success. I wish you the best.

David Trottier
Summer 2005

Note: For book updates, visit www.keepwriting.com and click the "Bible Updates" link.

HOW TO WRITE A SCREENPLAY

BOOK I

A Primer

How stories work

THE NEXT GREAT SCREENWRITER

You may have heard that breaking into the movie business is tough. It is.

However, if you write a script that features a character who has a clear and specific goal, and there is strong opposition to that goal, leading to a crisis and an emotionally satisfying ending, your script will automatically find itself in the upper 5%. Few would-be writers have mastered even the *basics* of screenwriting.

If your script also presents a well-crafted story with a strong story concept and an original character with whom people can sympathize, there are agents and producers awaiting the advent of the next great screenwriter.

You can be that next great screenwriter if you work hard, learn your craft, and develop discipline. You'll need to apply the fine art of pleasant persistence. And there are going to be disappointments. But you can do it! Now stop for just a moment and say that to yourself.

All screenwriters begin in the same way. All write one or more feature-length scripts of about 110 pages. Even if you want to write for television, your best means of entering the industry is a feature script that you can use as a sample.

Book I is designed to help you write that one spec script that's going to get you noticed. What is a spec script? It's the script you're writing now on the speculation that someone will buy it later. Book II gives you specific direction in the actual writing of the script. Books III and IV will help you with formatting and style. Book V helps you sell it. And Book VI provides additional resources.

THE STRENGTH OF THE SCREENPLAY FORM

A screenplay differs from a stageplay or novel in a number of ways.

A novel may describe a character's thoughts and feelings page after page. It's a great medium for expressing internal conflict. A stageplay is almost exclusively verbal. Soap operas and sitcoms fit into this category. A movie is primarily visual. Yes, it will contain dialogue. It may even deal with internal things. But it is primarily a visual medium that requires visual writing. I have seldom read a "first screenplay" that did not have too much dialogue and too little action. You may have that same common tendency to tell rather than show.

For example, picture a stageplay in which a babysitter cuts paper dolls with her scissors. The children are upstairs playing. From the other side of the room, a robber enters. He approaches her with a knife. Just in time, she turns and stabs him with the scissors. Not particularly exciting. In an actual stageplay, these people would probably talk to each other for ten minutes before the physical confrontation, because the conflict in a stageplay comes out in dialogue. That's the strength of the stageplay form.

A **novel** may focus on the thoughts and feelings of each character. That's the strength of the novel form—inner conflict. The babysitter contemplates suicide. And this is the robber's first job. He's not sure he can go through with it.

However, a **screenplay** will focus on the visual and emotional aspects of the scene. The scissors penetrate one of the paper dolls. The doorknob slowly turns. The babysitter doesn't notice. Outside, the dog barks, but the kids upstairs are so noisy that she doesn't hear the dog. A figure slides in through the shadows. His knife fills the screen. He moves toward her. The dog barks louder. The intruder inches closer. But she is completely absorbed in cutting paper dolls. He looms over her. His knife goes up. The dog barks louder still. She suddenly becomes aware, turns, and impales the man with the scissors. He falls. His legs twitch and finally become still. She drops the scissors and screams.

The focus here is on the action—the drama—because movies are primarily visual. Yes, there are notable exceptions, but you are wise to use the strength of the medium for which you have chosen to write. Inner conflict is great, dialogue is important to bring out interpersonal conflict, but make your screenplay visually powerful. Showing through action usually works better than *telling* with dialogue. Even in character-driven "dialogue" scripts, add visual touches.

THE IMPORTANCE OF BEING STRUCTURED

Your screenplay must be well structured because you want your story to survive once the director and other collaborators take your work of art and make it their own—you want the story to survive. This is one reason William Goldman emphasized in his book *Adventures in the Screen Trade* that "screenplays are structure."

Art—whether it's a painting, a vase of flowers, a rock ballad, or your story—is a union of form and content. Accordingly, the *content* of your story requires a dramatic structure or *form* to give it shape. Structure is the skeleton on which you hang the meat of your story. And without that skeletal framework, your story content falls flat like a blob of jelly, incapable of forward movement.

Most beginning writers just begin writing without any thought of story structure—where are their stories going, how will they end? Soon, writer's block sets in. One of your first writing steps will be to construct a skeleton, a structural model. Let's discuss that basic model.

Aristotle was right

Aristotle wrote in his *Poetics* that all drama (and that includes comedy, since comedy is drama in disguise) has a beginning, a middle, and an end. You've heard this before. Traditionally, the beginning comprises about 25% of the story, the middle is approximately 50%, and the end is about 25%. These are the basic proportions of the three-act structure. If you like to think in terms of four acts, then Act 1 is the beginning, Acts 2 and 3 are the middle, and Act 4 is the end. A seven-act structure still has a beginning, middle, and end. Shakespeare's five-act plays have a beginning, middle, and end, as does the five-act FOUR WEDDINGS AND A FUNERAL.

Because a screenplay is about 110 pages (120 pages at the most), the beginning is usually the first 15-25 pages. The middle is the next 50 pages or so, and the end is the last 10-25 pages. Obviously, the exact length can vary, but the middle will always be the biggest section.

Beginning, middle, and end

All great screenplays have a beginning, a middle, and an end. In the beginning, you set up your story, grab the reader's attention, and establish the situation for conflict. During the middle, you complicate matters and develop the conflict, which should rise to a crisis. In the end, you conclude the story and resolve the conflict. The end is the payoff for the reader, for the audience, and for you. Put your hero in the proverbial tree, throw rocks at her, and then get her out. Boy meets girl, boy loses girl and tries to get her back again, boy gets girl. Beginning, middle, and end.

What about DOA? It opens with the ending. Granted, it opens with the end of the central character's life, but not with the end of the story. What is this story really about? It is not about the central character's death, it's about who killed him. The dramatic premise is this: Can he find his killer before he dies? The story ends when he finds his killer. This is just a creative way of using the basic model.

In BACK TO THE FUTURE, the beginning takes place in 1985, the middle in 1955, and the end in 1985 again. A very simple overall framework.

THE TWO KEY TURNING POINTS

Twists and Turns
How do you get from the beginning to the middle and from the middle to the end? *Turning points.* They are also called *transition points*, *action points*, *plot points*, and *character crossroads*. Turning points are the twists and turns. They are the important events that complicate or even reverse the action, such as cliffhangers, revelations, and crises. Structure organizes these events into a story.

Your story may have dozens of turning points, but the two that facilitate the transitions from act to act are key to your story's success. The first big turning point ends Act 1 (the beginning) and moves the reader (and the audience) to Act 2 (the middle). It could be called the *Big Event* because it is usually a "big event" that dramatically affects the central character's life.

The second major turning point moves the reader into Act 3 (the end) and the final showdown. This is the *Crisis*. Of all the crises in your story, this is the one that forces the central character to take the final action, or series of actions, that will resolve the story. Let's look at some examples.

How big an event?
In CHINATOWN, detective Jake Gittes deals with extramarital affairs. A woman claiming that she is Mrs. Mulwray hires him to spy on her husband. So he takes some photographs of her husband with a girl. These are published in the *Los Angeles Post-Record*, and his job is done. He celebrates at a barber shop, where he hears a dirty joke. Cheerfully, he returns to his office and tells his buddies the joke. He doesn't see the beautiful woman standing behind him. The tension increases as Jake tells his joke because we know he's going to be embarrassed when he finally notices the woman. Jake tells the joke, gives the punchline, and turns. Surprise! The woman informs him that her name is Mrs. Mulwray and that she never hired him to spy on her husband, and now she's suing him. He's been embarrassed a second time. The first embarrassment foreshadowed the second. There's a beginning, middle, and end in this scene.

Is this not a big event in Jake's life? Jake has big problems now. If this is the *real* Mrs. Mulwray, who was the *first* Mrs. Mulwray? Who set him up and why? And how is he going to save his reputation?

Steven Spielberg said that, in the best stories, someone loses control of his/her life and must regain it. The Big Event causes that loss of control. In CAST AWAY, it's when Chuck Noland is cast away. In GHOST, the Big Event is the murder of Sam Wheat (played by Patrick Swayze). In THE SHAWSHANK REDEMPTION, Andy Dufresne (Tim Robbins) is incarcerated. In THE GREEN MILE, Paul Edgecomb (Tom Hanks) is healed by John Coffey. In THE INCREDIBLES, Bob Parr is lured to a remote island for a top-secret assignment.

The Big Event is the clincher in setting up your audience. They're now prepared for the long haul through the second and third acts. They want to know what happens next.

Crisis management
Now let's look at an example of the Crisis, or second major turning point, the one that moves the story from its middle to its end. In E.T. it is the moment when E.T. is dying, and the scientists converge on the house. Everything looks bleak. It is the moment when it looks least likely that E.T. will ever get home. This is the Crisis. What follows is the final struggle to get home. You have a similar low point in THELMA & LOUISE. How will they ever escape the law now? And, in THE INCREDIBLES, how will the Incredible family defeat Syndrome when he has apparently defeated them?

When you watch SLEEPLESS IN SEATTLE, you feel pretty low when Annie (Meg Ryan) announces that Sam (Tom Hanks) is history and that she's finally decided to marry Walter (Bill Pullman). You feel even lower when you see the physical distance between the building she's dining in and the Empire State Building Sam is headed for.

In TITANIC, the central character is Rose. The Crisis is precipitated by the separation of the lovers. Jack is arrested for stealing the Heart of the Ocean. (Is he stealing Rose's heart as well?)

Crisis in Cairo
In THE PURPLE ROSE OF CAIRO, Cecilia has a crummy life, a crummy husband, a crummy job, and lives during the Great (or Crummy) Depression. For relief, she goes to the local theater where, this week, THE PURPLE ROSE OF CAIRO is playing. She's seen it four times already, and at the fifth showing, one of the fictitious characters in the movie notices her in the audience and walks right off the screen and into Cecilia's life. The Big Event—right?

Let's take a closer look at THE PURPLE ROSE OF CAIRO. In the beginning, we are introduced to reality (Cecilia's husband and life) and then to fantasy (the fictitious character and movies in general). So what will happen next—in the middle? Can you guess? We'll have a rising conflict; in this case, fantasy vs. reality. This conflict will build to the Crisis. What's the Crisis going to be? It's the point when Cecilia has to choose between her husband (reality) and the fictitious character (fantasy).

The Crisis in this film is not just a low point, but an event that forces the central character to make a crucial decision. Once she decides, she can then move into the final act, the *Showdown* (or climax) and resolution of the story.

The crisis decision
As with THE PURPLE ROSE OF CAIRO, the Crisis often forces the central character to make a decision.

In THE GREEN MILE, Paul learns that John Coffey is innocent. What will he do now? Will he lead him to the chair so he can "ride the lightning"?

In ALIENS, the Crisis is precipitated when the little girl is kidnapped by the alien creatures, and the planet is about to explode. Ellen Ripley (Sigourney Weaver) must make a crucial, life-or-death decision. Will she abandon the planet and save herself? Or will she return for the little girl? She demonstrates her choice by igniting her flame-thrower.

Meanwhile, back in Casablanca
CASABLANCA: The Big Event, which seems subtle enough, is when Ilsa enters Rick's place and says, "Play it, Sam." Sam tells her that she's bad luck to Rick but plays "As Time Goes By" anyway. Then Rick enters and tells Sam, "I thought I told you never to play that song." Then Rick sees Ilsa. Obviously, there's a lot of history between these two people.

The Crisis in CASABLANCA occurs as follows: Ilsa must get the Letters of Transit from Rick. It's the only way she and her husband, Victor Laslow, can escape from the Nazis. One night, Rick returns to his room, and Ilsa is waiting for him. She pleads with him, but he will not give her the Letters of Transit. Finally, she pulls a gun on him. He says, "Go ahead and shoot, you'll be doing me a favor." Will Ilsa shoot him? That's her personal crisis in this story.

She can't and Rick realizes that she must still love him. They have their moment together and then Ilsa says that she can never leave Rick again. "I don't know what's right any longer. You have to decide for both of us, for all of us." Ilsa turns the responsibility over to Rick because he is the central character, and, as such, he should be the most active person in Act 3. Rick accepts by saying, "All right, I will." Here, Rick agrees to make the crucial decision about who will benefit from the Letters of Transit. The rest of the story—the end, the final act—is the unfolding of Rick's decision.

The perfect drama
Several years ago, I discovered the perfect drama: Charles Dickens' *A Christmas Carol.* We meet Scrooge, Tiny Tim, Bob Cratchit, and others. Each has a problem. Scrooge's problem, which he doesn't realize that he has, is that he lacks the Christmas Spirit. The Big Event is the appearance of Marley's Ghost.

During the middle of the story, three more spirits appear to Scrooge, but the Crisis comes when Scrooge sees his name on a tombstone, and he asks the crisis question: "Is this fate or can I change?" The story ends with Scrooge getting the Christmas Spirit and helping the others solve their problems.

We are allowed to catch our breath after each apparition. In other words, this story is well paced. Excitement and action are followed by reflection and reaction, and each major and minor turning point creates even more anticipation for the next, so that the story's high points get higher and higher until the end.

In terms of dramatic tension and conflict, *your* story also needs peaks and valleys. Remember that the peaks should get generally higher as the story progresses.

Of mints and men
I'll take a moment here and offer a letter from a student who thanked me for bringing mints to class and demonstrated her clear understanding of basic story structure. She writes:

> It was ironic that I met another writer who shared my addiction to starlight mints. In my case, it began as an innocent habit. I would keep a jar of mints beside my computer so I could have a little pick-me-up at any time during the day. THE SET UP. Then a trip to the dentist revealed I had my first cavity in 12 years. BIG EVENT. Things went from bad to worse as I missed dentist appointments, spent the housekeeping money on starlight mints, and couldn't even kiss my husband because of all the mints crammed into my mouth. PLOT COMPLICATIONS. Until the CRISIS MOMENT, when my husband told me that I had to choose between starlight mints or our marriage. I made the agonizing decision to give up mints. I'm happy now and my marriage is stronger than ever. RESOLUTION.

Comedy and story structure

Does comedy use story structure? Yes. Effective comedy is built on the same principles as effective drama. AIRPLANE! is the story of a man who has lost his nerve to fly and who must regain it to save the people on the airplane. Here's a quote from the writers of AIRPLANE! and THE NAKED GUN, David Zucker, Jim Abrahams, and Jerry Zucker.

> The movies appear to be a kind of screen anarchy, but believe me, the process of getting it up there is much different. I mean, we're not maniacs, we don't bounce off the walls when we write. It gets to be a very scientifically designed process, actually. We spend a lot of time . . . marking off the three acts, concentrating not on the jokes but on the structure and sequence of the story. It's a very dull first couple of months, but that's how we spend them. (*Hollywood Scriptwriter.*)

Situation, conflict, and resolution—the flow of the story

MAKE A GOOD FIRST IMPRESSION

The first thing your script should be concerned with is hooking the reader and setting forth the rules of your story. If the opening scene captures the reader's interest in some unique way, it is called the *hook*. Otherwise, it's just the opening scene.

Obviously, the opening image—the first thing we see—makes your first impression. It implies something about your story—the location, the mood, and even the theme.

BODY HEAT opens with "Flames in the night sky."

APOCALYPSE NOW opens with a jungle aflame and the surreal sounds of helicopters. Superimposed over this is the face of Captain Willard (Martin Sheen) watching a ceiling fan that reminds him of helicopter rotors. He is recalling his last mission. The writer/director is setting the standards by which we'll measure the rest of the story. He is defining the context of his story.

What is the context of your story? It will include the atmosphere or mood, the location, the emotional setting, and the genre. Genre refers to movie type: for example, action/ adventure, Western, thriller, romantic comedy, sci-fi, family drama, and so forth.

In SIGNS, first we see the farm, then we see the central character wake up. There's a sense that something is wrong. And then we see the crop circles in the corn. (Although crop circles are normally found in wheat fields and similar grains, Shyamalan used corn because it is scarier.) From this quick opening, we get an idea of who the story is about, where they live, the fact that they have a mystery at their farm, and the film's genre.

O BROTHER, WHERE ART THOU? opens with a Depression-era chain gang. SEABISCUIT opens with photos of Depression-era cars and assembly lines: "It was the beginning and the end of imagination all at the same time."

In SPIDER-MAN 2, Peter Parker is late delivering pizzas. He's fired. And then it's one problem after the other. He has money problems. He's late for class. And so on. Peter's situation is well established and we feel for him early on.

In GHOSTBUSTERS, we see a librarian scared by a ghost and we laugh our heads off. Supernatural comedy. Then we see Dr. Venkman (Bill Murray) hitting on a coed. There are probably a thousand ways to portray this, but the writers stay in the genre. Venkman pretends the coed has ESP and that she needs his tutelage and support to understand her gift.

In L.A. CONFIDENTIAL, we meet two Los Angeles police officers in the 1950s. The first few scenes define the story's tone, time, and location. And we see a particular police officer dispensing "justice" before an arrest.

BLADERUNNER opens with a "guided tour" of a definite future place while setting the mood of the story. JERRY MAGUIRE opens with an introduction to the world of sports-agenting.

SCREAM begins with a long sequence of Casey Becker (Drew Barrymore) at home alone. Someone calls her, terrifies her, asks her questions about horror movies. The caller tells her the consequences are deadly if she answers the questions incorrectly. She answers incorrectly. This interchange and resulting carnage establishes the film's genre as well as its hip style.

In Episode IV of STAR WARS (A NEW HOPE), the "rules of the game," the nature of the weaponry, the limits of the technology, and the two conflicting sides are all introduced early.

YOUR TWO KEY CHARACTERS

Early in your script, you'll want to introduce us to your *central character*, who is sometimes called the *pivotal character*. Often this person will appear in the opening scene. Obviously, the primary *opposition character* must be introduced as well. This person does not have to appear as early, but could. It's your dramatic choice.

The *protagonist* is the good guy or hero, while the *antagonist* is the bad guy. Usually the protagonist is also the central character, but sometimes the role of central character goes to the antagonist. In AMADEUS, Salieri, the bad guy, is the main cause of action and, therefore, the central character around whom the story is built. His opponent is Mozart, the good guy.

In THE HAND THAT ROCKS THE CRADLE, Peyton, the nanny, is the central character because it's her goal that drives the story. Claire, the wife, is the primary opposition character, even though she is the protagonist. Marlene is a secondary opposition character.

And certainly, in THE LADYKILLERS, the central character is Professor G. H. Dorr (Tom Hanks), and he is definitely the antagonist.

One key to making a story dramatic is to create a strong central character with a powerful goal, and then provide a strong opposition character who tries to stop the central character from achieving that goal. This assures us of conflict. And *conflict is drama.*

A DYNAMITE EXPERIENCE

Recently, my 17-year-old nephew saw NAPOLEON DYNAMITE and urged me to see it. "Uncle Dave, it's great. It's totally unique, and it doesn't even have a plot."

I watched it and loved it, especially the classroom "happy hands" scene, but I had "bad" news for my nephew. I said, "I hate to tell you this, but the writers used classic romantic-comedy structure for their story." He looked shocked. "Let me take you through the main turning points," I said. "A drama begins with things more or less in balance and then the *Catalyst* upsets the balance and gets the story moving. The Catalyst is when Deb meets Napoleon at his doorstep, where she tries to sell him beauty aids."

"But 'Dynamite' is a comedy, not a drama," Taylor said.

I explained that comedy has its roots in drama and then continued with the lecture. "The Big Event is when Deb sits down next to him in the cafeteria. And this is a big event if girls don't usually like you."

Even though my nephew doesn't have girl problems, he understood, having read the third edition of *The Screenwriter's Bible*. Encouraged, I blabbered on. "The *Pinch* is usually the moment toward the middle of the movie when the character becomes more committed, involved, or motivated. In NAPOLEON DYNAMITE, it's the dance. And who does Napoleon end up with at the dance?"

"Deb," Taylor said knowingly. And then he put the rest together. "The *Crisis* is when the two are pulled apart by a misunderstanding. She calls Napoleon a 'shallow friend.'"

"But the big guy bounces back," I interrupted. "He dances at the election assembly demonstrating his skill. Remember what he said earlier about girls liking boys with skills such as 'nunchuk skills' [referring to nunchakus]?"

My nephew laughed, recalling the moment, and then resolved the story for me: "So Deb returns to the tetherball court, where Napoleon delivers his immortal romantic line, 'I caught you a delicious bass,' and asks, 'Wanna play me?' So she plays him. That, combined with his earlier dazzling footwork, is the *Showdown* or climax."

"A dynamite experience," I quipped. "But it's not the whole story. Napoleon has not one but two goals that drive this movie. Remember, he's trying to help Pedro win the election for student-body president. In fact, that's the only reason Napoleon dances at the end, to win the election for Pedro. So his dancing is not only the Showdown for the get-Pedro-elected plot, it also sets up his climactic meeting with Deb at the tetherball court. That's when Napoleon realizes he's got himself a babe; we call that the *Realization*."

"Hey, don't forget the other romantic subplot of Kip and La Fawnduh," Taylor added proudly, emphasizing the last syllable "duh." My nephew scratched his head, thinking. "I guess the flick seemed plotless because the structure was handled in a fresh and original way."

"Exactly," I said, and then I put my hand on his shoulder and said, "Hungry?" He was. "I know a place that serves a delicious bass."

● ● ● ● ●

Let's review those key turning points, one by one.

THE CATALYST AND BIG EVENT

You've heard the horror stories of readers, agents, and executives reading only the first few pages of a script and then tossing it on the dung heap. One way to avoid that is for something to happen in the first ten pages. It pains me to be so pointed, but I do so for your own good: Readers need to know right from the get-go what kind of story they're reading, who to root for, and an idea of the direction of the conflict.

I recall how delighted my agent was when he told me about a script he had just read, REGARDING HENRY. "He's shot on page seven! Imagine, shot on page seven!" He emphasized "page seven" for my benefit because I was late getting things moving in the script of mine he was representing at that time.

Somewhere in the first 10 or 15 pages of your script, something should happen to give your central character a goal, a desire, a mission, a need, or a problem. I like to call this event the *Catalyst*, although it's often referred to by others as the *Inciting Incident*. Yes, it is a turning point. No, it's not usually the same as the Big Event, although it could be. This term and many other terms are used in a variety of ways by industry people. One person's Catalyst is another person's First Major Turning Point. The key is to understand the principle.

Here's the principle: When a story begins, life is in balance. Yes, your hero may have a problem, but it's a problem he's always had—his status quo. Luke Skywalker, in Episode IV of STAR WARS, wants to become a pilot, but he's stuck on the farm. It's a problem he's always had. Life is in balance.

Then the Catalyst kicks things out of balance and gives the central character a new problem, need, goal, desire. The central character spends the rest of the movie getting things back into balance. For Luke Skywalker, the Catalyst is when he tinkers with R2-D2 and accidentally triggers a holographic image of Princess Leia saying, "Help me Obi-Wan, you're my only hope." Now Luke has a desire to help Princess Leia and find Obi-Wan Kenobi (Old Ben). Luke's life will not find a new equilibrium until the Death Star is destroyed. The Big Event is Luke's return home to find that his aunt and uncle have been slaughtered. Now he joins with Obi-Wan to fight the empire.

In WITNESS, an Amish boy witnesses a murder. It feels like the Big Event, but it can't be because it doesn't happen to the central character, Detective John Book (Harrison Ford). Rather, it's the Catalyst. It creates a problem or desire for Detective Book. Now he wants to solve the murder. Now the movie's moving. In other words, the Catalyst begins the movement of the story. But the Big Event in WITNESS occurs later.

The little boy peers through the trophy case at the police office and spots a picture of the killer. Book realizes that the murderer is on the police force. He goes to the chief and reports this. The chief asks, "Have you told anyone else?" Book says, "I haven't told anyone." Then when Book goes home, he is shot. He knows they'll attempt to kill the boy next, so he rushes to the boy and his mother and together they escape to Act 2 and the world of the Amish.

Do you see that the Big Event is bigger than the Catalyst?

In CHINATOWN, the first Mrs. Mulwray who hires Jake is the Catalyst. She gives Jake a mission. But the Big Event is when the real Mrs. Mulwray shows up.

In MY BIG FAT GREEK WEDDING, Ian Miller enters Toula's restaurant. That's the Catalyst. She decides that the only way to land a hunk like Ian is to get away from her family and improve herself. The Big Event is when he walks into the travel agency where she works.

In PRETTY WOMAN, Edward (Richard Gere) and Viv (Julia Roberts) meet: the Catalyst. He pays her to stay with him at the hotel: the Big Event.

In TOY STORY, the arrival of Buzz Lightyear (Catalyst) creates a lot of buzz in the toy community. And now Woody has something of a problem to solve. But it's not until Buzz tumbles headlong out the window (Big Event) that Woody's life really changes.

JERRY MAGUIRE: He sees his client in the hospital, then writes a mission statement: the Catalyst. He is fired: the Big Event.

INDEPENDENCE DAY: The aliens arrive: the Catalyst. They blow up the White House: the Big Event.

THELMA & LOUISE: They leave town to go fishing: the Catalyst. Louise shoots Thelma's attacker: the Big Event.

You may ask, Can the Catalyst also be the Big Event? Sure. GHOST and REGARDING HENRY are two examples. Keep in mind that I am presenting guidelines in this book, not hard-and-fast rules.

A good Catalyst and/or Big Event, besides giving the central character a new problem or desire, will often reveal something of the main conflict or story premise. It may raise *the central dramatic question* for that film. For example, will John Book (in WITNESS) catch the killer? Will E.T. get home? Will Toula get Ian (in BIG FAT GREEK WEDDING)? What was CITIZEN KANE referring to when he said,

"Rosebud"? Will Police Chief Martin Brody (Roy Scheider) get Jaws? Will Edward and Viv find true love in PRETTY WOMAN? Can J. C. Wiatt (Diane Keaton) have it all—a family and a career—in BABY BOOM? Will Chuck Noland in CAST AWAY survive and return home?

FORESHADOWING

Because Act 1 is primarily devoted to setting up the story situation, foreshadowing becomes a vital tool. In the first act of ALIENS, it's established early that Ripley (Sigourney Weaver) can operate a combination loader/forklift. This large contraption is literally an extension of her arms and legs. That's the setup. At the end of the movie, she uses it to fight the big mama alien. That's the payoff.

The tetherball court is established in the first act of NAPOLEON DYNAMITE. Napoleon asks Summer Wheatley, "Wanna play me?" She rejects him. The payoff is the final scene when Napoleon asks Deb, "Wanna play me?" And she does. This new response is the measure of how things have changed for Napoleon.

You can get away with almost anything if you set it up, or foreshadow it, early in your story. Much of screenwriting is setting things up for a later payoff.

In most James Bond movies, Q gives James the gadgets he'll use later in the movie. They can be pretty ridiculous, but as long as they are established early, we believe them. However, if at the end of the movie James saved himself with a gadget that Q did not give him, perhaps a tiny missile that carried a 100-megaton nuclear warhead, we'd say, "Where did that come from?" And we'd feel ripped off—right?

HIGH NOON is a wonderful example of foreshadowing. The audience is made aware of the terrible thing that might happen at high noon. This foreshadowing helps motivate conflicts between Marshal Will Kane (Gary Cooper) and his wife, and with certain townfolk.

In an early scene in GHOST, Sam Wheat (Patrick Swayze) watches an airline disaster on the news and comments about how quickly life can end. Later he confides in Molly (Demi Moore) that he is afraid—every time something good happens in his life, something bad happens. This is a foreshadowing of his imminent death. There is also a suspenseful moment when a statue of an angel is moved into the apartment. Can you guess what this foreshadows?

Early in A BEAUTIFUL MIND, John Nash (Russell Crowe) witnesses the "presentation of the pens." This is the ceremony at which each professor in a department gives his or her pen to a member of the department in recognition of a lifetime achievement. When we see this presentation again, Nash is the recipient.

Here's a partial list of foreshadowing elements in TITANIC. Most are introduced early in the story.

> The sunken ship, rooms, fireplace, safe
> Rose's comb
> Nude drawing
> The automobile where they later make love
> How the *Titanic* would sink
> Heart of the Ocean necklace
> How freezing the water is (Jack points this out in the "suicide" scene)
> Spitting lessons pay off later when Rose hocks one up on her fiancé
> The number of lifeboats
> The gun
> Jack: "You jump, I jump."
> Jack: "You'll die warm in your bed." This foreshadowing comes late.
> The whistle. This is also introduced appropriately late, and its payoff is powerful.

Foreshadowing creates a sense of unity in a story and also becomes a tool of economy, providing more than one use for an element.

Look at all we learn in the first scenes of RAIDERS OF THE LOST ARK. The story is about lost artifacts, archeology, and high adventure involving World War II Nazis. We learn that both Belloq and Indiana are resourceful, that Indiana hates snakes, and that he must recover the lost Ark of the Covenant.

A word of caution on the first act taken as a whole: Don't provide too much background information or exposition at once. Only give the audience what they need to understand the story without getting confused. We'll discuss *exposition* at length in the dialogue chapter.

THE PINCH, RISING CONFLICT, AND CRISIS

The beginning of a story ends with the Big Event. The middle focuses primarily on the conflict and complications. The central character emerges from Act 1 with a desire to do something about the difficult situation created by the Big Event. Her action will likely fail, forcing her to take new actions. There will be many setbacks in Act 2 as well as some breakthroughs or temporary triumphs.

The long middle section (Act 2 of a 3-act structure) focuses on a *rising* conflict. Your reader will lose interest in a conflict that is merely repetitive; for example, when the central character and opposition character fight, then fight again, then fight again, and so on. Strong subplots that crisscross with the main plot will help you avoid repetitive conflict because they will create more complications that ratchet up the conflict. Thus, the conflict builds or intensifies.

At the *Pinch* of the story, about half-way through, another major event occurs. The central character often becomes fully committed. GONE WITH THE WIND'S Pinch is when Scarlet O'Hara makes her famous vow before intermission: "I'll never go hungry again."

The Pinch can also be the moment when the motivation to achieve the goal becomes fully clear, or the stakes are raised. In GHOST, this is when Sam, as a ghost, learns that his best friend is the one who had him killed.

In DAVE, the Pinch is when Dave defies the press secretary and acts as president. This is truly a *point of no return* for Dave, the point when he becomes fully committed.

In TITANIC, the Pinch comes when Rose decides to jilt her fiancé and go with Jack. Once she makes this decision to leave her social world, there is no turning back. Shortly after her decision, the ship strikes an iceberg.

From the Pinch on, the central character takes stronger actions, perhaps even desperate actions that threaten to compromise her values. One or more temporary triumphs by the central character arouse the opposition, who now shows his true strength. There may be a major setback, followed often by a new revelation or inspiration.

This is when Charlie Babbitt (in RAIN MAN) discovers that his brother Raymond is the Rain Man of his childhood, and that his dad protected Charlie as a baby by putting the Rain Man (Raymond) in an institution.

As a story's conflict intensifies, its pace quickens until the worst thing that could happen happens. This is the Crisis, the point when all seems lost, or when the central character faces a crucial decision. The worst thing that could happen to Indiana Jones is to be locked in a tomb with thousands of snakes while his enemies get away with the world's most important artifact. What's the worst thing that could happen to your character?

THE SHOWDOWN

As you know, the Climax or Showdown follows on the heels of the Crisis. Often, someone or something spurs the character on to the Showdown. The goal is on the line, including the theme or movie message (discussed later) and/or some important value.

In INDEPENDENCE DAY, the crisis is very dark, but a new revelation provides a glimmer of hope that moves our heroes to take one last gamble. Basic American values and global unity are at stake.

There's something you should know about the story's end: It's not mandatory to have car chases and explosions in it. In MOONSTRUCK, everyone simply gathers around the breakfast table. It's the big scene at the end—the biggest scene in the movie. It's the point when everything comes together. It's the Showdown, which is bigger than the Big Event. It's the biggest event (or series of events) in the movie because everything, up until now, has led up to it.

Although Hollywood loves a happy ending, some of the most effective and affective stories are bittersweet or end in some sadness: e.g., CAST AWAY, MY BEST FRIEND'S WEDDING, TITANIC, GONE WITH THE WIND, SLING BLADE, and CASABLANCA.

Avoid the *deus ex machina* ending (literally, "the god from the machine"). In ancient Greece, at the end of a play, the gods would enter in some sort of a contraption and solve all the mortals' problems. Easy solutions are not dramatic; better that your central character do his own rescuing in the end.

Likewise, don't end your screenplay by saying, *It was all a dream*. And bring closure to your story's end; don't leave its ending open or ambiguous. I realize there are exceptions to these guidelines. After all, THE WIZARD OF OZ was a dream, and the ambiguous ending of Hitchcock's THE BIRDS worked for me. But I advise you to wait until you're well past your salad days before attempting such an ending.

THE REALIZATION

During or just after a screenplay's climactic scene or sequence of scenes, the central character realizes something new about herself, or we're shown some visible or spoken evidence of her growth. The central character has been through a crucible, has shown great courage—physical, emotional, and/or moral—and now the final result must be revealed to the audience and understood by the central character. This is a story's moment of *realization*.

In GHOST, Sam's growth is demonstrated at the end when he's finally able to say "I love you" to Molly, instead of "ditto." Sam grows in another way—from mortal to guardian angel to heavenly being. Beginning, middle, end.

In A CHRISTMAS CAROL, Scrooge needs the Christmas Spirit. His attitude toward Christmas is neatly summed up in two words of dialogue: "Bah, humbug." The story is about transforming his attitude. In the end, the change in Scrooge is revealed through his charitable actions and words.

At the end of CASABLANCA, Louie observes, "Rick, you've become a patriot." Of course, the words by themselves are not enough. They simply confirm the meaning of Rick's recent actions. However, they work in the context of the story's theme that some things are worth sacrificing for.

In CITY SLICKERS, after Mitch Robbins (Billy Crystal) battles the river, he declares, "I know the meaning of life. It's my family."

When Ada goes (literally) overboard with the piano (in THE PIANO), she realizes she wants to live.

In THE MATRIX, Neo realizes that he can view the matrix as software code. Thus, he is able to destroy the antivirus code (Agent Smith). In this case, the realization is what gives the central character the ability to defeat the opposition.

JERRY MAGUIRE brings many elements together in the Realization. At Rod's interview after the game and on television later, he expresses gratitude to Jerry. It's then that Jerry realizes he has achieved his mission statement about integrity and providing personal attention. This realization is never directly stated, but the audience recognizes it when Rod thanks Jerry in the interviews. The audience also realizes that Jerry has succeeded with his outside goal when the terms of Rod's new contract are announced in the interview. Finally, during all this, Troy Aikman, quarterback for the Dallas Cowboys, mentions to Jerry that he likes his "memo," referring to the mission statement. Is Troy going to let Jerry represent him now? Looks like it to me.

In MR. HOLLAND'S OPUS, Mr. Holland is rewarded for his years of dedication to teaching when all of his students return and play his composition for him. He realizes that he has touched all of these students.

In GROUNDHOG DAY, Phil Connors (Bill Murray) goes through the five stages of grief—denial, anger, bargaining, depression (the Crisis), and acceptance—and then is presented to us at the town dance and bachelor auction. The town likes him, Rita likes him, and (at long last) he likes himself.

In the beginning of FALLING DOWN, we identify with William Foster (Michael Douglas), but soon lose affection for him as he declines. Detective Martin Prendergast (Robert Duvall), however, grows. So our affections shift to him. At the end, these two characters square off, both realizing what they've become. Prendergast has become a good cop and a man. Foster has a different realization. He says, "You mean I'm the bad guy?"

Sometimes, the Realization can be thought of as a "resurrection" of the hero. Oskar Schindler is presented with a ring at the end of SCHINDLER'S LIST. He realizes the good he's done (though he regrets not doing more) and that maybe he is a good man after all. He has grown from sinner to saint.

In A BEAUTIFUL MIND, the hero not only is recognized by his colleagues in a "presentation of the pens," but is awarded the Nobel Prize.

• • • • •

Finally, we have the *Denouement*, where all the loose ends are tied together and any remaining subplots are resolved. In BACK TO THE FUTURE, we see how Marty's family turns out, and the professor returns from the future with a stunning new outfit.

In summary, the six key turning points are:

1. The **Catalyst** kicks things off. It's part of your story's setup.
2. The **Big Event** changes your character's life. We move to Act 2.
3. The **Pinch** is a major moment in your story's middle; it's often a point of no return for your central character.
4. The **Crisis** is the low point or a moment that forces a decision that leads to your story's end. We move to Act 3 (the end).
5. The **Showdown** is the final face-off between your central character and the opposition.
6. The **Realization** occurs when your character and/or the audience sees that the character has changed.

Note: For a summary review of the function of each of these key turning points, see pages 92-94.

FORMULAIC WRITING

Now please don't internalize the above guidelines as a formula. This book is not intended as a write-by-the-numbers text. It is your handy guide for your writing journey.

Movies such as SHREK, NAPOLEON DYNAMITE, BEING JOHN MALKOVICH, SPY KIDS, AND O BROTHER, WHERE ART THOU? are fun to watch partly because they are so fresh and original. They use classic dramatic structure in inventive ways, in some cases bending the framework.

PULP FICTION tells two stories. One is about how Jules (Samuel Jackson) comes to believe that God has a mission for him. At the Showdown, he doesn't shoot the robber because he's going through a "transitional period." In the other story, Butch (Bruce Willis) refuses to throw a prizefight and comes to terms with his boss while escaping with his life. Each story has a beginning, a middle, and an end, but the events are not presented in exact chronological order. I wouldn't try something as tricky as this for my first script, but it illustrates an unorthodox and effective use of dramatic principles.

A BEAUTIFUL MIND is an episodic story that deals with a man's entire adult life. As with PULP FICTION, the story doesn't precisely follow the pattern we have discussed. At a key point during the second act, John Nash faces a crisis decision: He must choose between his wife Alicia and his imaginary life. It is here he realizes that his imaginary friends do not age; he now believes he has found the key to solving his schizophrenia problem. This leads to the main Crisis that determines his fate. Instead of placing that main Crisis in the hands of the central character, as I would normally recommend, it's Alicia who must make the key decision to sign the commitment papers. This is followed by a longer-than-normal final act. I have no quibbles with any choices made because they worked wonderfully! It's a beautiful and dramatic film.

Dramatic structure is at once firm *and* flexible. There are many ways to tell a story. Your basic structure may change or evolve as you write, so be open to new, creative insights. Keep in mind that every story has its own structure, its own life, its own way of unfolding. It uses you, the writer, to express itself.

The low-down on high concept

A TITILLATING TITLE

Every screenplay and teleplay needs a titillating title. Of course, from the very beginning you'll want a working title to inspire you. The title you choose for your completed work should be short enough to fit on the marquee. Ideally, it conveys something about the concept or theme. Like the headline in an ad, the title must stop the reader and pull him into the story. For example, the title STAR WARS instantly conveys something of the story.

SPY KIDS has a direct appeal to its primary audience. The premise is clearly implied: What if James Bond were a kid?

SCREAM is almost as good as PSYCHO as a title for a horror movie, and TOY STORY identifies its market as well as the story concept. DIE HARD and DIRTY DANCING were considered "million-dollar titles" at the time of their conception because they were so provocative.

SUPER SIZE ME was enough to grab my attention. That expression is well known by most people.

The title THE SIXTH SENSE clearly communicates the genre and main idea of the story.

Although a little long, HONEY, I SHRUNK THE KIDS is a superb title. It effectively conveys the idea of a fun sci-fi family comedy.

An example of an ineffective title might be RAIDERS OF THE LOST ARK. I heard Sydney Ganis, the marketer of this project, explain how much he worried about this title. Is this the football Raiders? Is this Noah's ark? How is this title going to fit on the marquee? Not to worry. The movie had good word-of-mouth and a heck of an advertising budget, so it didn't matter.

Nevertheless, in almost every case, an effective title can make an important first impression for your script, especially if it hints of a high concept.

IT'S GOTTA BE BIG

Jeffrey Katzenberg, in his now-famous and still-relevant internal memo to Disney executives (published in *Variety*, January 31, 1991), preached the following:

> In the dizzying world of moviemaking, we must not be distracted from one fundamental concept: the idea is king. If a movie begins with a great, original idea, chances are good it will be successful, even if it is executed only marginally well. However, if a film begins with a flawed idea, it will almost certainly fail, even if it is made with "A" talent and marketed to the hilt.

Leonard Kornberg said, "When a script comes in, it is the concept that gets it purchased."

And in the words of Jason Hoffs at Spielberg's company: "Probably 80% of the spec scripts this year were bought for concept and not execution."

According to Robert Kosberg, "Screenwriters usually focus on the craft of screenwriting . . . plot, developing characters, but these all fall aside if the initial concept is not clear. Find great ideas. Keep asking yourself, Do you have a good idea here?"

These quotes should not surprise you when you consider that producers, distributors, and exhibitors need a simple, easy way to sell the movie to their audiences. The concept sits at the core of every pitch, regardless of who is pitching to whom. So let's discuss what makes a good concept. Here are a few snippets I've gleaned from Hollywood pros.

- Easily understood by an eighth-grader
- Can be encapsulated in a sentence or two
- Provocative and big
- Character plus conflict plus a hook (the hook is often the Big Event)
- Sounds like an "event" movie with sequel potential
- It has legs—it can stand on its own without stars
- It will attract a big star
- A fresh and highly marketable idea
- Unique with familiar elements

May I summarize all of that? *When I hear a good concept, I immediately see a movie that I can sell.* Does your concept say, "This is a movie!"? I realize there is an element of subjectivity here, but that should come as no surprise.

There is an *implied structure* in good concepts.

For example, here's the concept of HOMEBOY, a spec script that Fox Family Films paid $500,000 for: *Two black brothers are out to adopt a younger brother to mold into an NBA player and get rich. They find only a white country bumpkin, then bring him to their neighborhood to make him a star.*

You can almost see the beginning, the middle, and the end. You see the conflict. You see the fun. It's a subjective evaluation to be sure, but that's a good movie concept.

Concept comes in many forms. For example, it can be presented as a *premise question:*

What if Peter Pan grew up? (HOOK)

What if you learned that your friends and work only existed in your imagination? (A BEAUTIFUL MIND)

What if the devil had a son? (ROSEMARY'S BABY)

What if super heroes were forced out of action due to lawsuits? (THE INCREDIBLES)

The concept can be expressed as a *logline.* The logline is the *TV Guide* one-sentence version of the story. *Terrorists hijack Air Force One* (AIR FORCE ONE). Here's the logline for CHAIN LETTER, a spec script sold to Touchstone for around a quarter of a million dollars.

A legal secretary, after being fired and getting dumped by her boyfriend, receives a chain letter, then sends it to the people who wronged her, only to find them dead the next morning.

You know it's a movie. It grabs you—hook, logline, and sinker. Most importantly, you (as a producer) know just how to sell it to the public. And that's the key. You know you can sell it to your particular market. You see the theater ad in the paper. You see the DVD jacket at Blockbusters.

The following logline became THE KID: *A 10-year-old boy time-travels 30 years into the future to save the overly serious man he will become.*

While doing research, I spotted the following sale description at www.scriptsales.com. The sale amount was reported to be in the "mid- against high-six figures." Here's the pitch for BLADES OF GLORY: *A pair of men's figure skaters are banned from the sport following a brawl during the Salt Lake Olympic Games. After three years of obscurity, they attempt to put aside their differences and exploit a loophole in their suspension, partnering to compete as pairs figure skaters.*

The concept is always a *hook*, which is any brief statement, premise, or logline that hooks someone into the story.

> *What's the worse thing that could happen to a babysitter? Lose the kids.* (ADVENTURES IN BABYSITTING)

> *TOP GUN in a firehouse.* (BACKDRAFT)

> *What would you do if you were accused of a murder you had not committed . . . yet?* (MINORITY REPORT)

> *A man dies and becomes his wife's guardian angel.* (GHOST)

> *DANCES WITH WOLVES goes to Japan.* (THE LAST SAMURAI)

> *Your girlfriend is able to have all memory of you blotted from her mind. What do you do?* (ETERNAL SUNSHINE OF THE SPOTLESS MIND)

These are very briefly presented concepts, but they grab your attention enough to make you want to get to the substance behind them.

Considering the large number of teenagers who go to movies, here's a strong concept: *A teenage computer hacker breaks into the Pentagon computer system. In the end, he prevents World War III.* (WAR GAMES)

Or how about this one? *A spoiled teenager realizes too late that she has wrecked everyone's life and jumps off a cliff.* I'm sorry, but I couldn't resist sharing my wife's reaction to CROUCHING TIGER, HIDDEN DRAGON.

The concept is important for another reason. It's what you lead with when you pitch your script or write a query letter. We'll cover all of that in Book V. What's important now is this: The concept is what hooks—or fails to hook—the agent or producer.

Some of the best concepts present something extraordinary happening to someone who is ordinary—someone just like us. That something extraordinary is often the Big Event, the first major turning point in the story.

A radio talk-show host is out to redeem himself after his comments trigger a psychopath's murderous act. This is the intelligent, character-focused FISHER KING.

The fish-out-of-water concept is always popular—a character is thrown into a whole new situation or lifestyle, as in BEVERLY HILLS COP. SPLASH, for example, is literally about a "fish" (mermaid) out of water.

As I mentioned earlier, successful concepts often combine something familiar with something original. The following concept helped sell THE ROTTENS for $150,000 to Avnet-Kerner. Here's the concept:

When the most rotten family moves into a small town and wreaks havoc, the family's youngest son starts to break his parents' hearts when he realizes that he wants to live a life of goodness and virtue. Instead of the familiar black sheep of the family, we have the white sheep of the family. It's a twist on an old idea. In fact, some people might see it as a twist on the ADDAMS FAMILY concept.

Speaking of a twist on an old idea, a high school version of *MY FAIR LADY* sold for low-six figures. It was produced as SHE'S ALL THAT.

Can you see why this next concept sold? *A teenager is mistakenly sent into the past, where he must make sure his mother and father meet and fall in love; then he has to get back to the future.* It presents a clear beginning, middle, and end. It's about a character with a problem.

Keep in mind that most of the scripts sold are not produced. In fact, only about one in 15 or 20 of the scripts purchased and developed are ever produced. Even million-dollar scripts are sometimes not made: e.g., THE CHEESE STANDS ALONE and THE TICKING MAN. But the money still changes hands.

A good concept has *universal appeal*. Most everyone can identify with it. Some concepts give us a peek into a special world. We all want an insider's look. Here's the concept of a script that sold for $1 million. It's called BLADES.

A news helicopter pilot is deputized by the police after the president's helicopter, Marine One, is taken over by terrorists. He has to save the president as the terrorists try to manipulate the news media to their advantage.

Of course, not all production companies are looking for high-stakes action. You would not pitch *DIE HARD in a mall* to a producer of art films. But regardless of the company, they all are looking for an angle they can use to sell the kind of movie they want to produce.

One of the many pluses of having a powerful concept is that the execution of the concept into a screenplay does not have to be superior. In other words, the higher your concept, the more forgiving producers will be with your script. Of course, you don't want it to be rewritten by another writer, so make that script the best it can be.

But what if you're writing a sweet little character-driven story with no car chases and bombs? Don't despair! LOOK WHO'S TALKING is just a simple love story, but the premise is *What if babies could talk?* And that's hot. In fact, a script entitled FETCH sold for the "mid-six figures" as LOOK WHO'S TALKING *for a dog instead of a baby.*

Also, keep in mind that stories are about characters with problems. For example: *A starving sexist actor masquerades as a woman to get a role in a soap opera.* As you can see, high concept does not necessarily mean high adventure. TOOTSIE is neither, but the concept is strong, and the character growth arc is implied.

Stories that are offbeat or provocative stand an excellent chance of being purchased if they're easily visualized and encapsulated in a few words. Regardless of how mainstream or non-mainstream your story is, ask yourself these questions as you begin the writing process:

> What is at the core of my story?
> What makes my story stand out?
> What is the concept that will help the people understand what it's about?

ADAPTATIONS

Don't adapt it until you own it. This is one of my few carved-in-stone rules. Don't adapt a novel or play unless you control the rights to the property. We'll discuss the acquisition of rights to true stories, books, and plays in Book V. There are three basic steps to writing an adaptation:

1. Read the novel or play for an understanding of the essential story, the relationships, the goal, the need, the primary conflict, and the subtext.

2. Identify the five to ten best scenes. These are the basis for your script.

3. Write an original script.

Adaptations are not as easy as that, of course; they're difficult assignments. A script cannot hope to cover all the internal conflict that the novel does, nor can it include all the subplots that a long novel can. Novels often emphasize theme and character. They are often reflective, but movies move. These are all reasons why novel lovers often hate movie versions. But Hollywood thrives on adaptations.

Jurassic Park is a novel that was adapted to the screen. The book's central character is the billionaire, with the mathematician as the opposition character. The book is science-driven, an intellectual experience as much as an emotional experience. Spielberg saw the high concept: *What if you could make dinosaurs from old DNA?*

It's interesting to note the changes that transformed this book into a movie. First, the central character becomes the paleontologist. This provided a more youthful hero. Our paleontologist is given a flaw he didn't have in the book—he doesn't like children. He grows to like them by striving for his goal. There is no love interest in the book, but Dr. Ellie Sattler (Laura Dern) fills that role in the movie. Although the character development in the movie is thin, the above changes make for a more visual and emotionally accessible film. The focus of the movie, of course, is on the dinosaurs, the T-Rex in particular. Hey, movies are visual.

My favorite scene in the book—the moment at the end when the paleontologist realizes that the velociraptors want to migrate—is simply not visual enough or emotional enough for the movie; plus it doesn't have a strong bearing on the main action plot. I think the right choices were made.

Story-layering, plot, and genre

Now that we have a basic understanding of how a story works, let's expand on that and deepen the story.

GOALS AND NEEDS

In every story, the central character has a conscious goal. The goal is whatever your central character outwardly strives for. Of course, opposition makes it *almost* impossible to reach the goal. That opposition usually comes in the form of a person who either has the same goal or who, in some other way, opposes your central character's goal.

Beneath it all lies a great unconscious *need*. The need has to do with self-image, or finding love, or living a better life—whatever the character *needs* to be truly happy or fulfilled. This yearning sometimes runs counter to the goal and sometimes supports or motivates it. The Crisis often brings the need into full consciousness.

Usually the need is blocked from within by a character flaw. This flaw serves as the inner opposition to the inner need. This character flaw is obvious to the audience, because we see the character hurting people, including himself. The flaw is almost always a form of selfishness, pride, or greed.

Where does the flaw come from? Usually, from the backstory. Something happened before the movie began that deeply hurt the character. Now he acts in inappropriate or hurtful ways. Let's see what we can learn about goals and needs from TWINS.

Vincent Benedict (Danny DeVito) is the central character. His conscious, measurable goal is $5 million. There is a strong outward opposition to this goal—a really bad guy wants the money as well. Vincent also has a need of which he himself is unaware. He needs the love of a family. Blocking him is his own greed and selfishness—he's out for himself. This is the character flaw, and it is motivated by his backstory. His mother abandoned him, and he learned early that all people are out to get him, so he'd better get them first. Vincent can never have what he truly needs until he gives up his selfish and self-pitying point of view.

This is a neat little story because the goal and the need happen to oppose each other at the Crisis. Vincent must choose between the two. He can escape with the money (his goal), but someone holds a gun on his brother (his need). What will Vincent decide?

At this crisis moment, he finds himself unable to leave his brother. Why? In a later scene, we learn that he really cared but didn't fully realize it until the Crisis. That's why he turned around and willingly gave up the money to save his brother's life. Vincent reformed. He gave up something he wanted for the sake of his brother. Fortunately, in the end, he gets both a family and the money. The writer gives the audience what they want, but not in the way they expect it. Don't you love those Hollywood endings?

TWO STORIES IN ONE

Screenplays often tell two main stories. The *Outside/Action Story* is driven by the goal. It is sometimes referred to as the spine.

The *Inside/Emotional Story* usually derives from a relationship and is generally driven by the need. It is sometimes referred to as the *heart of the story* or the *emotional through-line*. To find the Inside/Emotional Story, look in the direction of the key relationship in the story. Sometimes there is no inside story, no flaw, no need, as in many thrillers, action/adventures, and horror movies. James Bond has no flaw or need, only a goal and an urge.

Each story—the Outside/Action Story and the Inside/Emotional Story—has its own turning points and structure. One is the main plot; the other, a subplot. Hopefully, the two stories are intertwined synergistically.

Again, TWINS serves as a good example. The Outside/Action story is driven by the $5 million goal, and the Inside/Emotional Story is driven by his need for a family. The action is what keeps us interested, but the emotion is what touches us. Although there are exceptions, the Inside/Emotional Story is what the movie is really about. The movie is really about a relationship.

In GONE WITH THE WIND, Scarlet has several goals. She wants to be seen by all the boys. She wants to get married. She wants never to eat radishes again. She wants to save Tara. And she wants Ashley, which is probably her main goal. Rather complex.

It may even sound confusing until you realize that the story is really about what she needs—Rhett Butler. Scarlet is outwardly striving for all the things just named, but she is not consciously after Rhett. Nevertheless, the movie belongs to Scarlet and Rhett.

In ROMANCING THE STONE, what is Joan Wilder (Kathleen Turner) outwardly striving for? She wants to find the stone so she can save her sister. Is this a clear and visual goal? Yes. Is she consciously aware that this is what she's after? Yes. Is her goal opposed by anyone? Yes. Zolo wants it, as do the kidnappers. And Jack Colton (Michael Douglas) wants the stone so he can buy a boat and sail around the world.

What does Joan Wilder need? Romance. Is she striving for romance? No. She writes out her fantasies in her romance novels. Her flaw is simple indifference—she won't try. In this story, she gets what she needs by striving for the goal.

In my script-consulting work, I receive many scripts that are completely missing a goal. To illustrate, let's pretend I was a consultant for Diane Thomas when she first started writing. She tells me she has a script about a woman who goes on vacation to South America and falls in love with an adventurer. Sounds interesting, but it's not compelling enough. So I ask Diane about the goal.

"Happiness is Joan's goal," she responds.

"Happiness is not a goal. It's too vague."

"Well . . . romance is her goal. That's it."

"That feels more like a need than a goal. It's actually part of your Inside/Emotional Story. You need an action track for this inside story to roll on."

"Well, vacationing is her goal. She consciously wants to have a good vacation. She deserves it after all that writing."

Diane relaxes. It appears as though she has a complete story now, but I disappoint her. "Technically, vacationing is a goal," I say, "but it does not stir my heart, nor does it set up strong opportunities for conflict. Something has to *happen*."

"I know!" Diane states triumphantly. "What if her sister is kidnapped and she has to save her?" Now Diane has a strong Big Event and a story.

This problem is so common that I strongly urge you to stop and examine your story. Are you missing an action track for your wonderful inside story to roll on?

Variations on the action and emotion tracks

In BACK TO THE FUTURE, the outside story plot, as you would expect, is action-oriented. It is driven by Marty's goal to get back to the future. So far so good. The inside story plot, however, is driven not by a need, but by a second goal: Marty wants to get his mom and dad back together again.

This results in twin crises at the end of the story, side by side. First, can Marty get his parents to kiss before he disappears into oblivion? This is the Inside/Emotional Story built around a relationship. Once resolved, Marty races from the dance to the Outside/Action Story: Can Marty, in the DeLorean, hit the wire at the same moment that lightning strikes the tower?

Is there an inner need in this movie? Yes, Marty needs a better family, and that's just what he gets in the end.

In THE SIXTH SENSE, two characters go through a mutual healing. Dr. Malcolm Crowe wants to help Cole, but needs to communicate with his wife and accept his separation from her. His backstory is the first scene of the film; he is shot by a former patient. His flaw is that, like other dead people in this film, he only sees what he wants to see. He achieves his goal of helping Cole and meets his need by communicating with his wife and seeing the truth.

Cole wants to stop being scared by dead people, but his need is to communicate with them and also with his mother. Cole's flaw is that he won't share his secret with his mother for fear she'll think he's a freak. In this case, his flaw is not motivated by a specific backstory. What's interesting is that Cole's goal is achieved by satisfying the need. In other words, once he communicates with the ghosts, he's no longer afraid of them. We'll discuss this story in more depth in the chapter on "Theme."

MOONSTRUCK: Loretta's goal is to marry by the book. This goal is represented by Danny. She was married once before and it was unlucky because they didn't do it "right," so "this time, Danny, you've got to have a ring and get on your knees and propose, and we're going to a priest." She's doing this marriage by the book.

Loretta *needs* to marry for love. This need is represented by Ronnie. This is not fully in her consciousness until she goes to the opera with Ronnie. Blocking her need is her character flaw—she's going to marry someone she doesn't love. This character flaw is motivated by her backstory of having an unlucky marriage. At the breakfast-table scene in the end, she admits that the need is more important to her than the goal.

In SPIDER-MAN 2, the hero's main goal is to defeat Otto. He has a goal/need to find his identity. Underneath it all, there is a need for Mary Jane. His flaw is that he's too passive with Mary Jane and won't communicate with her because he wants to protect her. He has an additional flaw of not knowing his true mission.

HOME ALONE's Kevin strives to protect the house and himself from the Wet Bandits. That's the main action plot. The emotional story? He needs his family's acceptance, his mother's in particular. Two flaws block him: One, he's a brat; two, he is incompetent—he can't even tie his shoelaces. These are subplots. The first flaw hooks the parents in the audience—he becomes a son who learns to appreciate his mother and family. The second flaw hooks the kids—he becomes competent when fighting the adult bandits. This is a coming-of-age subplot.

The mother's goal is to get home. Her need and her flaw are similar to those of her son. In fact, they are mirrors of each other. Another subplot involves the man with the shovel who wants to become reconciled to his son. It's not hard to see that the underlying theme of this flick is family reconciliation.

MY BEST FRIEND'S WEDDING: Julianne wants to break up her best friend's wedding, but needs to accept it and let life go on.

KRAMER VS. KRAMER: The goal? Custody. The need? To be a loving father. In this screenplay, the goal and the need oppose each other, creating a crisis. Ted Kramer (Dustin Hoffman) loses custody in a court battle and wants to appeal. His attorney tells him: "It'll cost $15,000." No problem. Ted wants to go ahead. "You'll have to put Billy on the stand." Well, to put Billy on the stand could deeply hurt him. Ted loves him too much. He chooses to give up custody rather than hurt the child. He overcomes his selfishness and abandons his goal for custody.

There's another way to look at this. Think of yourself as the next great screenwriter creating this story from scratch. You know the story is going to be about Ted Kramer becoming a father, learning to love his son. So you, the writer, give Ted goals, behaviors, and desires that are flawed. You give him a main goal of gaining custody because you know it will eventually contrast with what he really needs, which is to unselfishly love his son. So Ted's goal in this story is flawed—seeking custody is not the best way to love his son or satisfy his inner drive to be a father. In the end, he becomes a father by giving up custody, by giving up the goal.

In THE WIZARD OF OZ, the main goal is Kansas; the need is to realize there's no place like home.

JERRY MAGUIRE wants a big contract for his only client, Rod. In the process of working with Rod, he manages to accomplish his mission and even finds intimacy with his wife. Let's take a closer look at this story, since it has not one but two flaws and two growth arcs. (Naturally, the flaws are related.)

	Action story	Emotional story
Flaw	Self-doubt.	Can't love and be intimate.
Catalyst	Client suffers in hospital; client's son accuses Jerry of not caring.	Meets woman who believes in him.
Big Event	Fired.	Goes on a date.
Pinch	Jerry accuses Rod of playing without heart; Rod accuses him of marrying without heart.	Proposes marriage.
Crisis	After refusing contract, Rod is apparently injured.	Wife separates from Jerry because he doesn't love her.
Showdown	Rod plays well, not injured, gets interviewed, and gets big contract.	Jerry returns to his wife.
Realization	At the two interviews, Rod recognizes Jerry: Jerry has fulfilled his mission, no longer doubts himself, and wants to be with his wife.	

PRETTY WOMAN: Here we have two people who need love, but who are prostituting themselves. Their behavior does not harmonize with their need. In the end, they give up their old ways and thus fill their needs. They grow.

My favorite romantic comedy is SOME LIKE IT HOT. Joe (Tony Curtis), posing as a millionaire, uses Sugar Kane Kowalczyk (Marilyn Monroe). He's after her body, but he *needs* to love her in the full sense of the word. Sugar's goal is to marry a millionaire. She chases after Joe because she thinks he is one. Her unconscious need, however, is to marry for love. The Crisis comes when Joe is forced by Spats Columbo, a gangster, to leave Sugar. At that point, Joe realizes he is actually in love with Sugar. He realizes what a jerk he is and vows to get out of her life. He'll do what's best for her and leave without her. Sugar, however, realizes that he's the one, even though he's not really a millionaire. She chases after him. Together for the right reasons, they sail off into the sunset.

In love stories (and even buddy movies such as MIDNIGHT RUN), one or both of the characters is willing to give up something in the end for the sake of the other. That something is often a goal related to their flaw. In PRETTY WOMAN, Edward not only gives up his questionable business practices, but he also overcomes his fear of heights. Love stories are essentially about two people transforming each other and learning to love each other. PRETTY WOMAN is pretty good at doing just that.

PLOT

Up until now, we've explained the Outside/Action Plot and the Inside/Emotional Plot. *Plot* is the structure of action and emotion. The verb *to plot* is a creative process that uses character development and story structure. When all the plotting is over, you end up with a *plot* and several *subplots*.

Plot comprises the important events in a character's story. The words *plot*, *structure*, and *story* are often used interchangeably. Plot grows from character because everything starts with a character who has a goal. Since the goal is opposed, the character takes action. The resulting conflict culminates in a crisis. Will she win? Will he lose? Will he grow? Will she decline? The answer to those questions determines the kind of story—the kind of plot—you're writing.

There are basically two kinds of stories: plot-driven stories (which I prefer to call goal-driven stories) and character-driven stories. In goal-driven stories, the focus is primarily on the character's goal and the action—the spine of the story. In character-driven stories, the focus is primarily on character dynamics, a need, and a key relationship—the heart of the story. First, let's look at some examples of goal-driven stories.

• **The character wins.** In this plot model, the character strives for a goal and wins. Very simple and very common. Examples include: THE INCREDIBLES, SHREK, INDEPENDENCE DAY, I, ROBOT, ROCKY, DIE HARD, THE FUGITIVE, MEN IN BLACK, THE SILENCE OF THE LAMBS, RUDY, TRUE LIES, NATIONAL TREASURE, and THE KARATE KID. In SAVING PRIVATE RYAN, Captain Miller achieves his goal, even though he dies. NAPOLEON DYNAMITE not only succeeds as a campaign manager, but he gets the girl, too.

• **The character loses.** With this plot, a moral victory of some kind often results despite the failure of a very sympathetic character. SPARTACUS fails to achieve his goal for the slaves and is crucified, but he sees his wife and child escape to freedom. In TITANIC, Rose loses Jack but her heart will go on. THELMA & LOUISE never get to Mexico, but in the attempt they achieve a certain freedom. In O BROTHER, WHERE ART THOU? Everett (George Clooney) never gets his wife back, and there's not much of a moral victory either except that he has a job with the governor, and that ain't bad in Depression-era Mississippi.

Other examples are BRAVEHEART, ONE FLEW OVER THE CUCKOO'S NEST, FROM HERE TO ETERNITY, THE MISSION (here, they flat-out lose), and JFK (the Jim Garrison character).

• **The character sows the seeds of his own destruction.** What Goes Around, Comes Around. Examples include: THE LADYKILLERS, FRANKENSTEIN, DANGEROUS LIAISONS, MOBY DICK, and SCREAM (the perpetrators). In Episode III of STAR WARS (REVENGE OF THE SITH), the Emperor molds Anakin Skywalker into Darth Vader; in Episode VI, it is Darth Vader who kills the Emperor.

The following plot models seem more focused on character dynamics, and on the Inside/Emotional Story.

• **The character grows by doing the right thing.** Here, the character is about to do the wrong thing, but transforms into someone who overcomes his or her flaw, and does the right thing. Very popular everywhere. In CASABLANCA, Rick wants to get even with Ilsa; in the end, he does the right thing and helps her and her husband escape. Charlie (Tom Cruise), in RAIN MAN, wants his inheritance; in the end, he tears up the check and does the right thing for his brother.

An ideal example is AN IDEAL HUSBAND where at least three characters grow by doing the right thing. Other examples include: HITCH, EMMA, ON THE WATER-FRONT, A BEAUTIFUL MIND (both John Nash and his wife, Alicia), MY BEST FRIEND'S WEDDING, JERRY MAGUIRE, SAINTS AND SOLDIERS, THE SCENT OF A WOMAN, BIG, AN OFFICER AND A GENTLEMAN, GROUNDHOG DAY, and SCHINDLER'S LIST.

Romantic comedies usually fit this plot model because one or more of the lovers gives up something for the other. In PRETTY WOMAN, both characters give up their careers. In SOME LIKE IT HOT, the lovers stop using each other. MIDNIGHT RUN is a love story without the romance—both Jack Walsh (Robert DeNiro) and Jonathan Mardukas (Charles Grodin) give up their goals for each other in the end.

• **The character grows up.** Here the character comes of age while striving for one or more goals that are either achieved or not achieved—it doesn't matter which. We don't really care whether the boys are first to find the body in STAND BY ME. What we care about is the relationship and growth of the boys. The goal is only there to give the relationship a track to roll on. In some character-driven stories, the goal may change. And that's fine as long as the conflict intensifies and rises to a crisis and showdown.

Here are more examples of characters growing up: GOOD WILL HUNTING, RISKY BUSINESS, HOOK (Peter Pan grows up), BREAKING AWAY, PLATOON, and AMERICAN GRAFFITI. In UNBREAKABLE, David Dunn grows from mere mortal, bad husband, and not-so-great father to a hero.

In a sense, Peter Parker, the central character in SPIDER-MAN 2, comes of age by affirming his identity as Spider-man. However, this could also be seen as a "character learns" plot. Let's look at that next.

• **The character learns.** Here, the character learns what he or she needs to be happy. George Bailey (Jimmy Stewart) realizes he has a wonderful life in IT'S A WONDERFUL LIFE. Bishop Henry Brougham (David Niven) learns what's important in life in THE BISHOP'S WIFE—that the people in the cathedral are more important than the cathedral itself. Harold, in HAROLD AND MAUDE, discovers that life is worth living. In THE SIXTH SENSE, Cole and Malcolm learn to communicate.

In THE GREEN MILE, Paul learns that "everyone must walk his own green mile." This knowledge does not necessarily make him happy, but it deepens his character and his appreciation for life.

In THE WIZARD OF OZ, Dorothy finds out there's no place like home. She also achieves her goal of returning to Kansas. (An argument could be made that the main plot is a Character-Wins Plot and that the realization of her need is merely a subplot that supports the goal.) Other examples: THE PRINCE OF TIDES—Tom Wingo (Nick Nolte) learns he wants to live with his family. In CITY SLICKERS, Mitch Robbins (Billy Crystal) finally figures out the meaning of life. In FINDING NEVERLAND, little Peter tells James Barrie that he (Barrie) is Peter Pan.

• **The character fails to learn.** Here, the character fails to learn what he or she needs to learn to be happy. In this plot, the character does not grow, but the audience learns the lesson. Examples include WAR OF THE ROSES, GOODFELLAS, and RAGING BULL. In BUTCH CASSIDY AND THE SUNDANCE KID, Butch and Sundance never figure out that they are in the wrong line of work and need to change with the times.

I suppose you could argue for O BROTHER, WHERE ART THOU? After all, even at the end, Everett (George Clooney) still wants to print up a dentist diploma and just get any old wedding ring for his wife. He's not very bright for someone who uses Dapper Dan pomade.

• **The character declines,** often by striving to achieve a worthy goal. Here are your examples: LAWRENCE OF ARABIA, UNFORGIVEN, CITIZEN KANE, and SUPER SIZE ME. In the beginning of THE GODFATHER, Michael (the central character) is something of a patriot who doesn't want a part of the family business. In the end, he *runs* the family business, but his rise is also his decline, which is demonstrated in the final scene where he lies, straight-faced, to his wife.

In virtually all stories, there is one main plot. Everything else happening in the character's life is a subplot. In addition to the central character's plot and subplot, each of the other characters in the screenplay has his or her own plot with a goal, action, crisis, and resolution. These are all subplots.

Furthermore, each character's crisis may come at a different juncture in the script, or may converge at the same crisis moment, depending on the story. The great secret to master-plotting is to bring the various subplots and main plot into conflict. In other words, most or all of the subplots should cross the central character's main purpose. One purpose of the step-outline on pages 99-100 is to accomplish this. You should find the Character/Action Grid on pages 105-109 to be helpful as well.

When two characters are at cross purposes, you have a *Unity of Opposites*. To ensure a conflict up until the story's end, you need a unity of the central character's main plot and the opposing character's plot. The unity exists when the two plots are in direct opposition to each other, and compromise is impossible, ensuring a struggle to the end. For example, in FATAL ATTRACTION, a married man has an affair with a beautiful blonde and wants to terminate the relationship with her, but he can't because she carries his baby and is fixated on him. There exists a *unity of opposites*. He wants to end the relationship. She wants the relationship to grow. Compromise is impossible.

GENRE

Another element to consider in plotting is genre. Each genre carries with it certain characteristics.

Love stories
In a romantic comedy, the lovers meet (Catalyst), are forced to be together or choose to be together (Big Event), fall in love (Pinch), are separated (Crisis), after which one or both will change in some way, reform, and return to the beloved (Showdown). Most often, this results in a Character-Grows-by-Doing-the-Right-Thing Plot.

This category includes "date movies," a term popularized by Jeff Arch and Nora Ephron's SLEEPLESS IN SEATTLE. In fact, in the film itself, *guy movies* are distinguished from *chick flicks*. A date movie is a movie that appeals to both guys and chicks. In the case of SLEEPLESS IN SEATTLE, women presumably see this as a love story, while men see a widowed father getting a second chance.

Action/adventure
These stories usually open with an exciting action sequence, followed by some exposition. Although these can be suspenseful, the key to this genre is exciting action. Make

sure there is plenty of it. These stories generally follow a Character-Wins Plot and usually end with a chase and/or plenty of violence.

William Martel, quoting Shane Black in *Scriptwriters Network Newsletter*, writes the following:

> The key to good action scenes is reversals. . . . It's like a good news/ bad news joke. The bad news is you get thrown out of an airplane. The good news is you're wearing your parachute. The bad news is the rip cord breaks. The good news is you have a backup chute. The bad news is you can't reach the cord. Back and forth like that until the character reaches the ground.

Thrillers

Thrillers focus on suspense more than on action. In a thriller, an ordinary man or woman gets involved in a situation that becomes life-threatening. The bad guys desperately want the *MacGuffin*, a name Hitchcock gave to the plot-device that often drives the thriller. In NORTH BY NORTHWEST, the MacGuffin is government secrets. In CHARADE, it's $250,000 in stamps.

Although the characters are after the MacGuffin, the audience cares more about the survival of the central character. This is because she cannot get help, has been betrayed in some way, and cannot trust anyone. The primary motivation is one of survival, so there's not much of a Character Realization in the end.

Many thrillers don't have a MacGuffin, but all thrillers isolate the central character, put her life at constant risk, and get us to identify with her fears.

Horror

Scary movies differ from the thriller in that the opposition is a monster, or a monster-like human. This genre leans heavily on shock and surprise. Examples include JAWS and SCREAM. ALIEN also relies on surprise, but the sequel, ALIENS, was wisely written as an action/adventure story, not another horror movie. Instead of scaring us, James Cameron thrills us with exciting action. Naturally there are horror elements in ALIENS, but the focus of the movie is on action.

Science fiction

Yes, ALIEN and ALIENS were science-fiction movies, but the horror and action/ adventure genres dominated in each respective case. Thus, we have hybrid genres: horror/sci-fi and action/sci-fi. BACK TO THE FUTURE is a fantasy family drama, or a sci-fi comedy, or a combination of all four. The point is that most science-fiction takes on the characteristics of another genre and moves it to another world or time.

Traveling angel

This is a story about a character who solves the problems of the people around him. He doesn't grow much himself because he's "perfect," but other characters do; and once they have done so, the angel rides off into the sunset. MARY POPPINS, SHANE, and PALE RIDER are examples. Percy in THE SPITFIRE GRILL redeems virtually everyone. In the case of THE BISHOP'S WIFE, the traveling angel really is a traveling angel.

In a way, Seabiscuit (in SEABISCUIT) qualifies as the only horse to be a traveling angel. The other characters in the story heal because of Seabiscuit, although Seabiscuit himself grows, too.

Detective/mystery

The murder mystery opens with a murder. Then, the police officer, private detective, or retired novelist solves the case. Since solving the case is primarily a mental exercise, there is often a voice-over narration so we can be privy to the central character's thoughts, as in MAGNUM, P.I. If this central character is a private detective, he will usually be portrayed as one who operates on the fringes of the law, such as Jake Gittes in CHINATOWN. Often, detectives uncover a small corruption that leads to a larger one. Many detective stories contain elements of "film noir."

Film noir

Film noir (literally, "night film") describes both a genre and a shooting style—shadowy, cynical, and realistic—and a storyline that features ordinary people in over their heads, no heroes and villains per se. In fact, there is usually a moral ambiguity, even though there may be a struggle between good and evil within the central character. Stories often end unhappily. L.A. CONFIDENTIAL, DOUBLE INDEMNITY, THE USUAL SUSPECTS, TOUCH OF EVIL, DOA, BASIC INSTINCT, PULP FICTION, FARGO, THE POSTMAN ALWAYS RINGS TWICE, and BODY HEAT are examples.

Fish-out-of-water

This is a popular genre because it creates so much potential for conflict and fun. A character is abruptly taken out of her element and forced to adjust to a new environment. Thus, Detective John Kimble (Arnold Schwarzenegger) becomes a kindergarten teacher in KINDERGARTEN COP. And Detective Axel Foley (Eddie Murphy) goes to 90210 in BEVERLY HILLS COP. In THREE MEN AND A BABY, three Peter Pans suddenly must care for a baby. PRIVATE BENJAMIN could be pitched as *Jewish American Princess joins the Army.*

I suppose you could say that Marty in BACK TO THE FUTURE is a fish-out-of-water when he drops into 1955 culture. So maybe that film is actually a sci-fi/fantasy/fish-out-of-water/family comedy.

Obviously, there are many genres and combinations of genres: Revisionist Western (DANCES WITH WOLVES), Screwball comedy (BRINGING UP BABY and WHAT'S UP, DOC?), Historical epic (SEVEN YEARS IN TIBET, LAWRENCE OF ARABIA), Buddy picture (OUTRAGEOUS FORTUNE), Milieu (ALICE IN WONDERLAND, MIDNIGHT IN THE GARDEN OF GOOD AND EVIL, and LORD OF THE RINGS), Action/romance (ROMANCING THE STONE), and on and on.

Once you choose your genre, watch several representative films. You will not be researching your story but learning more about what makes the genre work.

MYTH

Beyond genre and plot is myth. In any story you write, it may help you to understand the mythological journey. The "hero's journey," as presented by Joseph Campbell, follows a particular pattern that may be weaved into the fabric of any story, regardless of its genre. Many stories contain elements of this mythological journey, while a few, like Episodes IV-VI of STAR WARS, THE POLAR EXPRESS, and THE WIZARD OF OZ, can be called myths because the central character passes through each stage of the hero's journey. Briefly, these are the stages in the hero's journey:

The hero lives amid ordinary surroundings. The Catalyst is actually a call to adventure, but the hero is reluctant to heed the call. This could be the moment when the hero receives her mission. She is given an amulet or aid of some kind by an older person, a mentor. For example, Dorothy is given the ruby-red slippers by a good witch. Luke is given the lightsaber by Obi-Wan. Many stories feature mentors: e.g., Sean Maguire (Robin Williams) in GOOD WILL HUNTING, the train conductor in THE POLAR EXPRESS, and Agent K (Tommy Lee Jones) in MEN IN BLACK. In THE LORD OF THE RINGS, Frodo is mentored by Gandalf.

The central character travels to the extraordinary world. This is followed by a series of tests and obstacles. The hero often undergoes a death experience and enters the secret hideout, the witch's castle, the Death Star, the belly of the whale, or the innermost cave.

Finally, the hero seizes the treasure and is chased back to the ordinary world, where this treasure blesses the people. The grail heals the land. In THE POLAR EXPRESS, the little reindeer bell confirms the spirit of Christmas to all who hear it ring.

The hero may be resurrected in some way. Luke and Han are honored at an awards ceremony. Dorothy returns to her family. THE LAST STARFIGHTER is transfigured in front of the townspeople. Oskar Schindler is honored in a ring ceremony.

As a writer, you may have heard a call to action, a call to write, but hesitated. You must heed the call. As you struggle, as you learn, and as you write, you may very well walk the path of the hero, overcome obstacles, gain allies, and become the next great screenwriter. The hero's journey may very well become your personal odyssey.

Note: This is a good time to do Steps 1, 2, and 3 in the workbook (Book II).

Ten keys to creating captivating characters

Your central character requires ten things from a writer. Keep in mind as we review these that virtually all of them apply to supporting characters, and even minor characters, as well as to your main characters.

1. A GOAL AND AN OPPOSITION

Your character wants something. A dramatic goal is specific and measurable. Dealing with life is not a goal. Happiness is not a goal. Seeking $10 million worth of doubloons on an old Spanish shipwreck off the Florida Keys is a goal. Winning the Pan American Ballroom Dance Competition is a goal. Getting the broomstick of the wicked witch in order to return to Kansas is a goal. The nature of the goal reveals a lot about your character.

Whatever the goal is, it should not be easy to attain. There must be opposition to the goal. Opposition creates conflict, and conflict makes drama. Conflict reveals character and motivates people to learn. Ask yourself, *What does my character want and what does she most fear?* The opposition will force her to face her fear.

The opposition should be an individual. If it is an organization, let someone represent that organization. In GHOSTBUSTERS, the Environmental Protection Agency is represented by a man who makes it his personal business to bust the Ghostbusters.

To demonstrate the importance of an opposition, here's a story I'm paraphrasing from William Froug (*American Writers Review*, January 1997, p. 17). It concerns the classic

SOME LIKE IT HOT and how Billy Wilder and I.A.L. Diamond solved their writing problem. They had a funny idea of two men joining an all-girl band. They weren't able to develop a story from it because they didn't have a motivation for the two men to join the band, and they didn't have an opposition.

One day, Diamond walked into the office they shared on the studio lot to find Wilder waiting for him. As soon as he entered the office, Wilder shouted out, "St. Valentine's Day Massacre!" and Diamond shouted back, "That's It!" They made the two men accidental witnesses to the famous gangland killing. Now, in order to escape from both the law (represented by one individual cop) and the mob (represented by one individual mobster), they become cross-dressers so they can join an all-girl band. Once on the road with the band, they become opposition characters to each other (they both want the same woman). Now that's a movie!

In situations where a group opposes the central character, such as a gang, focus on one person in that group who stands as the greatest personal threat to the central character. Personalizing the opposition will create greater drama and will elicit the audience's sympathy for the central character. The hero is often defined by his/her opposition. And that opposition need not be evil; you just need someone who has a good reason to block your hero's attempt to achieve his goal, even if she is doing so subconsciously (as with the overprotective mother controlling her adult son's life "for his own good").

It is possible to have a nonhuman opposition, such as the forces of Nature, or even a monster (such as the Great White in JAWS). If you do have such an opposition, consider adding a human opponent as well. In JAWS, the mayor of Amity serves as a secondary opponent to Police Chief Brody. In ALIENS, Burke is a strong secondary opponent. In fact, a well-written story often features three opponents.

In addition to the goal, you may wish to give your character some related inner drive or yearning that either supports the goal or is in opposition to the goal. This inner need may be inwardly blocked by some character flaw. This was discussed more fully in the preceding section.

2. MOTIVATION

Your character must be motivated. Ask yourself this question: Why does my character want what he wants? The answer to that question is the motivation. And the more personal, the better. The more personal it is, the more the audience will identify and sympathize with the character. It's the emotional touchstone between your audience and your character.

What is Rocky's goal in the first ROCKY movie? His goal is very specific. He wants to go the distance with the champ—fifteen rounds. Why? *To prove he's not a bum.* It's the personal motivation that gives the story its power. Personally, I hate boxing. I couldn't care less who won the "Thrilla in Manila." And yet I've watched four of the Rocky movies. Why? Well, it's not for the boxing scenes. It's for the motivation *behind* those boxing scenes.

In the second ROCKY movie, his wife goes into a coma. Then she blinks her eyes open and says, "Win." Now Rocky has a motive for winning.

In ROCKY III, Clubber Lang (Mr. T) has a tiff with Rocky's manager, Mickey (Burgess Meredith). Mickey suffers a heart attack and dies. Does Rocky want to clean Clubber's plow? Absolutely, and so does everyone in the theater.

Another boxing movie, MILLION DOLLAR BABY (which is actually more of a character drama than a "boxing movie"), goes deeper. Frankie Dunn (Clint Eastwood) is motivated by guilt and by the fear of getting close to someone. He is lonely. Maggie Fitzgerald (Hilary Swank) grew up believing she was "trash." She wants to escape the past. She needs someone to believe in her. Boxing gives her life meaning. It's easy for people to identify with her personal motivation and with Frankie's; thus, people get "emotionally involved" with these characters.

Love is behind the desire to get well in A BEAUTIFUL MIND. John Nash is motivated to give up his *imaginary* life for a *real* life with his wife. Her love is his motivation.

And, in THE SIXTH SENSE, Dr. Malcolm (Bruce Willis) wants to help Cole because he was unable to save Vincent. He has a personal reason for wanting to achieve his goal.

In RAIN MAN, Charlie Babbitt's perception of his father's past harsh treatment of him motivates his goal of collecting the inheritance. In other words, he wants the inheritance to get even with his father.

JAWS is a horror movie complete with body parts and a monster. The only personal motivation needed here is survival, but the writer adds something very personal. When Brody fails to close the beach, a boy is eaten by JAWS. At the funeral, the mother slaps Brody's face in front of the entire town and says, "You killed my son." Now Brody wants not only to protect the town, but redeem himself.

In JERRY MAGUIRE, our character is fired and humiliated. He is also motivated by his employee/wife, who is the only person who supports him.

Like Jerry Maguire, Rose, in TITANIC, is motivated by two things: She is imprisoned by a lifestyle where no one "sees her" as she is, and Jack is the only person who really does "see her." This is why she literally reveals herself to him.

The motivation usually grows with the conflict. It becomes stronger as the story progresses. Often, the motivation deepens or becomes most evident at the Pinch or midpoint of the story. In AMADEUS, Salieri has many reasons for disliking Mozart. It seems that whenever they are together, Mozart finds a way to insult Salieri, even if it's innocently done. These accumulate over time.

The clincher, however, is when Mrs. Mozart visits Salieri. She brings her husband's work with her and confesses that they need money and wonders if Salieri will help them. Salieri scrutinizes the manuscripts, and sees that these are "first and only drafts of music," and notices no corrections. From Salieri's point of view, Mozart must simply be taking dictation from God. Salieri takes it personally. He goes to his private room and throws his crucifix into the fire. "From now on we are enemies," he says. Why? Because God chose a degenerate like Mozart over him, Salieri, whose only wish has been to serve God through music. So here, at the Pinch or midpoint, we have the goal—to fight God by killing Mozart—and the motivation—because God is unjust.

3. A BACKSTORY

Before page one of your screenplay, something significant happens to your central character. That singular event is called the *backstory*.

In ORDINARY PEOPLE, the backstory involves two brothers, teenagers, boating on a lake. A storm capsizes the boat and one drowns. The other blames himself and tries to kill himself. The script begins when he returns from the hospital.

IN SLEEPLESS IN SEATTLE, the backstory is the death of Sam's wife.

In the above examples, we are given quick glimpses of the backstory. Most often, the backstory is not seen by the audience, but it is there, haunting the central character and affecting his actions.

In THELMA & LOUISE, Louise was raped in Texas. It's what makes it possible for her to shoot Thelma's attacker. This backstory is not revealed to Thelma or the audience until much later in the story.

Hana in THE ENGLISH PATIENT is troubled by the notion that everyone she loves dies.

In UNFORGIVEN, Bill Munny (Clint Eastwood) was a killer before his wife reformed him.

In THE SPITFIRE GRILL, Percy's dark past involves the death of her baby and a five-year prison sentence.

Fox Mulder, in the X-FILES TV series, is haunted by a single, traumatic event. When he was young, his sister was (apparently) kidnapped by aliens. This event deeply affects his actions and personality. He's not just an FBI man, but a person with a life and a past.

Sometimes only the screenwriter knows the backstory (as in AS GOOD AS IT GETS), but because he knows it, the characters seem fuller on the page. Not every character has a single past event that haunts her, but every character has a past that influences that character's actions and dialogue.

Backstory, flaw, and need

The backstory can be subtle. For example, in FOUL PLAY, Gloria Mundy (Goldie Hawn) was once in love and it ended badly. It's as simple as that. At the beginning of the movie, we see a cautious Gloria, a person not quite ready for a new lover, particularly if it's Tony Carlson (Chevy Chase). It's easy to see how the backstory gives rise to the flaw that blocks the need. In the case of Gloria, she needs to feel safe with a man. She's not approachable because she's afraid.

In ORDINARY PEOPLE, Conrad's need is to forgive himself for his brother's accidental death. His flaw is that he tries to control his feelings too much and is self-accusing. This all emerges from his backstory.

In SIGNS, Rev. Hess's wife is killed tragically before the movie begins. This gives rise to his flaw of losing his faith and his need to regain his faith.

Del Spooner (Will Smith), in I, ROBOT, hates robots. This is because of his backstory: a robot saved his life instead of someone more deserving. He needs to stop blaming robots and overcome his bias.

In the CHINATOWN love scene, Mrs. Mulwray asks Jake why he avoids Chinatown. He explains, "I thought I was keeping someone from being hurt, and actually I ended up making sure she was hurt." Jake is referring to his backstory, a traumatic event that transpired before the movie began. In the climactic showdown, Jake tries to keep Mrs. Mulwray from getting hurt and, in so doing, inadvertently facilitates her death. The backstory foreshadows the resolution.

THE SILENCE OF THE LAMBS: When Clarice (Jodie Foster) was a little girl, her dad, a police officer, was killed. She went to live on a ranch. One night they were slaughtering lambs and they were crying. She picked up a lamb and ran, but she wasn't strong enough. They caught up with her and slaughtered the lamb. The need of her adult life was to silence those cries. When a woman is captured by Buffalo Bill and placed in a pit, that woman becomes a crying lamb that Clarice wants to save. But is she strong enough? She is. After she saves the woman, she gets a call from Dr. Lecter. "Well, Clarice, have you silenced the lambs?" That's the *Realization*. We know she hasn't. They'll always be crying, but now she is strong enough to save them. (Some of my students dispute this, maintaining she *has* silenced the lambs of her past. What do you think?)

Showing the backstory

Occasionally, the audience is actually shown the backstory. In FLATLINERS, we see each main character's backstory at the appropriate moment in the script. The films CONTACT, THE PHILADELPHIA STORY, BACKDRAFT, THE SIXTH SENSE, and VERTIGO open with a backstory.

In CASABLANCA, the backstory is revealed in a flashback, as is the case in many films. In NUTS, attorney Aaron Levinsky (Richard Dreyfuss) must unravel the backstory of his client Claudia Draper (Barbra Streisand) to win the case.

4. THE WILL TO ACT

How do you judge a person? By words? Or by actions? Don't actions weigh more heavily than words for you? As the saying goes, "What you do sounds so loud in my ears, I cannot hear what you say."

Action reveals character, and crisis reveals his true colors, because a person does what he does because of who he is. Problems and obstacles reveal what he's made of. Since actions speak louder than words, your character will generally reveal more through action than through dialogue. Yes, dialogue can tell us a lot, particularly about what is going on inside, but actions tell us more. Dialogue can be action. When Darth Vader tells Luke that he is his father and that he should join him, that's an action.

Running Bear is a Sioux hunting buffalo on the wide prairie. This is interesting action. The buffalo are the opposition. But how can we make this more dramatic? Suppose the white settler's son is in the buffalo's path. The white man is Running Bear's enemy. But now Running Bear must make a decision that will reveal his true character. He decides to save the boy. Now he has an action—to save the boy from the herd.

48

Okay, let's take this one step further. The boy's father looks through the window and sees his son, and the buffalo; then to his horror, he sees his enemy, Running Bear. He thinks Running Bear is trying to kill his son. He grabs his rifle and races outside. Now we really care about the outcome. This is drama—characters in willful conflict. Note that each character has a different view of the facts. That leads us to our next point.

5. A POINT OF VIEW AND ATTITUDES

Everyone has a belief system, a perception of reality that is influenced by past experience, a point of view that has developed over time. Our current experience is filtered through our past experience. This means that two people may react in totally different ways to the same stimulus. It depends on their perception. Their point of view is expressed in attitudes.

Some time ago, I was in a department store. I found a little two-year-old who was alone and crying. I tried to calm her down so I could find her mother. The problem was that her mother found me, and guess what she thought I was? That's right, Chester the Molester. Her perception was understandable, given the times we live in, but it was not reality. We don't see reality the way it is; we see it through the filter of our past experience.

Your character also has a past. We're going to discuss how to create that past shortly, but for right now realize that your character has a point of view expressed through attitudes. What is your character's point of view about life? What is your character's concept of love? How does he or she view the opposite sex? What is your character's attitude toward growing old? sex? falling rain? grocery shopping? dental hygiene and regular professional care? Is happiness a warm puppy or a warm gun?

Sol Stein recommends that you "give each character a separate set of facts. Don't give them the same view of the story." With different views of things, your characters will also have different attitudes. Your character will act from his or her point of view or belief system, regardless of how that point of view squares with reality. Salieri believes that great music comes from God. Therefore, Mozart must be God's creature on Earth.

A summary example

In STARMAN, an alien creature crash-lands in Wisconsin. He is a being of light who floats over to Jenny's house. Jenny has withdrawn from life because her husband was killed. The alien finds a lock of her husband's hair and clones himself a body. Now he looks just like her husband. He then makes her drive him to Arizona, which is where his mothership will pick him up. The alien's motivation for this goal is to get home. (This is "E.T. meets IT HAPPENED ONE NIGHT.") His point of view of life happens to be that *life is precious*.

Jenny's goal is to escape. Her motivation is to be safe from the alien and also to be safe from her past. And the alien looks just like her past. The writer has taken her inner problem and put it on the outside to make it visual. Jenny's point of view of life or belief is that life is scary: Husbands die (the backstory) and aliens kidnap you (the action story).

At the Pinch, Jenny observes the alien as he brings a dead deer to life. This action emerges from his belief that life is precious. Touched by this action, her goal of escape is displaced by a desire to help Starman. This new goal is motivated by his inspiring action. Her point of view of life changes as well. Life is not so scary.

This story uses the deer as a metaphor. Jenny is the dead deer that Starman brings back to life (the emotional story). Her perception of life changes. And that's the key. When a character's point of view changes, that's character growth.

6. ROOM TO GROW

Your central character also has a point of view of herself. This point of view of self is called self-concept. *I'm a winner, I'm a loser. I'm clumsy, I'm graceful.* All of us act from this point of view of ourselves, and so do your characters. Here's what happens in the well-written story:

Metaphorically speaking, your character is a fish. The Big Event pulls him out of the water. He tries to swim. It's worked in the past, but it doesn't work now. And so he is forced to take new actions, different actions, but things get more and more difficult right up to the Crisis. Mustering all the courage and faith he has, he takes the final action; then he emerges from the climax with a new self-concept—he's a fish no longer.

This moment is the Realization—the character realizes a change has taken place. Usually the Realization follows the Showdown (or climax), but it can take place during the Showdown or just before. It's a key emotional moment for your audience. We discussed the Realization at length in the second chapter, but here's a couple of additional examples.

Michael Dorsey (Dustin Hoffman) states his realization in TOOTSIE as follows: "I was a better man as a woman with you than I was as a man. I just have to do it without the dress." He has grown or changed.

In THE WIZARD OF OZ, Dorothy is asked pointblank, "Well, Dorothy, what did you learn?" And then Dorothy tells us all the ways her perceptions and attitudes have changed. Most important, her attitude toward home has changed. She realizes now that "there's no place like home."

How does growth come about? Only through adversity and opposition, and striving for a goal. Only through conflict, making decisions, and taking actions. "True character is revealed," the proverb goes, "when you come face-to-face with adversity." Part of the excitement of reading a script or viewing a movie is identifying with a character that grows and learns in the face of adversity.

In defining your character's growth arc, ask yourself how your character grows or learns. Often, your character will grow from some form of slavery to some form of freedom (TITANIC), but it can be from death to life (STARMAN). A character can learn to love (RAIN MAN) or overcome pride (DRIVING MISS DAISY) or become more principled (AN AMERICAN PRESIDENT). As already stated, all growth can be defined as a changed perception of self, life, others, or something else. Often that change is gradual. Often it comes with breakthrough events.

As a footnote, let me reiterate that in some action/adventures, thrillers, and other stories, the central character may not grow. James Bond doesn't grow; he just accomplishes his mission. However, in most genres, character growth of some sort is desirable, even essential. One reason I enjoyed DIE HARD was that the writer gave action hero John McClane (Bruce Willis) room to grow in his relationship with his wife.

7. BELIEVABILITY

One reason dramatic characters are interesting is that they are generally single-minded and focused. Humans have many things going on in their lives and tend to run off on tangents. Your job as the next great screenwriter is to make your dramatic and comedic characters seem as human as possible. In other words, your job is to make us care about them. Here are some ways to accomplish that.

Give them human emotions
As you know, people watch movies to feel emotion vicariously. Whether it's love, revenge, fear, anticipation, or what-have-you, you can only touch these moviegoers if they are able to relate to how your character feels. This doesn't mean that your character should blubber all over the place. It means that we need to see your character frustrated, hurt, scared, thrilled, in love, etc. Often, we empathize with a character more when she fights what she feels rather than when she expresses it.

RAIN MAN is a remarkable film because one of the main characters is incapable of emotionally connecting with another person. I admire the writers, who dealt with this problem by giving Raymond (Dustin Hoffman) a desire to drive a car. "I'm an excellent driver," he would say. If your eyes became misty, it was at the end, when Charlie (Tom Cruise) lets Raymond drive the car on a circular driveway.

Give them human traits
SPIDER-MAN 2 succeeds largely because the focus of the story is more on Peter Parker the human being than on Spider-Man the superhero. Peter has human emotions, traits, values, and dimension. And that's why we love him.

When SNOW WHITE AND THE SEVEN DWARFS was being developed, the dwarfs were seven old guys who looked alike and acted the same. Then Walt Disney decided to give each dwarf a human trait and to call him by that trait. What a difference a trait makes.

In creating characters, first focus on the core of your character—her soul. Who is she? What is her strongest trait? We'll call this her dominant trait. Look for a couple of other traits. Then look for a flaw that might serve as a contrast. That flaw, if it exists, will create an inner conflict.

Finally, determine if your character projects a façade. That fake persona is an element of the character and can be thought of as a trait. In THE PINK PANTHER series, we all love Inspector Clouseau's presumed competence. Children who watch THE POLAR EXPRESS gradually learn that the train conductor is not nearly as mean as he first seems. In AS GOOD AS IT GETS, Melvin Udall's articulate attacks and obsessive-compulsive behaviors are part of the scary façade he uses to fend off a scary world. Once he learns to deal with his fear, his hidden compassion begins to emerge and his obsessive compulsions become less intense. That is what is at the core of his growth arc.

In all, identify three to five specific traits for each of your characters, including a possible flaw, façade, or imperfection.

You don't have to reveal a character's traits all at once. Ideally, each scene reveals something new about your central character. Each contact with a new character sheds new light until the central character is fully illuminated. You will want to introduce your central character in normal circumstances before the Catalyst upsets that balance so that we have a feel for who this person is. Occasionally, this is done by other characters talking about the central character. For example, in CASABLANCA, everyone talks about Rick before we meet him.

It is also important to include characteristics, problems, and imperfections that are familiar to all humans. He's a grouch. She can't deal with people until she's had her morning coffee. Inconsequential human imperfections will make your dramatic or comedic character more believable and more human. An opposition character's imperfections might be more irritating than endearing.

Some writers determine their characters' astrological signs for them. You could give your character one of many psychological and personality tests. Is your character primarily visual, auditory, or kinesthetic? Since you want difficult people in your story, you might avail yourself of a copy of *Coping with Difficult People*. The book describes certain difficult personality types.

Give them human values
Now let's take a moment to consider the Corleone family. It's doubtful that you'd invite these guys over for dinner. And yet, in the GODFATHER movies, you actually rooted for them. Why? Well, for one thing, these guys are loyal. They have a code of honor, a sense of justice. They have families and family values just like you and me. We like people with positive values.

If *your* central character happens to be a *bad guy*, make sure he's morally superior to the others in the story. If your character breaks the law, make him less corrupt than the law. The Corleones had a code of honor—they didn't sell drugs. Sure, extortion, protection rackets, murder, prostitution, gambling, but hey—they didn't sell drugs.

Other ways to create a little sympathy for your character is to give her a talent for what she does, and/or an endearing personal style in how she does it. Give her a moment alone to reveal her goodness. In such a moment, Rocky moves a wino out of the street and talks to a puppy.

Confront your character with an injustice, or place him in a difficult situation or in jeopardy. Be careful not to make him too much of a victim. In GODFATHER II, the Corleones are immigrants in an unfair situation. We sympathize. They take action. We may not agree with their choices, but we admire their fortitude.

Give them human dimension
Your characters, and particularly your central character, should have dimension. Avoid cardboard characters and stereotypes. Occasionally a stereotype works, particularly in a comedy or action script, but your main characters will play better if they have depth. No one is totally evil or perfectly good. The bad guy loves his cat, while the good guy kicks his dog once in a while.

Writers have a tendency to make their favorite characters flat, lifeless, and passive. We're afraid to bloody their face or to give them flaws. Don't fall into that trap. By and large, the most-loved characters in film have depth and dimension. Yours should, too. Even sitcom characters tend to have some dimension to them. They may not be terribly deep, but you'd be hard-pressed to name a favorite TV character who is not flawed.

Heroes and villains

Depending on the nature of your story, your character lies somewhere between real life and a cartoon. Some heroes are swashbucklers with hardly a flaw. And some villains are bad all the way through. Often, that works for special-effects movies. (I say that without any intent to denigrate such movies. Each movie should do what it does best.)

Other films go deeper. In such stories, the hero is often an ordinary man or woman who becomes a hero on his or her way to something entirely different. An ordinary person becomes an extraordinary person or an extraordinary person comes to realize who he really is or finally finds his way.

Likewise, the opposition character does not need to be a classic villain. Who is the villain in AS GOOD AS IT GETS or GOOD WILL HUNTING or KRAMER VS. KRAMER? Yes, there is plenty of opposition, but no villain among the main characters, just people.

Generally, the best villains or opposition characters believe they are doing the right thing. In other words, they wouldn't characterize themselves as a villain. Even the fiancé in TITANIC (who is rather one-dimensional) would be able to justify his actions, but he cannot respect Rose's point of view. The opposition character often has difficulty recognizing another person's view of reality or her needs.

8. DETAILS

Details are the little things that mean a lot. Think of them as characterization tools or aspects of character. Idiosyncrasies, habits, quirks, imperfections (as discussed) and other characterizations will add a lot to a character. They help make the character a distinct individual. Who would Columbo be without his crumpled overcoat? Who would Melvin Udall be (in AS GOOD AS IT GETS) without his obsessive compulsions? Even when he's under pressure to get a coat so he can have dinner with Carol (Helen Hunt), he cannot bring himself to step on a line.

Personal expressions can make a difference. The Emperor in AMADEUS concludes his pronouncements with, "Well, there it is," and Raymond the Rain Man says, "I'm an excellent driver." Jane Craig (Holly Hunter) just cries periodically in BROADCAST NEWS, and Roger Rabbit has an endearing way of stuttering when he says, "Please."

In WHEN HARRY MET SALLY, Sally orders her food in a certain way, and she drops letters into the mailbox one at a time.

Napoleon Dynamite likes to draw. He considers himself an artist, but his drawings are terrible.

In CONTACT, Ellie Arroway (Jodie Foster) sits the same way both as an adult and a child. These are tiny characterizations that add to the believability and definition of a character. How does your character handle the little things?

If it seems right for your character, give him a specialized knowledge or skill, such as David Lightman's computer-hacking skill in WAR GAMES, and Luke's knowledge of The Force in Episodes V and VI of STAR WARS.

In THREE DAYS OF THE CONDOR, Joseph Turner (Robert Redford) is a full-time reader for the CIA. It's easy to believe in his intelligence and knowledge when he's forced to the streets.

In O BROTHER, WHERE ART THOU? Everett (George Clooney) is obsessed with his hair. He wears a hair net at night, says, "My hair" when he wakes up in the morning, and uses Dapper Dan pomade in the daylight hours. You can see how original, specific details can make a character memorable.

A prop becomes a character in THE LADYKILLERS. A portrait of Irma's husband always seems to have a different facial expression each time Irma looks at it. And she takes guidance from it.

When a prop takes on special meaning, it becomes especially effective. That is true for a beautiful detail in the movie A BEAUTIFUL MIND. Alicia gives John Nash her handkerchief for good luck. We see that prop on two other key occasions in the film, the latter on the occasion when he declares his love to her at the Nobel Prize ceremony.

Props have been used with good effect. Melvin's plastic baggies in AS GOOD AS IT GETS. Captain Queeg's ball bearings. Kojak's lollipop. Captain Hook's hook. James Bond's gadgets. The weapons in MEN IN BLACK. Whenever Indiana Jones gets into trouble, he has his whip. He uses the whip to get himself out of trouble. (The whip, of course, does not save him. He uses the whip to save himself. That's an important distinction.)

It follows that coincidences should generally work against your central character. Make it increasingly difficult for her to achieve her goal. Don't bail her out at the end (*deus ex machina*). She should be the most active character in the final act.

9. A WRITER WHO CARES

Every character hopes for a writer who cares. Your central character must have a life and a voice of his own. He can only get that from a writer who cares. You show that you care by researching.

The main purpose of research is to come to really know your characters. Once you know who they are, you can observe them emerging on the page as real. One of the most beautiful experiences you can have is when your characters take over your story and tell you what they want to do.

Research is observing people, taking notes in your little writer's notebook when things occur to you. Research is searching your mind, your own experience, people you've known who can serve as character prototypes, places you've seen, and so forth.

Research is investigating, exploring, and creating your character's background. For instance, your character has an educational background; ethnic, cultural, and religious roots; a professional (or work) history; past and present social connections; and a family of some kind. Your character also has a particular way of speaking.

What kind of character would Forrest Gump be if little thought were put to his background, psychology, traits, imperfections, idiosyncrasies, and moral character?

Research means trips to the library for information, or to a place of business to understand your character's occupation. Research is interviewing someone of a particular ethnic group, or even visiting a neighborhood. Don't assume you can get by because you've seen other movies that have dealt with the same subject matter.

It's easy to get interviews. Recently, I interviewed a petroleum geologist. I told him I'd buy him lunch if he'd let me ask him some questions. He was thrilled for several reasons. One, he could tell the guys at work, "Hey, I can't go to lunch with you tomorrow. I got a writer interviewing me for an upcoming movie." Two, he was getting a free lunch. Three, he's proud of the job he does. The benefit to me was that I learned many unexpected things that I could use in my screenplay to lend authenticity and authority to it.

A struggling student on the East Coast tells me that she didn't really understand her story until she interviewed a blackjack dealer in Las Vegas. Another from the Heartland benefited immensely from a quick jaunt to the library to investigate fencing and other kinds of sword-fighting. A client informed me that most private investigators are employed in family and marital disputes, and by insurance companies. They use clipping services. They sit on the passenger side of the automobile because there's more space. He also learned that it's legal to go through someone's garbage.

Research is writing a character biography or completing a detailed character profile. Of course, much of this information will never make it into your script, but since your character will be alive to you, he or she will appear more fully drawn on the page.

Although your character's physical description is very important to you, it will be of little importance to the script. All actors want to see themselves in the part, so only include physical details that are essential to the story. When you describe a character in your script, it will be with a few lines or words that really give us the essence of the character. Something the actors can act.

But you, the writer, the creator, need to see this person in detail, because a person's physiology affects his psychology. What kinds of emotions does your character have? What is her disposition? How does he handle relationships?

Identify complexes, phobias, pet peeves, fears, secrets, attitudes, beliefs, addictions, prejudices, inhibitions, frustrations, habits, superstitions, and moral stands. Is your character extroverted or introverted? aggressive or passive? intuitive or analytical? How does he solve problems? How does she deal with stress? In what way is he screwed up? And so on. Have fun with this!

Research is reflecting, and asking questions.
- What are my character's values?
- What does my character do when she is all alone?
- What's the most traumatic thing that ever happened to my character?
- What is his biggest secret?
- What is her most poignant moment?
- What are his hobbies?
- What special abilities does she have?
- What is his deepest fear?
- What kind of underwear does she wear?
- Which end of the toothpaste tube does he squeeze?
- What kind of car does she drive?
- What is the worst thing that could happen to my character? (Maybe this will be the crisis.)
- What is the best thing that could happen?
- What is my character doing tonight?

Research is creating unique aspects to your character that make her stand apart from all other movie characters. Part of this may consist in giving your character a contradiction or traits that exist in opposition, such as the beautiful woman who's as clumsy as an ox, or brave Indiana Jones' fear of snakes. You may wish to identify one or more loveable imperfections as well.

As this research progresses, certain things will stand out. After all, in the actual script, you will only be able to emphasize certain aspects of your character, so you will want to select those that say the most about your character and best relate to your story. The work you've done will reveal itself in the unique and multi-faceted character that you have created from the dust.

When do you do this research? Some writers like to do it early in the process; others prefer later in the writing so that the characters can be created to fit the demands of the script. Whenever you choose to do it, it's important to be thorough. A thumbnail sketch of the main characters is seldom sufficient.

10. A STRONG SUPPORTING CAST

A screenplay is a symphony and a symphony requires orchestration. Your character is just a lonely solo without other characters. In the well-written story, relationships are emphasized. Some relationships work because of opposite personalities. The ODD COUPLE is an excellent example. Some relationships work because each can fill the other's need and they transform each other. Others work because the characters are rivals. Still others work because of similar interests or goals.

In your cast of characters, you want one central character, at least one opposition character, and a confidant (or sidekick) your central character can talk to. This is one way to reveal your central character's thoughts, feelings, and intentions. The confidant sometimes performs the additional function of lending contrast to your central character. In dramas, the confidant sometimes creates necessary comic relief, although this function (if needed) can be performed by another character. Roy O'Bannon (Owen Wilson) is a superb sidekick and comic-relief character in both SHANGHAI NOON and SHANGHAI KNIGHTS; he also serves as a clear contrast or foil to Chon Wang (JACKIE CHAN). In REVENGE OF THE SITH (STAR WARS Episode III), R2D2 performs important duties while also serving as a comic-relief character.

You will probably want a love interest, who may function in another role as well, the way Eric Matthews (Benjamin Bratt) is both love interest to Gracie Hart (Sandra Bullock) and leader of the police investigation in MISS CONGENIALITY.

Occasionally, you see a thematic character, someone who carries the theme or message of the story, such as Uncle Ben in SPIDER-MAN 2. We'll discuss this in more detail in the upcoming chapter on "Theme."

Sometimes a shapeshifter adds a twist to the story. For example, the central character's friend betrays her. In THE MATRIX, Cypher betrays his fellow crewmembers to Agent

Smith. In THE VERDICT, one of attorney Frank Galvin's aids works for the opposition. In MINORITY REPORT, John Anderton's mentor/boss turns out to be the bad guy. You have a similar shapeshifter in L.A. CONFIDENTIAL when Captain Smith shoots one of his own police officers.

You want characters with contrasts, and you can contrast characters on many levels— from attitudes to methods to social status. As you add characters, remember that each character in your story must perform a specific function in moving the story forward.

Note: This is a good time to do Step 4 in the workbook (Book II). You will find plenty of character-building tools there. You will also find Step 7 to be helpful.

Theme

Did you know there is something inside you that is motivating you to write? There is something that you want to say. This thing inside you is not a little alien creature; it is the *movie message*, sometimes called the *premise*, sometimes called the *theme*.

Regardless of what it is called, think of it as the *moral* of your story. This moral is not a sermon and it is not preached. Often, you don't know what this moral or message is when you start scripting your story. Not to worry—you'll know before you're through. Just keep writing. CAUTION: There is a danger in focusing on the movie message. You run the risk of writing a preachy script.

The resolution of your story will verify the acceptability of your message. This message or theme could be expressed as a universal statement that could apply to anyone. It's something you've been wanting to say. For this reason, it can be thought of as the *point of view* of your story.

WITNESS has a point of view. *Love cannot bridge the gap of two different worlds.* In THE AFRICAN QUEEN, the opposite is true. *Love **can** bridge the gap of two different worlds.* As you can see, the movie message isn't necessarily true in real life, just true in your story. And it should never be communicated in a heavy-handed way.

Speaking of love, A BEAUTIFUL MIND proves that *love can overcome mental illness.* Or in the words of John Nash, as he addresses his wife at the Nobel Prize ceremony: "It is only in the mysterious equations of love that any logical reasoning can be found. I am only here because of you."

The message of CHINATOWN is this: *You can get away with murder if you have enough money.*

After Chuck Noland (Tom Hanks) is cast away on a deserted island and returns home (in CAST AWAY), he finds that he has lost the love of his life. He tells his friend that at one time on that island he wanted to kill himself. When that failed, he realized that he had to stay alive. And then the tide came in and gave him a sail. Then he explains to his friend that now that he has lost Kelly (his love), he knows what he has to do. He has to stay alive because *who knows what the tide could bring.* And that's the message.

WHEN HARRY MET SALLY suggests that *men and women cannot be "just friends."*

In MY BIG FAT GREEK WEDDING, the controlling idea is *My family may be obnoxious, but they're my family and they'll always be there for me.*

Times are a-changin', and you have to change with them if you want to survive. This thematic statement, or movie message, suggests characters who are fighting time (the conflict) and who will not succeed. Can you name the movie? BUTCH CASSIDY AND THE SUNDANCE KID.

In THE SPITFIRE GRILL, Percy is an apparent Christ figure who gives her life in the end. The theme is *Christ redeems and heals.* Notice how most of the characters have biblical names. And the name of the town is Gilead from the bible passage that asks, "Is there no balm in Gilead?" The Balm of Gilead is what heals, and that is what Percy becomes—a healing balm.

SEABISCUIT's theme also sums up the story: *Everyone thinks we found this broken-down horse and fixed him, but we didn't . . . he fixed us.*

John Truby suggests that theme is the writer's view of how people should act in the world. For example, in GHOST and ROMEO AND JULIET, *great love defies even death.* And in CASABLANCA, *self-sacrifice for the right cause gives life meaning.*

Theme is what your movie is about. According to Patrick Sheane Duncan, ". . . a movie is generally about one thing, one theme or idea, and every scene and every character is formed from that fountainhead." (*Screenwriter Quarterly*, Fall 1996)

In MR. HOLLAND'S OPUS, *life is what happens when you are making other plans.* Each scene and the conclusion in particular points to that idea. In NICK OF TIME, it is simply *how do I save my daughter?* That question is the controlling idea. And *life goes on* in MY BEST FRIEND'S WEDDING.

Sixth Sense

M. Night Shyamalan called THE SIXTH SENSE a "writer's final cut." That may be why I like it so much. It's a writer's movie about characters that *need* to communicate. Once they learn that, they are at peace.

Malcolm (Bruce Willis) wants to help Cole because Cole reminds him of another child that he was unable to help. So he seeks redemption. He has a second, lesser goal which is to save his marriage. His unconscious need is to communicate with his wife and accept his separation from her (his death).

Cole wants the ghosts to go away. His driving desire is to stop being scared. His need is to communicate with his mother. But he won't, because he is afraid she'll think he's a freak. So he has nowhere to go emotionally until Malcolm comes to him.

Things get scarier and scarier until Malcolm has a breakthrough and tells Cole that maybe the ghosts want something. Essentially, he tells Cole to try to communicate with them.

Along comes a very scary Kyra. Cole finds the courage to say, "Do you want to tell me something?" In other words, he opens the lines of communication. Once he does, everything goes well for him. The final two sequences serve well the theme of *Communication overcomes fear.*

In the first of these sequences, Cole finally tells his mother his secret, risking the relationship. Will she think he's a freak? It's an emotional, cleansing scene that is very touching. It is successful not just because it is a great scene, but because of what preceded it in terms of character development and story.

In the final sequence, Malcolm communicates with his sleeping wife. It is then that he realizes he is dead, but now he is able to accept it. The characters are healed, at peace.

Thematic material and thematic characters

A few stories may lack a theme. Some others deal with *thematic material.* For example, WITNESS explores themes of violence and non-violence. BROADCAST NEWS discusses substance versus style. BABE presents issues of self-worth, class structure, and personal identity. UNFORGIVEN compares false reputation (Bob and the kid) with true reputation (Will and Bill).

In a few stories, it may be effective to create a thematic or symbolic character: someone whose purpose is to carry a theme, a value, or even the story message. This character is seldom the central character. For example, the mathematician in JURASSIC PARK and Libby Holden (Kathy Bates) in PRIMARY COLORS are both thematic characters. They also serve as moral consciences. The same is true of Uncle Ben in SPIDER-MAN 2, who says, "With great power comes great responsibility."

Dialogue, subtext, and exposition

WHAT DIALOGUE IS

Dialogue is not real-life speech; it only sounds like it. It is more focused, less rambling than real-life speech. Yes, it contains fragments and short bits, but anything extraneous is pulled out, including the *ans* and *uhs*. You might say that dialogue is *edited* speech. It is organized and has direction, but it retains the style of real-life speech. It doesn't have to be realistic, just believable.

Dialogue should be lean. Avoid long speeches. Try to keep to one or two lines. Naturally, there are exceptions. However, remember that in a movie, people have to understand what's being said the first time through. In a novel, a passage can be reread, but a movie keeps "reeling" along. Avoid monologues. Dialogue should be conversational. Allow characters to interrupt each other on occasion. Let them lie to each other. Avoid having your character say the other person's name he is talking to.

Don't think too hard when writing dialogue. In fact, don't think at all. Write from the heart. You can always return to it later, read it out loud to hear how it sounds, and make adjustments. Take a look at your words and ask yourself: Is there a better, leaner way to say this? Am I writing more but the audience enjoying it less? I'm not saying you can't write long speeches; I'm only saying they must be justifiable.

Be patient in writing dialogue. Sometimes it takes a while for your dialogue to break through. With many professional writers, dialogue is often the last thing written, so don't panic if your dialogue isn't working at first. The key here is to know your characters well enough that they speak with a voice of their own. That voice consists of eight elements.

1. The text, or words
2. The subtext, or the meaning of the words
3. Grammar and syntax
4. Vocabulary
5. Accent and/or regional or foreign influences
6. Slang
7. Professional jargon
8. Speaking style, including rhythm and sentence length

IT'S NOT WHAT YOU SAY, BUT HOW YOU SAY IT

Mama was right—the *subtext* (how you say it) has more impact that the text. Of the eight elements of dialogue, subtext is the one that gives writers the most fits, and yet it is a key principle.

What is subtext? Subtext is what's under the text. It's between the lines, the emotional content of the words, what's really meant. Dialogue is like an iceberg. The text is the visible part. The subtext is below. Audiences seldom want to see the whole block of ice. Likewise, your characters should seldom say exactly what they feel. When an actor wants to know her motivation in a scene, she wants to understand the emotions going on within the character. She wants to know the subtext.

Usually, the dialogue's context in the story suggests the subtext. For example, in the "fireworks" scene of TO CATCH A THIEF, Frances Stevens (Grace Kelly) seduces John Robie (Cary Grant), a reformed jewel thief. That's the context. Does she talk about sex? Does she say, "Come on, John, let's go for a roll in the hay?" Of course not. This moment requires finesse. She talks about her jewelry, and wouldn't he do anything to steal such beautiful works of art? "Hold them," she says, "the one thing you can't resist." Clearly, she's not talking about jewelry here. The subtext is, "I'm the jewelry; you're the thief—take me." She says one thing by saying something else. The subtext is always obvious to the audience.

In a previous section, we discussed goals and needs—your character not only has an outside goal but some inner need. The goal is the *text* of the story and the need may be thought of as the *subtext* of the story, or emotional through-line. It follows, therefore, that the subtext of the dialogue in a scene will often derive from the character's underlying need or drive in the scene. Here's an example:

Late in SPIDER-MAN 2, Spider-man tries to convince Otto Ottavias to give up his dream. Here's the text: "Sometimes we have to give up the thing we want the most—even our dreams." The subtext: "I am going to have to give up the thing I want the most to be Spider-man, my dream of being with Mary Jane."

In MOONLIGHTING, one detective is romantically interested in the other. The two, David and Maddy, are hired by a woman to find her runaway husband. During their investigation, David and Maddy argue over the husband's motives for running away. What are they really talking about? Their own relationship. After all, isn't Maddy running away emotionally from David? It's more fun (and believable) to observe them spar over the case while they are investigating it than it is to listen to them talk about their personal problems directly in a restaurant.

Subtext has to do with the true intention of the character. THE PRINCESS BRIDE is the story of a grandfather who wants to convert his young grandson to a kissing book. A kissing book is one where the boy and the girl actually kiss in the end—yuk! The grandson is sick in bed and is forced to listen to his grandfather read him this kissing book. The grandfather begins reading something like this:

"Once upon a time, there was a boy and a girl. And the girl used to torture the boy by asking him to do things for her, and every time the girl asked the boy to do something for her, he would say, 'As you wish.' But what he was really saying when he said *as you wish* was *I love you*."

I can't think of a better explanation of the relationship between the spoken word and the subtext than this grandfather's explanation.

At the end of this movie, the grandson is converted to this kissing book—he likes it— and as the grandfather leaves, the boy asks him if he could . . . well, maybe . . . come by tomorrow and read it again. And the grandfather says, "As you wish." Wouldn't you agree that this indirect statement, loaded with subtext, is much more powerful than the more direct *I love you*? And it's a lot more fun as well.

Which works better? "I'm very fond of you, Ilsa." Or: "Here's looking at you, kid."

Here's a dramatic situation: A cop confronts a robber, who holds his gun to an innocent woman's head. Which line works better? "If you shoot her, I'll be real glad, because I'm gonna enjoy killing you." Or: "Go ahead, make my day." In this case, less is more.

In DOUBLE INDEMNITY, Walter Neff (Fred MacMurray), the insurance salesman, uses an automobile metaphor to express his sexual interest in Phyllis (Barbara Stanwyck). She replies, "There's a speed limit in this state, Mr. Neff. Fifty-five miles per hour." He asks how fast he was going and she tells him, "About ninety." Then he says, "Suppose you get down off your motorcycle and give me a ticket." She says, "Suppose I let you off with a warning." The subtext is steaming off the words. Of course, she's lying. She's interested even though she says she isn't; that's the subtext. When the text is a lie, the truth (the subtext) will be/should be understood by the audience.

How do you show that someone's parents don't understand their teenaged daughter? One client handled this with the following simple exchange.

                    GIRL FRIEND
          Did your parents like your poem?

                    SUZANNE
          They don't understand poetry.
          They think it's dumb.

When writing dialogue, keep in mind the character's attitudes, point of view, feelings, thoughts, and underlying need or drive. Try to say one thing by saying something else. This does not mean that every line of dialogue must have a subtext. However, most beginning scripts have too little subtext.

WRITING BETTER DIALOGUE

Here's a technique that will improve your dialogue. Read your dialogue out loud or have members of your writers' group read it to you. With the spoken word, it's easier to detect errors. You will hear what works and what doesn't. Is the dialogue too *on the nose*, too direct? Does it have an implied meaning or subtext?

Also be aware of the rhythm. Some characters are terse and staccato; some are lyrical and elegant. Each character has a style of speech. (If a character speaks with a dialect or accent, just give us a flavor of it.) Avoid VOICE OVER narration. Avoid chitchat. *Hi, how are you? Fine, and how about you?* Also, avoid introductions. *Hi, this is Clark. Clark, this is Lois.* In the well-written story, when introductions are made, there's some clear and overriding dramatic purpose. It's not just cheap exposition.

Dialogue should also move the story forward, just as scenes do, and reveal something about the character's attitudes, perceptions, traits, and values. Every dialogue scene should involve some conflict, even if it is just passive resistance. Back and forth, like a contest or competition.

The diner scene from FIVE EASY PIECES illustrates the essence of dramatic writing. Robert Dupea (Jack Nicholson) stops at a diner. He wants toast, he orders toast, but the waitress won't give him toast because it's not on the menu and she doesn't "make the rules." He tries several approaches. She fends him off every time, each time the tension building, the conflict escalating. Finally he orders a chicken salad sandwich, toasted. And he tells her to hold the butter, lettuce, and mayonnaise, and to hold the chicken between her knees. She kicks him out, so he clears everything off the table and onto the floor. The exchange of verbal blows creates the rising tension of this classic scene. The theme underneath the dialogue has to do with "the rules."

EXCITING EXPOSITION

Another purpose of dialogue is to communicate the necessary facts and background information of the story. These facts are called *exposition*. Your job is to make the exposition exciting.

Most of the exposition comes out in the beginning of the story. For example, the audience needs to understand how Indiana Jones' mission will benefit the world. Don't give the audience any more information than is necessary to understand the story. Be careful not to reveal too much too soon. Let your characters keep their secrets as long as they can. Often, saving up exposition and using it in crucial moments will make it more exciting, and even transform it into a turning point. At the same time, don't hold back so much exposition that the audience is confused rather than intrigued.

Some exposition can be creatively planted in love scenes, action scenes, or comedy scenes, because at those moments you already have the audience's attention. I love the sword fight scene in THE PRINCESS BRIDE for that very reason. You learn a lot about both characters in the dialogue exchange that accompanies the thrusts and parries of their swords.

Be careful not to get *too* exciting. In the second INDIANA JONES movie, the main exposition is presented through dialogue at a bizarre dinner. The food is so disgusting that the audience's attention is diverted from the characters' dialogue.

In the first INDIANA JONES movie, the exposition is handled more effectively. The opening sequence is so exciting that we are riveted to the screen for the succeeding sequence, where most of the necessary information about the Lost Ark of the Covenant is communicated through dialogue.

Exposition should come forth naturally and not be tacked onto a scene. Seldom should you allow one character to tell the other something he already knows. Her: "We've been married ten years now, honey." Him: "Yes, I recall. We were married under the great oak in the backyard, the one that your mother cut down a year later." Her: "I remember it well." It's forced and contrived. Please don't do that.

Another way to make exposition exciting is to have characters argue over it. Some exposition can be handled without dialogue. In the opening scene of UNBREAKABLE, David Dunn (Bruce Willis) sits on the train looking rather morose. A pretty woman sits next to him and he removes his wedding ring. That's exposition. It tells us he's unhappily married.

In the opening sequence of WAR GAMES, we are shown how the U.S. nuclear-missile firing system works. This information not only underscores the danger and prepares us for a thrilling ending, but also makes the story more believable.

Flashbacks

About 95% of the flashbacks in unsold scripts don't work. Usually, the flashback is used as a crutch, a cheap way to introduce exposition. This has given rise to the industry bias against them in spec scripts. Seldom does it move the story forward. And that's the key—use a flashback only if it moves the story forward.

If you watch THE FUGITIVE, you'll see dozens of flashbacks, but each pushes the story forward or wants you to know what's going to happen next. Don't give exposition in a flashback unless it also motivates the story, as in JULIA, MEMENTO, and CASABLANCA. Do not take us to the past until we care about what's happening in the future. Otherwise, a flashback becomes an interruption.

Avoid long flashbacks and dream sequences. They are high-risk. If you must have a flashback, use a transitional device: an object, place, song, visual image, color, phrase, or incident. Quick flashes are the safest, such as the momentary glimpses of the backstory we see in ORDINARY PEOPLE.

My advice on flashbacks is to find a more creative way to communicate exposition. To illustrate, put yourself in the place of the writer of STAR TREK II: THE WRATH OF KHAN. You have a problem: Khan, the opposition character, is Kirk's superior physically and mentally. How can you make it believable that Kirk can defeat Khan?

One solution is to *flash back* to the days when Kirk was a cadet. He takes a field test called the Kobiashi Maru, which presents a no-win scenario. Kirk, however, beats the no-win scenario by reprogramming the test computer so that he can win.

You, however, reject this idea of a flashback for one that is more creative. You decide to open the story with a starfleet captain on a ship that is in trouble. Soon we learn that this captain is really a cadet and that she is taking a test called the Kobiashi Maru. She is bothered by her performance. Kirk tells her not to worry, that there is no correct solution—it's a test of character. So she asks Kirk how *he* handled it. He won't tell her.

You have made it a mystery that is touched on throughout the story—how *did* Kirk handle the Kobiashi Maru? The audience wonders. You, the next great screenwriter, have created suspense.

CUT TO: Late in the story. It appears as though Kirk and his friends are trapped in an underground cavern with no way out, and with no apparent way to contact Spock, who is somewhere out in the universe. At that moment, the female cadet once again asks Kirk how he handled the Kobiashi Maru. Bones tells her that Kirk reprogrammed the computer. "You cheated," someone says.

Then Kirk surprises everyone by pulling out his communicator and contacting Spock: "You can beam us up now," he says. Ah-ha, so Kirk had it all pre-arranged, but to do it, he broke Federation rules. He has cheated Khan and has surprised everyone else. That's when Kirk explains: "I don't believe in the no-win scenario. I don't like to lose." Not only have you explained how Kirk could defeat a superior being, you have also given us the *key* to Kirk's character. And this plays better than a flashback.

Note: There are many sample scenes containing dialogue in Book IV.

How to make a scene

Screenplays are composed of acts, acts break down into sequences, sequences into scenes, and scenes into beats. A scene is a dramatic unit consisting of the camera placement (INTERIOR or EXTERIOR), a location, and time. When one of these three elements changes, the scene changes as well. In this discussion, I am using the term *scene* loosely. The points that follow could apply to any dramatic unit consisting of one or more scenes.

KEYS TO GREAT SCENES

- **Each scene should move the story forward** in terms of both plot and character. In other words, the scene you are now writing should be motivated by a previous scene, and it should motivate a scene coming up. One creates anticipation for another in a cause-and-effect relationship.

  If the central character gets more involved in some way, that means your scene is probably moving the story forward. All scenes should direct us to the Showdown at the end, which is the biggest scene, or sequence of scenes, in the movie. Ask yourself: What is the payoff for this scene? Why do I need this scene? What is my purpose for this scene? Does the scene reveal something new about a character and/or the story? At the end of this scene, does the audience want to know what happens next?

- **Never tell what you can show.** Be as visual as possible. Rather than two ladies at tea commenting on the fact that Darla skydives for relaxation, *show* us Darla actually jumping from a plane, or show her coming home with a parachute and trying to stuff it into the closet.

Do you recall the barn-raising scene in WITNESS? When the workers pause for lunch, the eyes of the elders are on Rachel Lapp (Kelly McGillis), who is expected to marry an Amish man, but who likes John Book (Harrison Ford). Without a word of dialogue, she makes her choice by pouring water for John Book first.

One scene in SEABISCUIT presents a key episode in the life of Charles Howard, the central character. We first see his young son reading *Flash Gordon*. Charles tells him to go fishing. That's about the only dialogue in the entire scene.

Next, his son sees his father's car. He gets his fishing equipment. He starts the car, and notices the birds and trees. He drives erratically; he's too young to be driving. We see another car approaching going the opposite direction. We sense there could be a collision.

Back at the house, the phone rings. Charles picks up the phone. We cut to the car; there's been an accident. Charles drives. Charles runs. Charles holds his dead son MOS (without any sound).

We cut to the graveside, then back to the house where Charles plays with his son's Flash Gordon puzzle. He cries. He locks the garage.

In MY BEST FRIEND'S WEDDING, Julianne (nicknamed Jules) and Michael (her best friend) have a moment together. The setting is visual: A boat on the Chicago River and not a couch in an apartment. They both want to tell each other how they feel about each other, but they fight it (which makes the audience empathize with their feelings more strongly than if both characters just blurted out what they were thinking).

Jules wants to tell Michael that she loves him. As they both approach the moment where they might say what they feel, they approach a bridge. The dialogue continues as follows:

```
                    MICHAEL
          Kimmy says, when you love someone,
          you say it. You say it out loud.
          Right now. Or the moment ...
```

```
He pauses. Jules wants to say. They are under the
bridge, silent for a long moment, and then past the
bridge. She's misty-eyed.

                    JULIANNE
          ... passes you by.
```

That visual cue of passing under the bridge tells us that the moment has passed for her to say that she loves him. The visual cue brings the message home and makes for a stronger moment.

- **Avoid talking heads.** John and Mary argue over breakfast. One head talks, then the other. Make this more interesting by beginning the argument at breakfast, continuing it while in the car racing to the club, and concluding it during a racquetball match. Each statement a character makes is punctuated by the whack of the racket or the whop of the ball slamming against the wall. Now the action complements the dialogue, plus you give yourself the opportunity to characterize your characters by how they play racquetball, how they drive, what they drive, etc.

- **Every dramatic unit has a beginning, a middle, and an end.**

- **Start the scene as close to the end of the scene as possible.** In other words, once your scene is fleshed out, evaluate it and lop off anything at the beginning that is unnecessary. (In fact, cut the fat anywhere you can.)

Imagine a cowboy riding up to a log house in the middle of the prairie. No one for miles around. He quietly dismounts, grabs his rifle, and gingerly approaches the cabin. He peeks through the window. There she is. Young, beautiful, and alone. Inside the cabin, the woman turns. The door is kicked in. The cowboy steps inside and points his rifle right at the woman. He wants the money and he wants her. She reaches behind for a knife and throws it at the cowboy.

Does this scene remind you of the opening scene of ROMANCING THE STONE? It is, except that the final version of the scene begins at the moment the door is kicked in. Everything preceding that moment was cut. The writer wisely started the scene as close to the end of the scene as possible.

In terms of scene length, challenge any scene that runs more than two pages. Many great scenes are long, and some scenes should be long. Nevertheless, if you challenge your long scenes, you may find ways to improve them and shorten them. This will strengthen the pace of the story. You may even find scenes that should be a little longer, and that's okay, too.

- **Pace your scenes.** Provide peaks and valleys of emotion and tension, with the peaks ascending toward a climatic conclusion. Follow action scenes with dialogue scenes. Contrast heavy scenes with light scenes. Make sure the pace quickens as you close in on the Crisis and Showdown. In HOME ALONE, we have the reflective scene in the church just before the madcap slapstick sequence at the house.

  Pacing does not need to focus on action and events, such as in LETHAL WEAPON; it can focus on details as in STEEL MAGNOLIAS. LETHAL WEAPON is plot-driven and must move fast, while STEEL MAGNOLIAS is character-driven and more leisurely paced; you can stop and describe the roses.

- **Scenes should culminate in something dramatic.** This could be a decision or an imminent decision. It could be a reversal, a cliffhanger, or a revelation—some event that makes us want to see what's going to happen next. Keep in mind that twists and turns in the plot are essential. You cannot allow your story to progress the way your audience expects it to. Scenes should end with a punch, with some kind of tension that leads us to another scene. For example, in TITANIC, Rose's mother orders her to never see Jack again. Throughout the scene, Rose's mother tightens Rose's corset. Note how that adds visually to the tension of the scene. The pressure is tightening around Rose.

  In GOOD WILL HUNTING, Will (Matt Damon) confronts a college kid who is hitting on a coed (Minnie Driver). After the long scene, Will flashes the coed's phone number at the college kid, showing he has won. It punctuates the scene. It brings the scene to a conclusion, but it also creates anticipation that more is to come.

  In dialogue scenes, generally the last line should be the strongest line. In the very last scene of SOME LIKE IT HOT, Jerry (Jack Lemmon), posing as Daphne, must convince Osgood Fielding III (Joe E. Brown) that she (Daphne) can't marry Osgood. The wonderful conflict is created by Osgood's subtle resistance to Jerry's attempts to achieve his goal of getting out of the wedding.

  First, he tells Osgood that he can't get married in his mother's dress because they aren't built the same way. "We can have it altered." Then Jerry (still posing as Daphne) confesses that he is not a natural blonde. "Doesn't matter." Then Jerry admits that he smokes all the time. "I don't care." Jerry tries another angle; he tells Osgood he's been living with a saxophone player. "I forgive you." With feigned remorse Jerry announces that he can never have children. "We'll adopt some." Finally, Jerry removes his wig, speaks in his male voice, and admits that he is a man. The response? "Well, nobody's perfect." And that's the *punch*line that ends the movie.

- **Strive to create effective transitions between scenes.** I'm not referring to tricky cuts and arty dissolves—leave editing directions to the editor. Find ways to fit the scenes together. For example, one scene ends with a roulette wheel spinning. The next scene begins with a car wheel digging into the mud.

  Early in 2001: A SPACE ODYSSEY, a prehistoric man throws his tool into the air. It's a bone that becomes a spaceship, a tool of modern man.

  Here's an effective transition from Bruce Joel Rubin's JACOB'S LADDER. In it, Rubin uses sound and images to move us from Vietnam to New York.

  ```
  As he spins around, one of his attackers jams all eight
  inches of his bayonet blade into Jacob's stomach. Jacob
  screams. It is a loud and piercing wail.

  From the sound of the scream, there is a sudden rush
  through a long, dark tunnel. There is a sense of
  enormous speed accelerating toward a brilliant light.

  The rush suggests a passage between life and death,
  but as the light bursts upon us we realize that we are
  passing through a subway far below the city of New York.
  ```

  This would be followed by INT. NEW YORK SUBWAY, and the scene would continue.

  This kind of transition is the exception rather than the rule. It is important in this screenplay because of the theme. This is the story of how a man comes to accept his own death, very much like Rubin's prior screenplay, GHOST.

  You are not required to link your scenes with transitions. You do this occasionally, when appropriate.

  Transitions can be visual, verbal, thematic, and so on. Is it okay to sharply contrast scenes? Absolutely. If it moves the story forward, use it. Keep in mind that a straight cut from one scene to the next is not only correct, but the norm. The object is not to get fancy but to give the story cohesion.

- **Each scene should contain a definite emotion or mood.** Focus on that emotion as you craft the scene. Ask yourself: What is my character's intention or goal in this scene? What is my character's feeling? What is my character's attitude? Asking this will help give the scene direction and the dialogue subtext.

- **Focus the scene on a well-motivated conflict.** Even in less-dramatic scenes, a conflict should exist, regardless of how minor or how subtle it is. Often, two people with the same goal will disagree over methods or procedure, or just get under the other's skin: Bones and Spock, James Bond and Q, Butch Cassidy and Sundance, Mr. and Mrs. Incredible, and Mr. and Mrs. Smith (in MR. AND MRS. SMITH). Even in love scenes, there may be some resistance at the beginning. Conflict is one of the tools you can use to build suspense.

- **Each scene should have a definite purpose.** See pages 204-207.

Note: For examples of scenes, see Book IV.

Suspense, comedy, and television

Building suspense is the art of creating an expectation of something dramatic that is about to happen. Since we go to movies to feel vicarious emotion, putting us in suspense simply builds emotion as we anticipate the outcome. Here are ten tools to thrill and manipulate us.

TOOLS FOR BUILDING SUSPENSE

Evoke emotion
Create characters we like. They must be believable since they act as a conduit through which emotion can pass to us. We need to sympathize with them and feel what they feel.

Create conflict
As mentioned earlier, rising conflict creates suspense. Since conflict is drama, two committed forces in conflict will always heighten suspense. Remember grade school? Two boys would start fighting and everyone would make a circle around them. No one tried to stop the fight. (This is very irritating if you're the smaller boy.) No one stopped it because we were all in suspense, wondering if blood would squirt out someone's nose, and betting on who would win.

Provide opposition
Give your central character a *powerful opposition*; then force your character to battle this foe. The opposition should be in a position of strength, capable of doing damage.

In STAR TREK II, Khan serves as an excellent example, because he is superior to Kirk physically and mentally. We all go through the extreme mental duress of wondering how Kirk is going to survive, let alone defeat, this "giant."

The "giant" in FATAL ATTRACTION is Glenn Close, the lover. She is in a position to do damage to Michael Douglas.

The formidable foe in MY BEST FRIEND'S WEDDING is Kim, the fiancée. She has the emotional leverage on Michael, Julianne's best friend. Besides, she's adorable. How can Julianne compete with that?

In THE SIXTH SENSE, the dead people seem infinitely more powerful than little Cole. Since we know so little about the aliens in SIGNS, they seem formidable. And Otto Ottavias is made more powerful when Spider-man appears to be losing his powers. It creates an expectation of trouble, our next point.

Build expectation
Create an *expectation for trouble*. Do you recall the baby carriage in THE UNTOUCH-ABLES? In this scene, Elliot Ness must face off with Capone's boys at the train station. He's ready and in position, but a woman is having difficulty moving her baby carriage up the stairs. We get nervous—we just "know" she is going to get in the way. The suspense builds.

Consider also the scene from FATAL ATTRACTION where Dan Gallagher (Michael Douglas) returns home and finds his wife conversing with his lover. There is an expectation that the wife might realize that this blonde she is talking to is actually a woman who is having an affair with her husband. In this case the jeopardy is emotional, not physical. When the wife introduces the lover to Dan, the subtext is powerful because they have already met. The lover says such lines as, "Don't I remember you?" "We've definitely met." "I never forget a face." The subtext is, *You're not getting away from me. I'm going to make you pay.*

At the Showdown of GHOSTBUSTERS, our heroes confront the goddess Gozer. Gozer tells them that the Destructor will come in whatever form they choose with their thoughts. Dr. Stantz (Dan Aykroyd) has obviously thought of something, and the other characters try to figure it out because they, and the audience, know the Destructor is coming, but they don't know what form it will take. Comedic suspense builds as Stantz points to his head and says, "It just popped in there." What just popped in there? We catch glimpses of something huge and white moving past the buildings, but we still don't know what it is. Stantz babbles, "It can't be, it can't be." The anticipation peaks and finally Stantz admits, "It's the Stay-Puft [sic] Marshmallow Man." And then we see the huge figure lumbering down the avenue.

Increase tension

Put the audience in a *superior position*. Take, for example, a couple we care about. While they are out to dinner, someone sneaks into their apartment and places a bomb under their bed. Later, our happy couple returns and they hop into bed. We know the bomb is there, but they don't. We, the audience, are in a superior position.

Imagine a small child playing in the yard. The mother steps inside the house. The child wanders toward the busy street. We are in a superior position to the child and to the mother. We are the only ones who are aware of the danger, and that builds suspense.

In THE GREEN MILE, a tremendous amount of tension is created when Percy purposely doesn't wet the sponge prior to the execution of an inmate in the electric chair. We know the sponge is dry, but no one else in the movie realizes it until it is too late.

Use surprise

Throw in an occasional nasty twist, or sudden turn of events. The first surprising appearance of a dead person in THE SIXTH SENSE creates a great deal of suspense. The sudden collapse of the house in LEMONY SNICKET'S A SERIES OF UNFORTUNATE EVENTS puts us on edge.

In PSYCHO (the classic 1960 version), Norman Bates kills Marion Crane early in the now-famous shower scene. This nasty twist serves the purpose of creating an expectation of *more* violence. Indeed, Hitchcock once remarked, "At this point I transferred the horror from the screen to the minds of the audience." Interestingly enough, there is only one more violent act in the entire movie, and yet we are held in suspense throughout.

Create immediacy

When *something vital is at stake* for the character, that *something* becomes vital to us, the audience, as well. It can be the physical safety of the world or the moral redemption of a juvenile delinquent. It can be the emotional fulfillment of two lovers who find each other, the protection of a secret document, or the triumph of a value. In SPIDER-MAN 2, it is both the safety of Mary Jane and New York. The higher the stakes, the more intense the suspense.

Establish consequences

Closely related to the above is the establishment of terrible consequences if the central character does not achieve her goal. When the Challenger space shuttle exploded, there was a lot of grief and sadness. A couple of years later, we sent up another shuttle. Do you recall the suspense you felt as the countdown proceeded on this later shuttle mission? That heightened suspense was due to the prior establishment of terrible consequences.

Limit time
Put a ticking clock on it. "You have only 24 hours to save the world, James. Good luck." Deadlines create suspense because they introduce an additional opposition—time. You can probably think of a dozen movies where a bomb is about to explode, and the hero must defuse it before the countdown reaches zero. The torpedo-firing sequences in THE HUNT FOR RED OCTOBER were particularly thrilling because of the element of time.

Likewise, when the wicked witch in THE WIZARD OF OZ captures Dorothy, she turns over the hour glass. "This is how long you have to live, my little pretty." Although we are never told how Dorothy is going to die, we still worry. Apparently, Hitchcock was right when he said that "the threat of violence is stronger than violence."

You can easily create an artificial deadline. The damsel is tied to the railroad tracks. Can Dudley Do-Right save the damsel before the train runs over her? Here you have an implied deadline. Other effective uses of the ticking clock include HIGH NOON, the rose petals in Disney's BEAUTY AND THE BEAST, and the prediction that John Anderton (Tom Cruise) will murder someone in 36 hours in MINORITY REPORT. In TITANIC, can Rose reach Jack and get him out of his handcuffs before the room fills with water?

Maintain doubt
Finally, if there is a reasonable doubt as to how the scene or movie is going to end, the suspense is intensified. How is Cole going to get away from his "dead people" problem in THE SIXTH SENSE, especially if Dr. Malcolm stops trying to help him (as he decides to do in one scene)?

In the opening scene of THE UNTOUCHABLES, one of Capone's boys leaves a brief-case full of explosives in a store. A little girl picks it up and it explodes. At this point, we realize that anyone in this movie can die, and we fret over Elliot Ness's little girl and wife the entire movie. Why? Because this scene has left us in genuine doubt about their safety.

LEAVE 'EM LAUGHING

Have you ever watched a comedy, laughed for about 20 minutes, and then grown restless? The probable reason for this is that the comedy had a weak story structure and poorly drawn characters. The comedy may have relied more on gags than on character and story. Virtually all of the humor in SHREK flows from the characters and the situation, which is one reason the story is so effective.

Comedy is drama in disguise. And there is no comedy without conflict. This means that virtually everything in this book applies to comedy as well as to drama. Here are a few points that apply particularly to comedy.

Comedy requires clarity and good timing—a *sense* of humor.

Love situations and other personal situations are easy for us to identify with and are ripe for comedy. That's one reason the family situation comedy has done so well. As psychologist Abraham Maslow stated, "That which is most personal is most general." Comedy reveals our secret desires and yearnings so that we can laugh at them.

Comedy makes good use of surprise and reversals, in revealing the truth about people, situations, and life.

Comedy generally takes an unusual point of view through use of exaggeration, deception, overstatement, understatement, contrast, parody, a ridiculous point of view, or obsession.

Comedic characters need to present the same contrasts that dramatic characters do. In GHOSTBUSTERS, we have a rational, cerebral type (Harold Ramis); an emotional, enthusiastic child (Dan Aykroyd); and a cool dude who understates almost everything (Bill Murray). This is a good mix. The fourth ghostbuster doesn't really add much to the comedic mix and, thus, is less effective as a comedic character.

Comedy presents people with pretenses or façades, then removes those pretenses one by one or little by little. One scene from PLAY IT AGAIN, SAM features Allan Felix (Woody Allen) preparing for a blind date (a situation we can all relate to—right?). He goes to extremes to impress her. He thinks he can score the first night, and that's his pretense. He impresses her, all right, but not the way he had hoped. It's a reversal of what he expected. He's brought back to earth. And it's funny.

Another example of two characters with a pretense appears in CELEBRITY WEDDING, a screenplay by Yours Truly and Greg Alt. Sam and Natalie pretend not to like each other (that's the pretense). They have just seated themselves on a plane, thinking they have escaped from the bad guy, Novaks.

Immediately, Sam spots Novaks, who hasn't yet spotted them. Somehow, Sam must find a way to hide Natalie's face so that Novaks doesn't recognize her. They have to act quickly. Watch how the pretenses are removed and the truth of their feelings for each other are revealed.

(As you will read in Book III, the dash is normally used for interruptions of thought and the ellipsis for continuation of thought. An ellipsis at the end of a sentence normally means the character did not continue her thought.)

```
INT. PLANE - DAY

Sam and Natalie quickly throw themselves into two back
seats. Sam leans into the aisle and spots Novaks headed
their direction, searching the passengers.

                    SAM
          He's coming.

Sam turns to Natalie. Gets eye contact. She responds with
a short gasp. He kisses her long and hard, hiding her face
from Novaks.

Novaks glances at them in disgust, then turns back.

Sam releases Natalie, who is momentarily paralyzed.

                    SAM
          Ah sorry. I -- ah, couldn't
          think of anything else.

                    NATALIE
          Right -- I mean, I mean under the
          circumstances it was good. I
          don't mean good good, I mean,
          well....

                    SAM
          We really didn't have any other --

                    NATALIE
          -- Exactly. And if we had --

                    SAM
          -- We certainly would've -- or
          wouldn't've....

                    NATALIE
          Absolutely.
                    SAM
               (overlapping)
          Naturally.

A brief, unbearable silence. Face to face. Instantly, they
both reach for the same in-flight magazine.
```

```
                    SAM AND NATALIE
                 (simultaneously)
             Go ahead.
```

Disgusted with himself, Sam rips the magazine from the seat pocket and buries himself in it.

Natalie pulls out the emergency flight card and fans herself.

In this scene, the kiss comes as a surprise. The situation is readily identifiable in the sense that we've all embarrassed ourselves at one time or another in the presence of someone we were interested in. The scene ends with a visual subtext that implies Natalie is "hot."

TELEVISION

As you can imagine, television comedy writing is less visual than screenwriting, with less action. There may be only one or two locations. And so the emphasis is on interpersonal conflict and dialogue. The best situation for a sitcom is one that forces the characters to be together. They live together, work together, or belong together.

Sitcoms thrive with a *gang of four*, four main characters where each can easily be at cross-purposes with any of the others, creating more possibilities for conflict. In other words, they can play off each other.

Structurally, the sitcom opens with a teaser that says, "Boy, this is going to be really funny. Don't change the channel during the next two minutes of commercials!" Act 1 introduces the secondary storyline and the primary storyline in succession. (Sometimes one of these is introduced in the teaser.) Act 1 ends on a turning point that is either the most hilarious moment in the episode or is very serious. The second act resolves the primary story, then the secondary story. This is followed by a tag at the end that usually comments on the resolution. Some sitcoms present three stories or plotlines.

The hour-long TV drama or comedy also opens with a teaser or prologue. Act 1 establishes what's going on, Acts 2 and 3 develop it, Act 4 pays it off. Most shows add an epilogue. If the show is relationship-driven, an arena is created in which the story can play. The arena for ER is a hospital emergency room.

The *long form*, or Movie-of-the-Week (MOW), contains seven acts and about 105 pages. This means that six turning points must be carefully planned. It might be simpler to write this as a screenplay. In fact, the best way to break into television of any kind is with a feature script that you can use as a sample. It shows that you can create characters from scratch and write a story around them. Being the next great screenwriter, it's a challenge you can meet.

It goes without saying that the principles of drama that we have covered up until now apply to writing for television as well.

Note 1: For more on television writing, see "How to format TV scripts" in Book III *and "Television and Hollywood's back door" in* Book IV.

Note 2: This is a good time to do Step 5 in the workbook, Book II. *Next, read the formatting and style guide (*Books III and IV*). Then do Steps 6 and 7 in the workbook. Finally, use the marketing plan in* Book V *to sell your screenplay, consulting the resources in* Book VI.

7 STEPS TO A STUNNING SCRIPT

BOOK II

A Workbook

About this workbook

This workbook takes you through the seven steps of the writing process. I've tried to make it simple and easy to follow.

Each step is marked with checkpoints to keep you on track. In all, there are 26 checkpoints and more than 150 key questions to help you evaluate your progress. Not every question needs to be answered. Not every checkpoint needs to be reviewed in the order it's presented. These are not hard-and-fast rules, but fluid guidelines to help you craft a stunning script. In fact, many writers like to begin the process by developing their characters; if you are one of those, you may want to do Step 4 before Steps 2 and 3.

This workbook becomes a more effective tool if you've studied the primer (Book I) first and have started or have the nascent concept for a script.

Take a moment now to congratulate yourself. You are embarking on a great journey. I hope you enjoy the adventure of creating movie people and plotting the events of their lives. May success be yours.

Step 1—Summon your Muse

At the start of the workshop, two writing students were arguing. Sheila insisted that writing was purely a creative endeavor, while Sam argued that screenwriting was a scientific process. Back and forth they went. Finally, Robert, my teacher's pet, chimed in. "Stop! You're both right. Screenwriting is both an art and a science. The professional writer uses the head as well as the heart." Both wondered how Robert could possibly be right. But he was, and here is why.

The writing process begins with the creative urge, a desire to express something. Like a tiny seedling, an idea emerges from your heart and pushes its way through the soil of your subconscious. Often, several ideas will sprout. Like any birthing process, this can happen at any time and any place. And with the emergence of your idea comes that wonderful creative feeling.

How do you nurture that young seedling of an idea? What makes it grow? Thought and hard work make it grow. You think about the possibilities. Then, you blueprint the core story, which consists of a beginning, a middle, and an end. All this head work will act like a shot of adrenalin to your heart. More ideas will flow, and the story will evolve until it matures.

Every writer has two natures: the heart and the head. The heart is the passionate creator, the emotional artist, the child, the intuitive subconscious. The head is the detached critic or editor, the parent, the logical and analytical scientist or surgeon. And quite conscious.

Good writing utilizes both natures, but operates like an alternating current between the two. When you're in the creative, artistic mode, you shut off the head. You encourage the creative flow. You don't correct the spelling or improve the grammar. You just play in your sand box. There are no rules or restrictions. But once that energy is expended, the parental side takes over and cleans up the mess.

Back and forth you go. You write from the heart. You edit from the head. Back and forth until the head and heart agree (or you've become a schizophrenic).

The good Lord gave our brain two hemispheres. Both are important. Sheila is right-brained and focuses on the intuitive, artistic side of creativity. Sam is left-brained and focuses on the analytical, scientific side of creativity. Each should use his or her greater talent without abandoning his or her lesser talent.

I sometimes worry about writers who search for formulas, who want to make writing purely a science so that they can write by the numbers. They may want inflexible rules so they can be in control of the process. This is to be expected. Our educational system inculcates this into our brains. The secret to great writing is to be part of the *process*. You can't control it. In truth, the story knows from the beginning where it's going. There is no sweeter moment than when your characters take over and tell you what they want to do and say.

I also worry about the purists who may insist that anything written from the heart is perfect just the way it comes. That which comes easily is not necessarily good. They may be loathe to edit their work for fear of breaking some divine law. If it were true that everything pouring from the heart is perfect, no one would ever revise anything. There would be no second drafts, no rewriting. Just because it felt good when you wrote it doesn't mean that it is ready for market.

Writing is an evolutionary process that must be trusted. You must believe that there is a story within you. You must believe that it will find its way out. And you must believe in your talent to nurture it into a stunning script. If you believe, and act on your belief, your Muse will come to you.

THE WRITING PROCESS

Becoming part of the writing process is like "getting religion." For some writers it is almost a mystical experience. Let me provide a suggested framework for this process.

First you start off with a creative jolt, an idea that's about a 7.0 on the Richter scale. Then you do a lot of hard thinking—hammering out a good dramatic premise—beginning, middle, and end. You write the *TV Guide* logline in terms of character, action, opposition, and resolution. What's the concept?

Then, on wings of song, your Muse comes down from Mt. Parnassus and whispers sweet things. You write all these gems down.

You visualize the one-sheet, the poster that will adorn the movie theater walls in just a couple of years or so. You ask: Do I have a story? Do I have an original concept that will pull people in? If everything feels right up till now, you begin your research.

You develop your characters using both sides of your brain. Remember, even though your characters are within you before you ever begin, once they emerge, they must take on a life of their own.

With an understanding of your story and characters, you now construct the all-important story outline. This outline, sometimes called the step outline, is comprised of paragraphs, one paragraph for each scene, anywhere from 30-100 steps in all. (This figure can vary, depending on genre.) Many writers use 3" x 5" cards, a card for each scene, and pin these cards against the wall. This is when you chart the sequence of your story, alternating between your creative/intuitive nature and your evaluative/ practical nature.

Whenever you think you're getting off base, you write a short synopsis—about three pages—to get back on track.

By now, your creative pump is primed. You write your first draft from the heart. Some of these scenes are already written from previous bursts of creative joy. Intuitively, creatively, the draft takes shape. The second draft is written from the head, analytically.

Even as you approach the end of the process, the story is fluid, evolving into what it eventually wants to be. Don't force the process by being too rigid about scenes you have fallen madly in love with. Don't feel confined by your original outline. Remain open to your Muse.

This is just one way to write a script. With experience, you will find the way that works best for you. Some writers prefer to just write and allow things to manifest themselves in the writing. The most important thing is to trust the process and believe in yourself. The story is inside you; you must let it out in one way or another. So what are you waiting for? Come on. Let's create a masterpiece!

Step 2—Dream up your movie idea

What if you don't have any ideas? Here are a few tips that will help you get those creative juices flowing.

1. Put your mind in a relaxed state through meditation or deep breathing. Visualize a natural setting where you feel safe, or drift off to the setting of your script. The right brain, the Inner Creator, always works best when the left brain, the Inner Critic, has been tranquilized.

2. Rely on the Inspiration Cycle: Input, Incubation, Inspiration, Evaluation. After a few days of jamming your brain, relax and tell yourself that you need a breakthrough, then incubate. In other words, wait. It may take a few days. Soon enough, while falling asleep or taking a shower—Eureka!—the inspiration comes. You're flying. It may continue to flow for some time. But don't stop when it does. Evaluate it (the Inner Critic has been waiting for this moment) as a means of bringing on the next cycle of inspiration.

3. Stimulate the senses. Engage in a physical activity such as gardening, chopping wood, shoveling snow, fishing, dancing, aerobics, kneading clay, washing the dishes, tinkering with the car, and so on. Physical activity not only relaxes you, but it stimulates the senses and sensory details will stimulate your writing. It also occupies the left brain, freeing your child-like right brain.

4. Stir your creative desire by inventing writing rituals. Acquire a ball cap and imprint or embroider the word "writer" on it. Whenever it's time to write, you can tell your loved ones, "I'm wearing my writer's cap tonight." I know a writer who begins every session with an herb tea ceremony, instructing her "analytical brain to sleep so that the creative brain can come forth with a masterpiece." Speaking of ceremonies, why not conduct opening and closing ceremonies for the Writer's Olympics, starring you? Writing should be fun, so have a good time.

When I need to drop into the creative mode, I often play stimulating music, usually soundtracks and classical music, because they stir my emotions and imagination. You may find it helpful to look at a painting, photo, or object that suggests theme, character, or location to you, something that pulls you into your story. I know someone who closes her eyes and types as she visualizes.

5. Reflect on and dip into your past. The research has already been done on your life and your world. It's all inside you. You can draw from this well, especially when you need to feel the emotion your characters are feeling. But beware: There are pitfalls in autobiographical writing.

I'm often asked: Is it true I should write what I know? Can I base my script on something that happened to me years ago? How true to life should my characters be? Can I use myself and people I know? The answer is you need just enough distance from these characters and incidents that they can take on a life of their own.

Writing that is too autobiographical is usually flat, with the central character often becoming an observer of life instead of an active participant. Once I read a script about a wife who was abused by her husband. The wife did nothing but complain for 90 pages. On page 100 a neighbor rescued her. The only reason I read this all the way through was because I was paid to evaluate it. I thought to myself, "This is often how real people behave, but movie people are willful and active."

The writer had painted herself into a creative corner. She was too close to the truth. She needed to use the energy of her personal experience and create a drama with it. Even "true" stories combine characters and condense time for dramatic purposes.

The problem with autobiographical writing (and all writing, of course, is partly autobiographical) is that we love our central character. We make her perfect. We're afraid to bloody her nose. Solution? Use yourself and people you know as a basis for the fictional characters you create. Be as autobiographical as you want—you need that energy—but create enough distance to be objective. It's a razor's edge that every writer must walk.

6. Carry around a tape recorder or notebook. (There's scarcely been a writing instructor or adviser who hasn't recommended this helpful tip.) When you carry around a notebook or a microcassette recorder, you are asking your subconscious to find ideas for you. Armed with one of these tools, you'll be more observant and open to wandering ideas looking for a home. Write down, or record, these ideas and bits as they occur to you.

7. See movies in your genre. In fact, see eight good films and two dogs. Read a screenwriting book. Read screenplays—yes!—read screenplays. Page through old movie books or books of foreign films. Attend a seminar or workshop. Remember, don't stop learning in order to write; and don't stop writing in order to learn.

8. Steal. Shakespeare did. Are you greater than he? Look to the classics for plot and character ideas. Creativity is not creating something out of nothing; it's a new twist on an old idea. It's making new combinations of old patterns. It's converting the Big Dipper into the Little Ladle. Creativity is disrupting the regular thought patterns to create a new way of connecting. Gutenberg took the wine press and the coin punch and created the first printing press.

Read fairy tales, folklore, mythology, and history. Many classic plots can be easily adapted. *Romeo and Juliet* became WEST SIDE STORY and TITANIC. *Faust* became DAMN YANKEES, ROSEMARY'S BABY, WALL STREET, and BLUE CHIPS. Homer's *Odyssey* became FALLING DOWN and O BROTHER, WHERE AR THOU? *The Tempest* has been transformed into several movies. *Pygmalian* became MY FAIR LADY, which became SHE'S ALL THAT. *Moby Dick* became THE LIFE AQUATIC WITH STEVE ZISSOU.

How many *Frankenstein* plots can you identify (including a subplot of SPIDER-MAN 2)? How about *King Midas, Jack the Giant Killer,* and *Cinderella*/PRETTY WOMAN plots? Maybe it's time for your character to take the Hero's Journey (page 42). Try variations and twists of plots. How about a modern update of *Lord of the Flies* or some other classic? Just make sure that any work you adapt is in the public domain. (Refer to the index to find more information on adaptations.)

9. Visit parks, airports, parties, court rooms, crisis centers, or other places where people are likely to congregate or be in some kind of transition. This will help you look for character and story details. You may even find someone to be a character in your script.

10. Read the news. "Giant White Caught Off New England Coast" was the headline that inspired JAWS. "80-Year-Old Widow Weds 17-Year-Old Boy" inspired HAROLD AND MAUDE. TV and radio talk shows can give you ideas for topics that are current.

If you are aware of a true story that would work for a Movie-of-the-Week (and if it's not a big story that has already attracted producer-types), then buy an option to the rights of that story and write the script.

11. Understand dramatic structure. This needs to be emphasized. Sometimes you're stuck because you've violated some principle of dramatic structure. Use this in connection with #7 above. I've heard many writers credit a book or seminar for helping them work through a writing problem.

12. Be open to radical change. Be flexible. I once changed the gender of my central character to awaken a tired story. Maybe you should open your story on your current

page 30 instead of page 1. Ask questions. Ask the "what if" question. What if an alien child was accidentally left behind on Earth? What if my central character's mother is a jackal? Be open to any ideas, and any criticism. Everything goes. Nothing's written in stone until the shoot wraps.

13. Write what you care about, what you have passion for. What type of movie do you like to watch? This may be the type of movie you ought to write. Discover and follow what fascinates you.

Use the energy from pet peeves and gripes. Writing what you feel strongly about will help you keep going when the going gets tough. And keep in mind that the process of writing one script will generate ideas for other scripts and will grease the works for future creative success.

14. Try clustering. It's a technique that naturally summons your creativity and eliminates anxiety. Get a clean sheet of paper and write your story problem, concept, or character about half way down the page. Draw a circle around it.

Now brainstorm, using free-association. Whatever comes to mind, write it down, circle it, and connect it to its parent (or simply make a list). Go with any ideas that float by, regardless of how bizarre or strange. Keep your hand moving. If you have a moment when no idea comes, doodle in the corner until it does. Within about five minutes, you'll have a feeling of what you're supposed to do. An insight will come, the solution will be revealed, or a new idea will leap into your mind. If nothing happens, just stay relaxed. This is something that can't be forced.

15. Confront your blocks. List all your barriers to writing and communicate with them; that is, turn your barrier into an object or person and write a dialogue. In this free-writing exercise, an insight will come to you. Yes, you can overcome the barrier.

Keep in mind that the master key to overcoming writer's block is to realize that it's no big deal, just an occupational hazard. The real problem is when you panic. Blocks are just part of the writing process. In fact, a block is a blessing in disguise because now that your "head" is stymied, your subconscious is free to break through. So relax. Have fun. Trust the process.

Once you have a hat full of story ideas, you can search for the nuggets, the genuine movie concepts, the premises that have commercial potential.

CHECKPOINT 1

- How solid is your story idea, premise, or concept?
- Will it appeal to a mass audience?
- Is it fresh? original? provocative? commercial?
- Does hearing it make people say, "I want to see that!"?
- Is it large enough in scope to appear on the silver screen?
- Does it have "legs"—stand on its own as a story without big stars?

CHECKPOINT 2

- Do you have a working title that inspires you?
- Will this title titillate the audience? Is it a "grabber"?
- Does it convey something of your story concept or theme?
- Does it conjure up an image or an emotion?
- Is it short enough to appear on a marquee? (Not always necessary.)

CHECKPOINT 3

Imagine how your movie will be advertised. Then on a sheet of paper, sketch out the one-sheet (movie poster) for your movie.

- Is there a striking visual image that will stop passersby?
- Is there a headline that plays off the title or conveys a high concept?
- Will people want to see this movie?

Step 3—Develop Your Core Story

What is your story about? You need to know this and you need to know it now. There are producers who believe that if you can't tell them your story in a sentence or two, there isn't a story. They may be right. (For more help on script development based on the principles of this book, visit www.myscreenwriting.com or my site at www.keepwriting.com.)

A story presents a character who wants something and who is opposed by at least one other character. This opposition causes conflict and a series of critical events, all leading to the Crisis and Showdown at the end. What follows is a quick review of the critical events in virtually all dramas and comedies. (See Book I for a complete explanation of each.) Keep in mind that not all movies follow this exact pattern, and yours may not as well. The point is to create a brief outline of the main events of your story.)

CATALYST

Your story starts out in balance, but the Catalyst upsets that balance (hopefully by page 10-15), giving the central character a desire, problem, need, goal, mission, or something to do. The story now has direction and movement. In WITNESS, the Catalyst is the Amish boy witnessing the murder. It gives Detective John Book something to do—try to find the killer.

BIG EVENT

This is an event that changes your central character's life in a big way, thus the Big Event. It comes in around pages 20-30. This is where Marty travels to 1955 in BACK TO THE FUTURE. This is when John Coffey heals Paul Edgecomb of his urinary infection in THE GREEN MILE.

PINCH

About half-way through the script, there is another major plot twist. It is often a point of no return for the central character, or the moment when the character becomes fully committed, or when the motivation is strengthened or becomes clear. It's when Scarlet O'Hara vows never to go hungry again in GONE WITH THE WIND.

CRISIS

This is an event that forces a crucial decision. Often it is simply the low point in the story, the moment when all looks lost (as in E.T.), or when the lovers are separated (as in PRETTY WOMAN). It's when Benjamin Franklin Gates is abandoned underground by Ian in NATIONAL TREASURE.

SHOWDOWN

Commonly called the climax, this is when the central character and opposition character square off. It's the final battle or fight in each of the STAR WARS movies, the breakfast-table scene in MOONSTRUCK, and the final struggle between the Incredible family and Syndrome in THE INCREDIBLES.

REALIZATION

Just after the Showdown, or during it, or occasionally before it, the audience realizes that your central character has grown, changed, or figured something out. This is when the scarecrow asks Dorothy what she has learned. She knows now that there's no place like home. It's when the family admires and accepts Kevin at the end of HOME ALONE. Let's look at examples from five movies.

DAVE

Catalyst:	Dave is asked to pretend he's president.
Big Event:	The real president dies; Dave "becomes" president.
Pinch:	Dave acts as president and defies the press secretary.
Crisis:	The press secretary implicates Dave in a scandal.
Showdown:	Dave defeats the press secretary at a joint session of Congress.
Realization:	*I can help people find jobs*—Dave runs for office.

I, ROBOT

Catalyst:	Death of Dr. Lanning. Del wonders why Dr. Lanning would kill himself.
Big Event:	Del finds Sonny, and believes he is Dr. Lanning's killer.
Pinch:	Del survives the robot attack and wonders, "What do you want from me?"
Crisis:	NS-5s come online. Humanity is subject to the robots.
Showdown:	Del battles and defeats his true opponent, VIKI.
Realization:	*I no longer feel a bias against robots.*

Note: There's a strong subplot of Sonny finding his purpose.

TWINS

Catalyst:	Vincent meets his brother Julius.
Big Event:	Vincent is saved by his brother, so he takes him in.
Pinch:	Vincent meets the scientist; believes Julius really is his brother.
Crisis:	Vincent must choose between his brother and $5 million.
Showdown:	Together, Vincent and Julius trick the bad guy.
Realization:	*I'm not genetic garbage*—Vincent finds his mother.

MY BIG FAT GREEK WEDDING

Catalyst:	Ian walks into the restaurant.
Big Event:	Ian sees Toula working at the travel agency.
Pinch:	Ian proposes to Toula.
Crisis:	Toula's father says, "This won't work."
Showdown:	Wedding and Reception.
Realization:	*My family may be obnoxious, but they'll always be there for me.*

THE HAND THAT ROCKS THE CRADLE

	Peyton (Central Character)	Claire (Protagonist)
Catalyst:	Hub's suicide; no family	Molested by doctor
Big Event:	Gets Claire to hire her	Hires Peyton
Pinch:	Gets Solomon kicked out	Fires Solomon
Crisis:	Kicked out of the house	Asthma attack
Showdown:	Battle with Claire	Battle with Peyton
Realization:	None	*I trust my instincts* (trusts Solomon w/child)

CHECKPOINT 4

Write the *TV Guide* logline for your story.
- Who is your central character?
- What is his/her main goal? (This is the goal that drives the story.)
- Why is the goal so important to him/her?
- Who is trying to stop your character from achieving the goal?

CHECKPOINT 5

Identify the parameters of your story.
- What is the genre? (Action/adventure, thriller, romantic comedy, etc.)
- What is the time and setting?
- What is the emotional atmosphere, and the mood?
- What, if any, story or character limits exist?

CHECKPOINT 6

- What is the Catalyst that gives your central character a direction?
- What Big Event really impacts your character's life?
- Is there a strong, rising conflict throughout Act 2?
- Does the conflict build? or just become repetitive?
- Is there a Pinch, a twist in the middle, that divides Act 2 in half and more fully motivates your character?
- What terrible Crisis will your character face?
- Will the Crisis force a life/death decision, and/or make the audience fret about how things will turn out in the end?
- How does your story end? What is the Showdown?
- In the end, does your character learn something new?
    Or, is his/her growth (positive or negative) made apparent?
    Or, does he/she receive any recognition in the end?

CHECKPOINT 7

Now write out your core story in three paragraphs, one for the beginning, one for the middle, and one for the end. Paragraph 1 will end with the Big Event; paragraph 2 with the Crisis. Obviously, you cannot include all of the characters in this brief synopsis. Once this is done, re-evaluate your story.

Step 4—Create your movie people

Your central character wants something specific. That something is the goal. The character, who is conscious of this desire, strives for it throughout most of the story. Of course, the character is opposed by at least one other person.

In most stories, the character also has an inner need, something she may not be consciously aware of until the Crisis. This need is a yearning for the one thing that will bring true happiness or fulfillment to the character. The need is blocked by a flaw, usually a form of selfishness. The flaw emerges from a past traumatic event—the backstory.

The main plot of most movies is driven by the goal. It's the Outside/Action Story.

The main subplot is driven by the need. It's the Inside/Emotional Story. It is usually focused on the primary relationship in the story. It's concerned with character dynamics.

The Outside/Action Story is the spine; it holds things together. The Inside/Emotional Story is the heart; it touches the audience. To make the Outside/Action Story and Inside/Emotional Story work, you need to understand your movie people and how they function. (See pages 30-35 for a detailed explanation.)

CHECKPOINT 8

Does your central character have the following?

- An outside goal that the audience will care about?
- A powerful, personal motivation for achieving the goal?
- An opposition character in a position of strength, capable of doing great damage?
- The will to act against opposition, and to learn and grow?
- Human emotions, traits, values, and imperfections that people can identify with?

- A particular point of view of life, the world, and/or self, giving rise to attitudes?
- Details, extensions, idiosyncrasies, and/or expressions that are uniquely his/hers?
- A life and voice (dialogue) of his/her own?
- A key event from the past that has given rise to a character flaw?
- An inner need that he/she may be unaware of at first?

CHECKPOINT 9

Evaluate your other main characters (and especially your opposition character) by the criteria of Checkpoint 8. Each should have at least a goal or intention in the story. The more depth you can give them, the more interesting they will appear.

CHECKPOINT 10

Your movie people have sociological, psychological, and physiological characteristics. Use the following to provoke your creative thought.

Sociology

Occupation	Education	Criminal record
Birthplace/upbringing	Ethnic roots	Religion
Past/present home life	Political views	Social status
Hobbies	Affiliations	Private life
Work history	Work environment	Personal life

Physiology

Height/weight	Build or figure	Attractiveness
Appearance	Hair/eyes	Voice quality
Defects/scars	Health/strength	Complexion
Clothing	Physical skills	Athletic ability

Psychology

Fears/phobias	Secrets	Attitudes
Prejudices	Values/beliefs	Inhibitions
Pet peeves	Complexes	Addictions
Superstitions	Habits	Moral stands
Ambitions	Motivations	Temperament
Personal problems	Imagination	Likes/dislikes
Intelligence	Disposition	

CHECKPOINT 11

These are questions to ask of any of your movie people:

- How do you handle stress, pressure, relationships, problems, emotion?
- Are you extroverted or shy? intuitive or analytical? active or passive?
- What's your most traumatic experience? most thrilling experience?
- Essentially, who are you? What is at your core?
- What is your dominant trait?
- What do you do and think when you're alone and no one will know?
- How do you feel about yourself?
- How do you feel about the other people in the story?
- Who are the most important people in your life?
- How do you relate to each?
- What's the worst (and best) thing that could happen to you?
- What are you doing tonight? tomorrow?
- Where do you want to be ten years from now?

CHECKPOINT 12

- How does your central character grow or change throughout the story?
- How is your character different at the end of the story?
- What does he/she know at the end that he/she did not know at the beginning?
- What is your character's perception of reality?
- Does that perception change by the end of the story?
- What is each character's perception of the other characters in the story?
- Is your protagonist likeable?
- Will the audience identify with your central character on some level?
- Does your central character have depth, with both strengths and weaknesses?
- Will the two key roles attract stars?

CHECKPOINT 13

- What is the theme or message of your story?
- What are you trying to say?
- Will the end of your story say it for you without being preachy?
  (The theme may not be evident to you until later in your writing.)

CHECKPOINT 14

Revise your three-paragraph synopsis to incorporate any changes to your story.

Step 5—Step-out your story

This is where you find out if your story is going to work or not. Here, you outline your story. This work will make the actual writing much easier than it would ordinarily be.

CHECKPOINT 15

Plot the action of your story. Identify your central character's action plot and emotional subplot. Look at your other movie people; identify their goals. Their goals will drive their individual plots (actually subplots). Do these various plotlines intersect, resulting in adequate conflict for drama or comedy?

CHECKPOINT 16

Write a four-page synopsis or treatment (double-spaced). Summarize the beginning of your story in one page, the middle in two pages, and the end in one page. Focus on two to four main characters, the key events (plot points), and the emotional undercurrent of the story. Although somewhat difficult, this exercise will help tremendously in laying a strong foundation for your story. Now answer these questions:

- Is the central conflict of the story clearly defined?
- Are the character's goal and need clear?
- Are the stakes of the story big enough for a commercial movie?
- Does the story evoke an emotional response?
- Will the audience cry, get angry, laugh, get scared, fall in love, get excited, etc.?
- What makes this story unique, fresh, and original?
- Is your story too predictable? Have we seen this before?
- Are the facts of the story plausible? (They don't have to be possible, just plausible.)
- Will people be emotionally satisfied at the end?

CHECKPOINT 17

Step-out your script. This is a crucial step. Traditionally, the step outline consists of a series of 3" x 5" cards, one card for each scene or dramatic unit. Consider attaching these cards (or Post-it notes) to a wall, table, or corkboard to see the entire story at once.

At the top of each card write the master scene heading, then summarize the action of the scene in a sentence or short paragraph, emphasizing the essential action and purpose of the scene. Some writers like to list the characters appearing in the scene in the lower left-hand corner of the card. That way, they can see who is where at a glance.

You can use the lower right-hand corner for pacing and tracking plots. Some writers use a highlighter and identify plots by color. Blue is the action story, red is the love story, and so on.

You can identify scenes as fast or slow, action or dialogue. If you discover that you have four dialogue scenes in a row, all with the same characters, you can adjust this pacing problem by moving scenes around, cross-cutting with action scenes, condensing, or even omitting an unnecessary scene.

If additional ideas come to you, jot them down on blank cards. You'll end up with 30-100 cards, depending on the nature of the story.

Of course, you don't have to use 3" x 5" cards. You can step-out your story on your computer—whatever works for you. Once completed, your step outline will become the basis for writing your script.

Visit my web site at www.keepwriting.com for a PowerPoint tool for storyboarding and organizing your scenes.

CHECKPOINT 18

Now that your step outline is complete, ask yourself these questions:

- Are your scenes well-paced?
- Do the major turning points come at about the right time?
- Do things just happen, or is there a cause-and-effect relationship between character actions?
- Do the subplots intersect with the main plot, creating new complications?
- Are your characters' actions motivated, or do they exist just to make the story work?

- Do action, conflict, and dramatic tension build, or just repeat and become static?
- Are your central and opposition characters forced to take stronger and stronger actions?
- Does the conflict rise naturally to a crisis/climax?

Step 6—Write your first draft

Write your first draft from the heart. Keep your head out of it as much as possible. It's okay to change the story. It's okay to overwrite. It's okay to include too much dialogue. Everything goes, everything flows.

Once this draft is completed, you may wish to register it with the Writers Guild of America. This is optional since you will register it again after your final polish.

CHECKPOINT 19

It is absolutely imperative that you do the following upon completion of the first draft:

1. Take at least two weeks off from your script. Let it ferment for a while. You will be much more objective for the pre-revision analysis (Checkpoints 20-24). During this time you may want to read a book, go to a seminar, see movies of the same genre, or read scripts, or turn your attention to other things.

2. Reward yourself in some way that makes you feel good about being the next great screenwriter.

Step 7—Make the necessary revisions

Before writing the second draft, consider letting your hot property cool off. Sit on it a couple of weeks, then craft your second draft from your head. Here, you become a script surgeon. Whittle down the dialogue; remove unnecessary narration, flashbacks, dream sequences, and so on. You become an analyst in every way you can define that word. Once this work is completed, polish your script until you are ready to present your wonder to Hollywood. The following checkpoints will help you evaluate your revisions.

CHECKPOINT 20

Review Checkpoints 1-19. Do not skip this checkpoint.

CHECKPOINT 21 (THE SCRIPT ITSELF)

- Is your script too technical, too complex, or too difficult to understand?
- Will your script require a huge budget with unshootable scenes, such as herds of camels crossing the San Diego Freeway? Other possible big-budget problems: special effects, period settings, exotic locations, too many arenas or locations, large cast, water, and animals.
- Is your script's budget about right for its market?
- Have you followed the rules of formatting and presentation as described in Book III?
- Have you written thoughts, feelings, memories, or anything else that cannot appear on the screen?
- When you read you script, do you stop reading? At that point, there is likely to be a problem.

CHECKPOINT 22 (DIALOGUE)

- Is the dialogue "too on the nose"?
- Do your characters say exactly what they feel?
- Does each character speak with his/her own voice, vocabulary, slang, rhythm, and style?
- Is the dialogue crisp, original, clever, compelling, and lean?
- Are individual speeches too long or encumbered with more than one thought?
- Does the story rely too heavily on dialogue?
- Are your dialogue scenes too long?
- Are there too many scenes with talking heads?
- Are you telling when you could be showing?
- Is the comedy *trying* to be funny, or is it naturally funny?

CHECKPOINT 23 (EXPOSITION)

- Are you boring your audience by telling too much too soon?
- Are you confusing your audience with too little information?
- Are you giving your audience just enough exposition to keep them on the edge of their seats?
- Is your exposition revealed through conflict or through static dialogue?
- Have you used flashbacks as a crutch or as a means to move the story forward?

CHECKPOINT 24 (CHARACTER AND STORY)

- Will the reader root for your hero?
- Will the reader have an emotional identification with the hero?
- Are your characters believable? Are they humans with dimension?
- Do your characters come across as retreads whom we've seen before?
- Do any of your characters grow or change throughout the story?
- Is there a moment at the end when this growth will be recognized by the reader?
- When will the reader cry?
- Is the story too gimmicky, relying too heavily on nudity, violence, shock, or special effects?
- Will the first 5-10 pages capture the reader's interest?
- Do the first 20-30 pages set up the central conflict?

- Does the middle build in intensity toward the Showdown at the end?
- Is the story, plot, or ending too predictable?
- Are all the loose ends tied up in the Denouement (the resolution after the Showdown)?

CHECKPOINT 25

Sometimes it just doesn't work. You have story problems, character problems, and you're not quite sure how to solve them. When you are blocked or you sense something is wrong, what can you do?

1. Don't panic. We all go through this. Realize that you have the ability to solve your problems.

2. Take two weeks off. Don't worry about it. You may get inspiration during this period because you will be more relaxed.

3. Read a book; go to a seminar; flick-out. Many of my "breakthroughs" have come on a plane while reading a book about writing.

4. Often you actually know where the trouble is. You have a gnawing feeling inside about something in your story, or perhaps a sense that "something" is wrong, but you ignore it because you don't want to do a major rewrite. In my script-analysis work, I don't know how many times a writer has told me the following: "I kinda knew what was wrong, but I guess I needed you to confirm it." The point is this: You have an inner sense that you must learn to trust, even when it makes the writing process uncomfortable and the rewriting painful. When you read your script through, if you naturally stop reading at some point, that often signals a problem.

5. Get feedback from other writers or consider using a script consultant.

6. Study mythology (Christopher Vogler's *Writer's Journey*) and understand your genre.

7. Revise your four-page synopsis. Sometimes this helps you focus and get back on track.

8. Ask stupid questions. Don't be afraid to challenge your own ideas. Ask "What if?" Nothing is sacred. Anything goes. Maybe your hero should be the villain.

9. When revising, if solving one problem also solves another problem, you're on the right track.

10. Create a Character/Action Grid. Essentially, this is a mini step-outline, constructed on a few sheets of paper. Use it to identify each character's purpose and actions in the story. Most writers use it for their five to seven main characters.

On the next three pages you will find a format for the Character/Action Grid, developed by Donna Davidson and me. When Donna read the first edition of my book, she expanded my original tool for her own use. Donna has since published four novels and used the Grid for each. Feel free to photocopy these three sheets for your personal use. As you can see, the Character/Action Grid has two sections: 1) Character and Story (page 106), and 2) Actions (page 108).

Character and story

The sheet on page 106 allows you to develop four main characters on one page. The sheet on page 107 is exactly the same, except it is designed for just one character—it gives you more room to write. Not every cell in the grid needs to be filled. Make this tool *your* tool. Create your own categories. Better yet, create your own Grid.

At the bottom of the Grid page 106, you have room to think through your main turning points in terms of each character. Obviously, not each character will be involved with each turning point.

Actions

You will not be able to plot your entire screenplay on just one sheet of paper (page 108). You may need two or three of these sheets. In the second row of the Grid, write the names of your five main characters. Then in the remaining rows and columns simply list each action a character takes. Dialogue can be considered action when it constitutes or creates movement. When Rose tells Jack in TITANIC (after Sunday service) that she cannot see him again and is returning to her fiancé, that is an action.

The Grid allows you to see the entire story on just a few sheets of paper. It helps you notice if a character is static or uninvolved in the action, or if a character's actions are repetitive rather than building. In other words, you can more readily see if you have a rising conflict or a stagnant story.

The Grid helps with pacing and spacing. Is there a major twist every so often? Are the subplots supporting the main plot? Are character actions crisscrossing throughout the story? Are all of your other major characters fully involved in the story? Does a character disappear for half the story? (That can be good or bad, depending on the story.)

I recommend use of the Grid after the first draft or whenever you are stuck. But you are the captain of your ship. Use it when you wish or not at all.

CHARACTER/ACTION GRID — Character and Story				
Title, genre, concept				
Theme or message				
CHARACTERS				
Role, purpose in story				
Occupation				
Conscious goal				
Personal motivation				
Inner need				
Flaw blocking need				
Backstory				
Dominant, core trait				
Other good & bad traits				
Imperfections, quirks				
Skills, knowledge, props				
Point-of-view, attitudes				
Dialogue style				
Physiology				
Psychology, Sociology				
Relationship w/others				
Catalyst				
Big Event				
Crisis				
Showdown				
Realization				
Denouement				

CHARACTER/ACTION GRID — Character and Story	
Title, genre, concept	
Theme or message	
NAME OF CHARACTER:	
Role, purpose in story	
Occupation	
Conscious goal	
Personal motivation	
Inner need	
Flaw blocking need	
Backstory	
Dominant, core trait	
Other good & bad traits	
Imperfections, quirks	
Skills, knowledge, props	
Point-of-view, attitudes	
Dialogue style	
Physiology	
Psychology, Sociology	
Relationship w/others	
Catalyst	
Big Event	
Crisis	
Showdown	
Realization	
Denouement	

CHARACTER/ACTION GRID — Actions				

Ferdi Strickler, a Swiss client of mine, told me that he used the Character/Action Grid to create a Character/Character Grid. In this Grid, "every character tells what he thinks about the other characters, and of course, what he thinks about himself." I like this idea and any idea that adapts a tool for your specific purpose.

Below, you will find an example of a partially completed Character/Action Grid.

Character/Action Grid example
I designed the following story idea as a small example of how to use the Grid. I created only three characters. I won't take you through the entire grid with them, nor will I outline the entire story. I just want to give you a feel for the Grid's use. You will want to list every important action of your main characters from the beginning to the end of the story.

CHARACTER/ACTION GRID — Character and Story

Char:	JIM	SALLY	MAX
Role:	Central character/hero	Love interest, 2nd opp.	Main opposition
Occ:	Investigative journalist	Animal-rights advocate	Circus owner
Goal:	Exploit Blimpo the Elephant for a story	Save Blimpo the Elephant from exploitation	#1 Circus Act in U.S.
Motive:	Salvage career	Blimpo saves her life (later)	Prove he's not a loser
Need:	Be more caring	Trust and love Jim	Respect animals
Flaw:	Anything for a story	Only trusts animals	Inhumane

CHARACTER/ACTION GRID — Actions

JIM	SALLY	MAX
Fired, but then gets last chance		
Dumped by Sally	Dumps Jim; can't trust him	Whips Blimpo
	Kidnaps Blimpo; chased	Chases Sally
	Hides Blimpo in Jim's yard	
Next morning: Finds Blimpo		

Continue outlining your characters' actions to the end. When the Grid is completed, you will be able to see your entire story on 1-3 pages. The structure, pacing, motivation, and plotlines will be easier to work with.

CHECKPOINT 26

Before you submit your script, do the following:
- Get feedback from writers' group members.
- Consider hiring a professional reader or script analyst.
- Review Checkpoints 1-24 one last time.
- Make adjustments. Is your script a "good read"?
- Be sure the script looks 100% professional and that it is formatted correctly.
- Register your script with the Writers Guild of America.
- Create a strategic marketing plan (see Book V).

PROPER FORMATTING TECHNIQUE

BOOK III

A Style Guide

How to use this guide to craft a compelling and professional screenplay

This book shows you how to correctly format your *spec* screenplay, TV drama, or sitcom script. The word *spec* means you are writing it on *speculation* that you will sell it later; in other words, you are not being paid to write it. This Book (and Book IV) also teaches you about writing and writing *style*.

Formatting is a key element of screenwriting, and is inseparable from it. You will find that as your formatting knowledge increases, the quality of your writing will improve. Rather than viewing proper format as a limiting burden, see it as an integral part of the writing process that frees you to communicate your story clearly to other professionals. Anyone can define formatting "rules." Both this book and Book IV show you how to apply proper formatting technique to your spec story project.

Professional scripts sometimes vary slightly in formatting style, and yet they all look basically the same. There are surprisingly few absolutes, and professionals often disagree on this point or that. These formatting guidelines are like accounting principles—they are "generally accepted" by the industry. They will increase your script's chances of being accepted by agents, producers, directors, and talent (actors and actresses).

This book is both a user-friendly guide and a reference book. It contains clear, how-to instructions and dozens of sample scenes and other examples. You can easily find information in any of the following ways.

1. Use the **index** (pages 195-197) to quickly find any subject area or term. Those subject areas and terms can also be found in the index at the end of the book.

2. Read the entire **book** from beginning to end as a style guide. (This is what I recommend.) The book contains numerous how-to instructions, explanations, and clear examples.

3. Read the three-page **sample script** on pages 118-121. It contains *reference codes* identified by letters of the alphabet. Each reference code that you see can be cross-referenced to the same reference code later in the book. For example, the reference code [T] can be found next to the use of OFF SCREEN in the sample script on page 121; that reference code corresponds to an explanation of OFF SCREEN on page 171. These codes appear in alphabetical order in the body of the text, making them easy to find.

4. Study specific areas of interest to you. Here is how the book is laid out.

5. Check the glossary on page 194 for terms not defined elsewhere.

Marking pages with paper clips or Post-it flags will give you fast access to information of particular interest, such as the first page of the formatting index, for example.

All sample scenes and excerpts appear just as they would in an actual script, right down to the 12-point Courier New font. The format used for feature-length screenplays is also used for TV movies and hour-long TV dramas. One last thing to keep in mind before going on—you are writing a *spec* script. Let's discuss that in detail.

THE *SPEC* SCRIPT

The *spec* script is the *selling* script, sometimes called the *writer's draft*. You write it with the idea of selling it later or circulating it as a sample. Once it is sold and goes into pre-production, it will be transformed into a *shooting* script, also known as the *production draft*. The *spec*-script style avoids camera angles, editing directions, and technical intrusions. You may use these tools, but only when necessary to clarify the story. Scenes are not numbered in the spec script; that's done by the production secretary after your script is sold.

All the camera and editing directions in the world cannot save a bad story, but too much technical intrusion can make even the best story a chore to read. The main reason you write a *spec* script is to excite professional readers about your story. So concentrate on the story and leave the direction to the director and the editing to the editor. In this Book, and especially in Book IV, I will show you how to direct the camera without using camera directions. That is how you show professionals that you are capable of writing a shooting script version of your spec script.

Virtually every script you buy from a script service or bookstore, or view in a script library, is a *shooting* script or a variation thereof. Many screenwriting books contain formatting instructions for *shooting* scripts only, and some professional writers and producers still recommend the *shooting* script format because it's what they've always used and it's what working writers use when they are hired to write directly for a production.

However, the *shooting* script is not a joy to read for agents, executives, and readers who must plow through dozens of scripts every week, week after week. The technical directions clutter the script and intrude on the reading experience. That's fine if the script is about to be produced, but it works against you if you want your story to flow smoothly to the reader, enticing him/her to buy or recommend it to the higher-ups.

Both script styles (spec and shooting) utilize the same standard screenplay formatting rules—master scene headings in CAPS, double-space to narrative description, dialogue indented, and so on. And the *spec* script occasionally employs some *shooting* script terms: MONTAGE, FLASHBACK, INSERT for notes and letters, and INTERCUT for telephone conversations.

The essential difference between the two styles is this: The *shooting* script format requires specific technical instructions so that the director, crew, and cast can more easily perform in the shoot. The *spec* script format emphasizes clear, unencumbered visual writing to sell agents and producers on a great story. The following two examples illustrate the difference.

Shooting script example #1:

```
ANGLE ON JIM

He bats his eyes at Alicia.

ANOTHER ANGLE

He winks.
```

Spec script example #1:

```
Jim bats his eyes at Alicia, then winks.
```

Shooting script example #2:

```
Steve takes a puff from the pipe.

FX. - WE SEE STEVE LEVITATE SLOWLY ABOVE THE FLOOR, STILL IN
HIS SQUATTED POSITION.

STEVE'S POV — We then SEE the muted COLORS of the room begin
to BRIGHTEN intensely.
```

Spec script example #2:

```
Steve, sitting cross-legged on the floor, takes a puff from
the pipe.

Slowly he levitates in the same cross-legged position.

He sees the muted colors of the room brighten intensely.
```

Do you see how much easier the spec examples are to read? In effect, the writer directs the camera without using camera directions and identifies special effects without using special language.

SCREENWRITING SOFTWARE

Most screenwriting software is designed for (and promoted by) professional writers who write shooting scripts. Thus, spec writers sometimes find that they must disable some functions.

For example, the term CONTINUED does *not* need to appear at the top and bottom of each page of a spec script. When a character speaks, is interrupted by action, and then continues his speech, neither the term "continuing" nor the terms "CONT'D" or "cont'd" need to be used. They are shooting-script conventions. However, if your software automatically inserts these terms and you absolutely can't find a way to disable them, you'll probably be fine. This is not a major issue, and your script is not likely going to be thrown out just for that little peccadillo.

Whatever screenwriting software you own, it will probably work just fine for you. There are several that I like, including *Movie Magic Screenwriter.* For the *spec* scriptwriter (you),

I have designed easy-to-use, reasonably priced screenwriting software called *Dr. Format Screenwriting Software*. For information, visit my web site at www.keepwriting.com.

A personal note on the following sample script: In response to owners of past editions of the Bible *who have written me concerning the content of the sample script that follows, I feel compelled to explain that the scenes romanticize my occasional teaching practice of tossing a candy mint to any student who makes a brilliant comment or asks a profound question.*

THE PERSPICACIOUS PROFESSOR

by

David Trottier

1234 William Goldman Dr.
Hollywood, CA 90028
213/555-6789
dave@keepwriting.com

THE PERSPICACIOUS PROFESSOR

FADE IN: [A]

[F]
EXT. UNIVERSITY CAMPUS — DAY

A sign on an old ivy-covered building reads: "CINEMA DEPT." [K]

[C]
INT. SMALL CLASSROOM - DAY [B]

Twenty students sit in rapt attention while the buff DR. FORMAT [I]
scrawls "FORMATTING" on the board. Slung over his shoulder is a
"Sea World"-type pouch filled with candy mints rather than fish.

[I]
CHARLIE kicks back near a window, raises his hand. Two BUZZING [L]
flies vie for territorial rights to the chocolate on his face.

                    CHARLIE
          How do you handle phone calls?

The professor moonwalks to Charlie's desk carrying a demo phone.

          [R]   DR. FORMAT
          Excellent question, my man.

He tosses the grateful boy a candy mint. Charlie catches it on
his nose and barks like a seal, looking for laughs. [M]

Outside Charlie's window, CALCUTTA COTTER (19) in pigtails and [G]
a pinafore yanks someone out of the phone booth and steps in.

EXT. CLASSROOM - DAY [H]

                    [J]
With phone in hand, she turns to the classroom window and frowns at
what she sees -- the professor doing cartwheels down the aisle. [G]

                    WOMAN'S VOICE (V.O.) [U]
          Make him pay, Calcutta.

INTERCUT — CALCUTTA'S PHONE BOOTH/DEAN ZACK'S OFFICE [V]

The voice belongs to DEAN ZELDA ZACK who stands at her polished
desk with a swagger stick tucked under her arm.

                    CALCUTTA
          It'll work?

                    DEAN ZACK
          Stumps him every time.

2.

The dean chortles. Calcutta smiles, then SLAMS the receiver.

INT. CLASSROOM - DAY
                    [N]
The professor's hand SLAMS the receiver of his demonstrator phone.

The students simmer with interest.

The door swings open. Calcutta steps in and shuffles to her desk.

                    DR. FORMAT
        [W] Remember. It's gotta be lean.
            Description ... dialogue.
                (arching his brow)
        All lean, my pets -- lean!

He pirouettes and clicks his heels, to his students' delight.

Calcutta raises her arm and wags it aggressively.

                    CALCUTTA

        The tabs. Where do I set them?

A hush fades into silence. Dr. format wilts.

The students exchange questioning glances as Dr. F. stumbles
dizzily to his desk. He gazes blankly ahead to a spinning room. [O]

MONTAGE - THE PROFESSOR'S TRANCE [D]

-- The room spins.

-- He jabs at a giant tab key on a keyboard to no effect. In
   frustration, he hurls the computer out the window.

-- Dean Zelda Zack rides up to the same window on her swagger
   stick. She transforms into a witch, cackles, and rides off.

-- The spinning room slows to a stop. [M]

BACK TO THE CLASSROOM

The students are horrified. Calcutta smiles gleefully.

Dr. Format looks like he's just been hit by a Mike Tyson punch.

                    CHARLIE
        Our dear professor. What's wrong?

120

Several students clench the edges of their desks. Can he do it?

                    CHARLIE (O.S.) [T]
          He's done for.

Murmurs of agreement. The professor stares at his shoes and
makes an attempt at moonwalking. His feet start remembering.

                    DR. FORMAT
          Where to set your tabs. Assume
          a left margin at ... um ... at fifteen.

The students brighten in their seats. Calcutta frowns.

The professor is now in a serious moonwalking stride.

                    DR. FORMAT [S]
                  (the master)
          Dialogue at twenty-five.
          Wrylies at thirty-one ...

Calcutta nervously chews a pigtail.

                    DR. FORMAT [S]
          ... And then the character's name
          in caps! At thirty-seven!

Cheers and kudos. The professor's moonwalk has taken him to
Calcutta's desk, where he towers over her limp form.

                    DR. FORMAT [S]
          But why, Calcutta? Why?

                    CALCUTTA
          Cuz everyone else always gets a
          candy, even Charlie, and I don't.

Her shoulders heave in heavy sobs.

INSERT - THE PROFESSOR'S POUCH [E]

His fingers deftly lift a candy mint.

BACK TO THE CLASSROOM [E]

Calcutta lifts her head just as he flicks the candy into the air.
She catches it on her nose, barks like a seal, and consumes it
greedily. The students cheer.

As the professor pats her head, her pigtails rise as if to extend
her radiant smile.

Formatting in a nutshell

There are three parts of a screenplay: *headings*, *narrative description*, and *dialogue*.

1. Headings (slug lines)
There are three types of headings.
     A. Master scene headings, which consists of three main parts:
          1. Camera location (EXT. or INT.)
          2. Scene location
          3. Time (DAY or NIGHT)
     B. Secondary scene headings
     C. Special headings for flashbacks, dreams, montages, series of shots, and so on.

2. Narrative description
The word "narrative" loosely means *story*, and it consists of three elements:
     A. Action
     B. Setting and character (visual images)
     C. Sounds

3. Dialogue
The dialogue block consists of three parts.
     A. The *character cue*, or name of the person speaking, which always appears in CAPS.
     B. The *parenthetical* or *actor's direction* or *wryly*. This is optional.
     C. The *speech*.

What follows is an example of the three parts of a spec screenplay, the three parts of a master scene heading, the three elements of narrative description, and the three parts of a dialogue block.

```
EXT. FOREST — NIGHT

The moon shines on the pale, serene face of ELEANOR SAWYER.

                    ELEANOR
             (softly)
        Midnight.

She mounts a horse and rides into the darkness, the hoof
beats muffled by the leaves and flora on the forest floor.
```

Overall screenplay appearance

THE COVER AND CONTENTS

Physically, a screenplay consists of a front cover (of solid-color index stock, at least 65-pound, preferably 110-pound), a title page (or *fly page*), the pages of the script itself (printed on one side only), and a back cover—all 8½" x 11", all three-hole punched. That's it.

Nothing should appear on the front cover—not even the title. Once an agent or producer receives your script, the script will be placed horizontally on a stack. Someone will write your title on the side binding with a magic marker. Don't do it for them.

THE BINDING

To bind the script together, use Acco (or similar brand) No. 5 round-head brass fasteners, 1¼" in length. (Some people like to use No. 6.) It is fashionable to place the fasteners (or "brads") in the first and third hole and leave the middle hole empty. Do not use flimsy brads. A very distant second choice for binding is the screw-in brads. Do not bind a script in any other way. The above method makes it easy for producers and others excited about your work to make photocopies to pass around, which is something you want.

SCRIPT LENGTH

Your script should be about 100-120 pages—ideally, about 100-105 for a comedy and 110 for a drama.

THE 17 COMMANDMENTS

Certain things turn off most professional readers, agents, and producers. Here's a list of things to avoid.

1. Don't include fancy covers, artwork, illustrations, or storyboards.
2. Don't number the scenes. This is done after the script is sold.
3. Don't use fancy fonts or proportional-pitch fonts, only 12-point Courier or Courier New.
4. Don't justify right margins. Leave the right margin ragged.
5. Don't bold or italicize.
6. Don't use camera and editing directions unless necessary to move the story forward.
7. Don't date your script in any way. Scripts get old fast.
8. Don't write "First Draft," "Final Draft," or any draft.
9. Don't include a suggested cast list or character list with bios, unless requested.
10. Don't include a list of characters or sets.
11. Don't include a synopsis unless requested—you are selling your ability to write.
12. Don't include a budget.
13. Don't put the title or your name at the top of each page (as a header).
14. Don't ignore errors in spelling, grammar, and punctuation.
15. Don't "cheat" by using thinner margins, by squeezing more onto a page, by using a smaller typeface, or by widening dialogue lines beyond the standard 3 to 3.5 inches. (See "When to break the rules" in Book IV.)
16. Don't use CONTINUED or CONT'D unless your software leaves you no choice.
17. Don't send out a script that is over 120 pages.

The above rules may seem nitpicky, but they're easy to comply with, and adhering to them places you in the realm of the professional writer in the know, and helps you make a good first impression. Obviously, if your script is wonderful, but breaks one of these commandments, it is not going to be rejected. But why not give yourself every advantage to make sure that your script is read in the first place?

In addition, some agents and producers may make a request that violates one or more of these conventions. In such a case, give the agent or producer what he or she requests.

THE TITLE PAGE

The title page you see in the sample script is correct for a script that has not yet found an agent. You may add quotation marks around the title if you wish, or underscore it, or both. If there are two or more writers and they worked together and contributed equally, use an *ampersand* instead of the word *and*. For example:

"NAZIS IN SPACE"

by

Bart Snarf & Buffy Bucksaw

When the word *and* is used, it means a writer was brought in later to rewrite the first writer's script. In other words, they didn't work together.

Your address, phone number, and e-mail address (if you have one) should appear in the lower right corner where it can be easily seen. Nothing else needs to be on the title page. Once your script has found an agent, then the agent's contact information will appear on the title page. Your agent will be able to show you how to do that.

If you register your script with the Writers Guild (WGA), you may indicate your registration on the lower left corner of the title page of your script, as follows: Registered WGAw. (Use "WGAe" if you registered with the East Coast office.) However, you do *not* need to type your WGA registration number, *nor* do you need to type a notice on your script to validate your registration rights. Thus, there is no reason to include that information on your title page. If you register your script with the Copyright Office, then place your copyright notice in the lower left corner. (Note: The Writer's Guild and copyright will be discussed at length in the first chapter of Book V.)

TYPEFACE

Always use Courier or Courier New 12-point font. Why must it be just that font? Because Courier 12-point is the industry standard. Prior to the advent of the computer, screenwriters used the regular PICA typewriter font. It was a 10-pitch font, meaning that no matter what characters you typed, those characters would be equally spaced so that any ten characters strung one after the other would equal one inch. It also retained the "one page equals one minute of screen time" industry standard of the time. And

Courier 12-point does the same today. For that reason, even today's screenplays look like they were typed with a typewriter.

Virtually all other fonts are *proportional-pitch* fonts. They compress characters together to get more words on a line, such as what you see in magazines and books. With a proportional-pitch font, each character has a different width or *pitch*. Here's an example.

1234567890 — This is a Sabon 12-point font. It is a proportional-pitch font. Ten characters measure less than an inch in width.

```
1234567890 -- This is a Courier 12-point font. It is a non-
proportional font, or fixed-pitch font. You can choose any
ten characters in this font, and they will measure one inch
in width. This is what you use in a screenplay. It looks
like it's typed using a typewriter. Also, please notice that
the right margin in this example is ragged.
```

All of the examples in this format guidebook are in Courier New so that they appear exactly the way they would appear in a script.

MARGINS

Because scripts are three-hole punched, the left margin should be 1.5 inches, the right margin a half inch to 1.25 inches. I recommend one inch for the right margin. The top and bottom margins should be one inch each. Assuming the standard ten characters per inch (Courier 12-point font), that would mean a left margin at 15 spaces (1.5 inches from the left edge of the paper). The right margin can be anywhere from a half inch to 1.25 inches from the right edge of the paper. As already stated, the right margin should be ragged.

If you live outside the U.S. and use standard A4 paper, just add another 5/8 inch (about 15mm) to the bottom margin.

TABS

Although variations abound, let these standards guide you in setting your tabs:

- Left margin at 15 spaces (1.5 inches) from the left edge of the page.
- Dialogue at 25 spaces (2.5 inches); that's 10 spaces from the *left margin*.

- Actor's instructions at 31 (3.1 inches); that's 16 spaces from the *left margin*.
- Character's name at 37 (3.7 inches); that's 22 spaces from the *left margin*.

Make sure your dialogue does not extend beyond 60 spaces (6.0 inches) from the left edge of the page (in other words, a line of dialogue should be no wider than 3.5 inches, although some writers limit themselves to 3.0 inches), and actor's instructions beyond 50 spaces.

Parentheticals (actor's direction) should not be wider than 2 inches.

```
                    DR. FORMAT
            (spinning around in
              his chair)
        A dialogue block should appear
        like this.
```

The above guides are not written in stone—some writers indent 12 or 14 for dialogue, some indent 7 or 8 for actor's instructions, etc. As mentioned, a ragged right margin is preferred to a justified right margin.

LINE SPACING

A script page should contain about 54 to 55 lines. This does not include 2 lines for the page number and the line after the page number. If you add many more than that, the page will look cramped. If your software program allows for one or two lines more than the standard, don't be concerned. For more information on line spacing, see "When to break the rules" in Book IV.

PAGE NUMBERS

Page numbers should appear in the upper right, flush to the right margin, a half inch from the top edge of the page. No page number should appear on the first page of the script.

[A] THE FIRST PAGE

(Note: The reference code [A] and all future alpha codes refer back to examples in the sample script on pages 118-121.)

The title of your script may be centered at the top of page, CAPPED, and underscored. This is optional.

A screenplay almost always begins as follows:

```
FADE IN:
```

That is followed by a master scene heading or narrative description, after which normal script formatting rules apply.

Some movies begin with a BLACK SCREEN, which is followed by some words superimposed over the black screen, which is followed by the familiar FADE IN. For information on how to format superimposed words, see SUPER on page 156.

Some writers type their screenplay title at the top of the first page, but there is no reason for doing so.

CREDITS AND TITLES

Don't worry about where to place your opening and closing CREDITS. They're *not* required for the spec script. Besides, it's very hard to judge just how long it will take the credits to roll. If you have written this beautiful opening segment that is perfect for CREDITS or TITLES to roll over, the reader will recognize that fact without any special notation placed there by you. If you feel strongly about including credits, then use this format:

```
ROLL CREDITS
```

Or . . .

```
BEGIN CREDITS
```

And after the last opening credit . . .

```
END CREDITS
```

In the above example, CREDITS is treated as a "heading." However, it can also be included in the body of the narrative description. The word TITLES is often used in place of CREDITS. Again, I strongly advise against indicating CREDITS or TITLES.

THE LAST PAGE

There are two general ways to end a screenplay. My personal choice is to write THE END at the end. Some writers like to fade out, as follows:

`FADE OUT.`

Or:

`FADE TO BLACK.`

Notice that FADE IN is flush to the left margin and FADE OUT appears flush to the right margin (or at a tab 6 inches from the left edge of the paper). Thus, FADE IN is the only editing direction (or *transition*) that appears flush to the left margin.

Headings (slug lines)

Screenplays and TV scripts consist of three parts: 1) Headings (sometimes called *slug lines*), 2) Description, and 3) Dialogue. This section deals with headings.

Headings always appear in CAPS. There are three types of headings: A) Master scene headings, B) Secondary scene headings, and C) Special headings.

(Note: The reference code [B] below and all future alpha codes refer back to the sample script on pages 118-121.)

[B] MASTER SCENE HEADINGS

A master scene heading consists of three main parts, and a rarely used fourth.

1. Camera location
If the camera is located outside or outdoors, then use EXT. for EXTERIOR. If it is indoors, then use INT. for INTERIOR. Please read the brief section "Camera Directions" on page 145; it will provide a helpful example.

Occasionally, the action moves back and forth through a doorway or opening. This can create a large number of master scene headings. Sometimes a scene begins outside, but quickly moves inside (or vice versa). In such cases, the following camera location notation is permissible:

```
INT./EXT. CAR — DAY
```

2. Scene location
The second part of a master scene heading is the location of the scene, the place where everything is happening. Usually one or two words will suffice.

Occasionally, I see incorrect scene locations such as RUNNING or GRABBING LUNCH or CHRISTMAS MORNING. These are not locations. A STREET is a location. A DINER is a location. SMITHS' LIVING ROOM is a location, and that's where the Christmas tree is.

At code [C] on page 119, the location is a small classroom. I use the word "small" only because I don't want the director using one of those large, semi-circular auditoriums. I want a more intimate scene and perhaps a modest budget. Generally, you want master scene headings to be short and specific.

3. Time of day
Most often this will be DAY or NIGHT. Avoid terms like DUSK, DAWN, LATE AFTERNOON, EARLY EVENING, HIGH NOON, GLOAMING, or the time on the clock. Use these only if helpful to the story. Keep in mind that virtually all movie scenes are shot for DAY or NIGHT. If it is a morning scene, they'll use a tweeting bird to imply it is morning or a quick shot of the sun rising, but the scene itself will be shot for DAY.

Occasionally, SAME is used to indicate that the scene takes place at the SAME time as the previous scene. CONTINUOUS is occasionally used for a similar purpose—to show that one scene follows right on the heels of the other, without any lapse of time.

```
EXT. BACK YARD — NIGHT

Two dark figures sneak up to the kitchen window.

INT. KITCHEN — CONTINUOUS
```

```
Phil chops onions on a block.
```

If it is already obvious that one scene follows the other continuously without any time gaps or lapses, then it is not necessary to use CONTINUOUS. This may be the case for the above example. In fact, the time would also be obvious, so you could probably get away with the following:

```
INT. KITCHEN
```

When in doubt as to what to do, always opt for clarity. Make it easy for your reader. Thus, I recommend that you always include all three parts of the master scene heading.

Sometimes LATER is used to indicate passage of time.

If the scene is out in space, then it's neither DAY or NIGHT, so you may not need to indicate anything.

```
EXT. SPACE
```

However, if you have an interior scene, you may want to indicate DAY or NIGHT depending on whether the characters are working or sleeping. Of course, your characters' activity is a clue, so DAY and NIGHT may not be needed even then. The main thing is to not confuse or lose the reader.

4. Special notations

If a scene requires further identification because it is a dream, for example, such a clarification may be added as a fourth part of the master scene heading. Here is an example:

```
INT. ROOM OF MIRRORS - NIGHT - MARTY'S DREAM
```

or

```
INT. ROOM OF MIRRORS - NIGHT (MARTY'S DREAM)
```

Suppose your screenplay jumps all over time. In that case, you could additionally indicate the date (or the season) of the scene, as follows:

```
EXT. TOKYO BAY - DAY — 1945
```

or

```
EXT. TOKYO BAY — DAY (1945)
```

If you want the audience to see "1945" superimposed on the movie screen, you will need to use a SUPER. See page 156 for information on SUPERs.

Scenes presented out of sequence

If the scenes of your screenplay are not presented in chronological order, as in PULP FICTION, RUN LOLA RUN, and SLIDING DOORS, then use the fourth part of the master scene heading ("special notations" section) to keep the reader oriented. For example, I saw one script that alternated between "DREAM STATE" and "REALITY."

Scene changes

Technically, if any of the three (or four) elements of a master scene heading change, you have a new scene, and must type in a new master scene heading and include the change.

Master scene heading conventions

A master scene heading should appear as follows:

```
INT. CLASSROOM - DAY
```

As usual, variations abound, but the general form remains the same.

Occasionally, I have seen some scripts with master scenes bolded. Don't bold or italicize anything in a screenplay. Nor should a scene heading end with a period.

Recently, I saw the following master scene heading:

```
INT. CHILE — PUNTA ARENAS — HOTEL — CARMEN'S ROOM — EVENING
```

As discussed, a scene heading should indicate the *specific* location of the scene, not everything you know about that location. Also, as a general rule, use DAY or NIGHT. Thus, I would revise the above example to the following:

```
INT. CARMEN'S HOTEL ROOM — DAY
```

Or perhaps:

```
INT. HOTEL — CARMEN'S ROOM — DAY
```

Carmen's hotel room is the specific location of the scene. All the other information should come out in narrative description or previous scene headings. Here's an example of what I mean:

```
EXT. CHILEAN TUNDRA — DAY
```

The vast Southern Chilean tundra extends for miles.

SUPER: "SOUTHERN CHILE."

The city of Punta Arenas is visible in the distance.

EXT. PUNTA ARENAS HOTEL

A five-story red-brick monolith dominates the smaller shops that surround it.

INT. CARMEN'S HOTEL ROOM

[C] SPACING BETWEEN SCENES

Do you space twice or three times before a new master scene heading? I recommend two spaces.

Double-space (hit "Enter" or "Return" twice) before and after any kind of heading, including secondary scene headings. Most software programs double-space for you automatically. If you have a driving desire to triple-space before each new master scene heading, that's okay.

As mentioned in the "17 Commandments," do not number your scenes in a spec script. This is done by a production person after the final draft is sold and the script has gone into production.

Try not to end a page on a heading. Move the heading to the top of the next page.

SECONDARY SCENE HEADINGS

Master scenes often contain more than one dramatic unit, each of which could require a heading. These can be individual SHOTS (although you will seldom, if ever, use the term SHOT), or side locations, or specific instances that require highlighting. They provide you with ways to break up master scenes. Most of the rules regarding master scene headings apply to these as well.

In CASABLANCA, much of the action takes place at Rick's Cafe. These scenes can be quite long unless they are broken up into smaller scenes. For example, the master scene would be as follows:

INT. RICK'S PLACE - NIGHT

A few paragraphs into the scene and we go to a specific spot at Rick's place.

```
AT THE BAR
```

or

```
IN THE GAMING ROOM
```

We are still at Rick's Cafe. If we cut to the same location, but time has passed, we normally have a new master scene, and write:

```
INT. RICK'S PLACE - LATER
```

But we can probably get away with just:

```
LATER
```

If you are so disposed, you could write the first master scene heading of the above example like this:

```
INT. RICK'S PLACE — THE BAR — NIGHT
```

And then later in the master scene, go to

```
GAMING ROOM
```

And so on.

Directing the camera

Another advantage of using secondary headings is that you can direct the camera without using camera terms. In effect, your goal in spec writing is to direct the mind's eye of the reader.

Suppose you want to focus on characters in an intense scene. Instead of the common shooting-script notation ANGLE ON LARRY or CLOSE ON LARRY, you simply write:

```
LARRY
```

```
reaches behind his back and produces a dagger.
```

```
OLGA
```

```
laughs heartily.
```

Now you are using character names as headings, and the story flows easily without being encumbered by camera directions.

Of course, the above could also have been written as follows.

```
Larry reaches behind his back and produces a dagger.

Olga laughs heartily.
```

Here is another example of how to use secondary scene headings. The scene opens with a master scene heading that establishes the master location.

```
INT. CONVENIENCE STORE - NIGHT

A man wearing a werewolf Halloween mask enters.

AT THE COUNTER

the clerk freezes in fear.

IN THE AISLE

a young couple faints together.

AT THE COUNTER

the masked man opens a large paper sack.

                    MASKED MAN
          Trick or treat.
```

The same scene could be revised for a cleaner look. That's because, in the above example, the secondary scene headings are not needed to break up the short scene. So even though the above example is correct, the following is also correct, and probably preferred.

```
INT. CONVENIENCE STORE - NIGHT

A man wearing a werewolf Halloween mask enters. The clerk at
the counter freezes in fear.

In one of the aisles, a young couple faints together.

The masked man steps toward the clerk and opens a Halloween
sack.
```

                        MASKED MAN
            Trick or treat.

Action scenes
Secondary headings can become especially helpful in action scenes.

EXT. BLUE SKY - DAY

An enemy plane gets behind Billy's fighter (Eagle One). To
his left, Jimmy's fighter (Eagle Two) cruises. Below them is
the Mediterranean Sea.

INSIDE EAGLE TWO

Jimmy looks to his right at EAGLE ONE.

                        JIMMY
            Look out, Billy!

JUST ABOVE THE WATER

The enemy closes in.

                        JIMMY (VO)
            He's on your tail!

Eagle One dodges and weaves while the enemy fires at him,
missing.

INSIDE EAGLE ONE

Billy pulls up on the stick.

                        BILLY
            Thanks for the tip!

Allow your prose to flow
Avoid ending a sentence with a scene heading.

Rick struts into the

GAMING ROOM.

Omit that period after GAMING ROOM and write something like this:

Rick struts into the

```
GAMING ROOM
```

```
where he spots a discouraged young man near the roulette
wheel.
```

Let your prose flow.

SPECIAL HEADINGS

Other common secondary headings are the MONTAGE, the SERIES OF SHOTS, the INSERT, the FLASHBACK, DREAMS, DAYDREAMS, and so on. All follow the same basic formatting pattern, although variations abound.

[D] MONTAGE AND SERIES OF SHOTS

If I didn't use the MONTAGE sequence at [D] on page 120, I would need more master scene headings than Carter has pills. A MONTAGE is a sequence of brief shots expressing the same or similar idea, such as a passage of time, or a stream of consciousness. The MONTAGE is based on a concept.

MONTAGE examples
Here's a common format for the MONTAGE.

```
MONTAGE - SUZY AND BILL HAVE FUN TOGETHER

-- They run along the beach. Suzy raises her countenance
   against the ocean spray.

-- They bicycle through a park.

-- Bill buys Suzy ice cream at a small stand. She stuffs it
   into his face. The patrons chuckle.
```

And, of course you would end the montage with BACK TO SCENE or END MONTAGE appearing flush to the left margin, or you could type a new master scene heading if the MONTAGE is short. It's okay to include dialogue in a MONTAGE sequence, but generally the focus is on beats of action.

That same MONTAGE could be written without the double indent, with everything flush to the right margin, as follows:

```
MONTAGE - SUZY AND BILL HAVE FUN TOGETHER
```

-- They run along the beach. Suzy raises her countenance against the ocean spray.

-- They bicycle through a park.

-- Bill buys Suzy ice cream at a small stand. She stuffs it into his face. The patrons chuckle.

Some studios and production companies prefer a MONTAGE format that lists location, followed by action.

MONTAGE - SUZY AND BILL HAVE FUN TOGETHER

-- A beach - They race across the sand. Suzy raises her countenance against the ocean spray.

-- A park - They bicycle down meandering paths.

-- An ice cream stand - Bill buys Suzy an ice cream cone. She stuffs it into his face. The patrons chuckle.

The above locations could be placed in CAPS. That would be correct as well. Here's still another version.

MONTAGE - SUZY AND BILL HAVE FUN TOGETHER

-- EXT. BEACH - DAY -- They race across the sand. Suzy raises her countenance against the ocean spray.

-- EXT. PARK - DAY -- They bicycle down meandering paths.

-- EXT. ICE CREAM STAND - NIGHT -- Bill buys Suzy an ice cream cone. She stuffs it into his face. The patrons chuckle.

Other variations on the above styles would likely work. All of these styles are correct and can also be used with the SERIES OF SHOTS.

SERIES OF SHOTS example
Similar to the MONTAGE is the SERIES OF SHOTS, consisting of quick shots that tell a story. They lead to some dramatic resolution or dramatic action, whereas a MONTAGE focuses on a single concept. Here's an example of how to format the SERIES OF SHOTS.

SERIES OF SHOTS — JOHN GETS EVEN

A) John lifts a .38 Special from his desk drawer.

B) John strides down the sidewalk, hand in pocket.

C) John arrives at an apartment building.

D) Mary answers the door. John pulls the trigger. A
   stream of water hits Mary in the face.

Those letters numbering the shots could be replaced with dashes, as with the MONTAGE.

MONTAGE vis-a-vis SERIES OF SHOTS

Generally, the MONTAGE is used more than the SERIES OF SHOTS. Even when the sequence is a true SERIES OF SHOTS, the MONTAGE format is often used. Sometimes the heading MONTAGE is used and then the shots are numbered exactly like the SERIES OF SHOTS example above. The rules are fluid here, and the terms are often used interchangeably. Use both devices sparingly.

Generally, a MONTAGE in the script is scored to music in the movie. For example, the above MONTAGE of Suzy and Bill could be lengthened to be accompanied by a love song—the MONTAGE concept would be "falling in love." The training MONTAGE from ROCKY is another example. Thus, the word MONTAGE often means: *Put the hit song here.* But don't *you* indicate the musical selection you prefer. (For more on music, see page 162.)

FLASHBACKS AND DREAMS

Since the FLASHBACK is often abused by beginning writers, make sure that your use of it pays off dramatically.

In terms of formatting, handle a FLASHBACK like a MONTAGE. (Note that secondary headings are often followed by a space-hyphen-space and then an explanation of the heading, as with the example below.)

FLASHBACK — TRAIN ACCIDENT

David sees the train coming and jumps on the train tracks.
He laughs; he's playing chicken with the train.

With the train nearly upon him, he tries to leap from the
tracks, but his foot catches on a rail tie.

BACK TO PRESENT DAY

If the flashback takes place at only one location, you may write the heading as follows:

```
FLASHBACK — EXT. TRAIN TRACKS — NIGHT
```

Another way to handle the above is to write the master scene heading as follows:

```
EXT. TRAIN TRACKS - NIGHT - FLASHBACK
```

Or

```
EXT. TRAIN TRACKS - NIGHT (FLASHBACK)
```

If you use one of the above notations, then the next scene heading would look something like this.

```
INT. PSYCHIATRIST'S OFFICE - DAY — PRESENT DAY
```

Or

```
INT. PSYCHIATRIST'S OFFICE - DAY (PRESENT DAY)
```

FLASHBACK sequence
If a FLASHBACK covers several scenes, then the following example might work best.

```
EXT. WOODS — NIGHT — FLASHBACK SEQUENCE
```

And then continue writing FLASHBACK SEQUENCE at the end of each master scene heading in the sequence. Once the FLASHBACK SEQUENCE concludes, indicate PRESENT DAY at the end of the next master scene heading.

```
INT. CLASSROOM - DAY - PRESENT DAY
```

Or simply write:

```
BACK TO PRESENT DAY
```

Another way to handle a FLASHBACK SEQUENCE is to write the following heading:

```
FLASHBACK SEQUENCE
```

And then write out all the scenes in sequence, just as you would normally write scenes, and then end the sequence with this:

```
END OF FLASHBACK SEQUENCE
```

Quick flashes

On rare occasion, you might have a situation where a character recalls a series of quick flashbacks in succession. Handle that with the same format you'd use for a MONTAGE or a SERIES OF SHOTS.

```
QUICK FLASHES — DUKE'S BASEBALL MEMORIES

-- Duke slides home safe. Jubilant teammates scramble to
congratulate him.

-- Duke, playing shortstop, snags a hot grounder, and tosses
the man out at first.

-- Duke swings at a fast ball and watches it sail over the
left-field fence.
```

FLASHBACKS, DREAMS, and DAYDREAMS are written in present tense. In fact, all the conventions that apply to FLASHBACKS also apply to DREAMS, DAYDREAMS, IMAGININGS, and VISIONS.

Dreams, daydreams, imaginings, and visions

Handle these events the same way you handle flashbacks.

```
DREAM — SID IN THE JUNGLE
```

If your character has a dream sequence, format it as you would a flashback sequence.

If your character has a vision, the formatting is the same:

```
DAME NOSTRA'S VISION — WORLD WAR FIVE
```

Label all dreams, visions, daydreams, nightmares, flashforwards, and flashbacks as such. It's not usually in your best interest to hide the fact from the reader to surprise him, although there are exceptions to this advice. And please don't open your movie with a dream and have your character awaken bolt-upright in her bed; that has become cliché. If you must use the cliché, give it a fresh twist.

Animated scene

Suppose you have a short animated segment in one of your scenes. Use the same formatting pattern we have been discussing.

```
ANIMATION — SILLY BILLY MEETS THE MONKEY MAN
```

or

```
EXT. PET STORE — DAY - ANIMATION
```

[E] INSERT

The INSERT (also known as the CUTAWAY) is used to bring something small into full frame. This can be a book, news headline, sign, contract, letter, or a leather pouch filled with mints. You use the INSERT because it is important to draw special attention to the item. In the case of a letter or a document with a lot of text, you may wish to use the INSERT as follows.

```
INT. LIMO - LATE NIGHT

As Sylvester steps into the limo, the chauffeur hands him a
letter and bats his eyes like an ostrich.

                    CHAUFFEUR
          Your wife, sir.

Sylvester tears the letter open as the door SLAMS shut.

INSERT - THE LETTER, which reads:

          "Dearest Darling Sylvester,

          I am leaving for Loon City to start
          a turkey ranch. Don't try to follow,
          my peacock, or I'll have your cockatoo
          strangled. There's plenty of chicken
          in the refrigerator. I love you, you
          goosey duck.

                    Your ex-chick, Birdie"

BACK IN THE LIMO

Sylvester smiles like the cat who ate the canary.

                    SYLVESTER
          So long, Tweetie Pie.
```

Note that the contents of the note are indented like dialogue; however, quotation marks are used to quote the letter.

Once you have written the INSERT, it is good manners to bring us BACK TO SCENE (see code [E] on page 121), although this can also be done with a new master scene heading or secondary scene heading. In any situation like this, opt for clarity and a smooth flow of the story.

Here's an example of an *unnecessary* INSERT:

```
INSERT — COLT .45 AUTOMATIC ON THE TABLE

BACK TO SCENE
```

Although the above is technically correct, you can avoid the use of CAPS (which are hard to read) and write the above as narrative description, as follows:

```
A Colt .45 automatic lies on the table.
```

It is more important to be readable and clear than to use formatting conventions that might encumber the "read."

On page 121, you'll see an example of an INSERT. Here is perhaps a more efficient way to write it.

```
Her shoulders heave in heavy sobs.

The professor dips into his leather bag and deftly snatches
a candy mint.

Calcutta lifts her head just as he flicks the candy into the
air.
```

STYLE SIMILARITIES OF SPECIAL HEADINGS

Notice that all special headings may be formatted using the same or similar style. They name the special function first and then they state what it involves. Here's a list:

```
MONTAGE - SUZY AND BILL HAVE FUN TOGETHER

SERIES OF SHOTS — JOHN GETS EVEN

FLASHBACK — EXT. TRAIN TRACKS - NIGHT

DREAM — SID IN THE JUNGLE

DAME NOSTRA'S VISION — WORLD WAR FIVE

INSERT - THE LETTER

INTERCUT - TELEPHONE CONVERSATION
```

INTERCUT

A full explanation of this special heading plus examples can be found under "Telephone Conversations" on pages 176-179. As you view the examples, keep in mind that you can INTERCUT any two scenes, not just two scenes that are part of a telephone conversation.

[F] ESTABLISHING SHOT

Often, at the beginning of a movie, sequence, or scene, there is an establishing shot to give us an idea of where on earth we are. There are two ways to present an establishing shot.

Incorrect:

```
EXT. NEW YORK CITY - DAY - ESTABLISHING
```

Correct:

```
EXT. NEW YORK CITY - DAY

Manhattan sparkles in the sunlight.
```

The second "correct" example is preferred because it is more interesting, plus it directs the camera without using camera directions. It's obviously a long shot of the entire city that establishes where we are.

In our sample script, we are at a university campus classroom. Note that master scene heading code [F] in the script example on page 119 does not end with the word ESTABLASHING. It's not necessary to add it, even though it does establish the master location.

Also notice, in the same example [F], that the description runs from general to specific, from long shots down to a close-up. In effect, I am directing the camera from a long, establishing shot of the university campus to a building, and finally to a close-up of a sign on that building. And I do it without using camera directions.

[G] CAMERA PLACEMENT

In the scene beginning at reference code [B] on page 119, the camera is inside the classroom. We know this because the master scene heading is INT. SMALL CLASSROOM - DAY. The INT. means that the camera is inside the classroom. However, the camera can SEE (at the first reference code [G]) out through the window to the young woman in pigtails and a pinafore.

Likewise, in the next scene, the camera is outside the classroom (by virtue of the EXT.) "looking" into the classroom as the professor performs cartwheels down the aisle (at the second reference code [G]). Thus, the window is used as a transitional device between scenes.

[H] The master scene heading for this scene (at [H]) is EXT. CLASSROOM - DAY. It could as easily have been EXT. PHONE BOOTH - DAY. The reason it isn't is that I felt the relationship between the phone booth and classroom would not be quite as clear. The choice, as always, is yours. Always strive to write clearly so that the reader can easily visualize the images and actions of your scene.

THE STORY'S THE THING

Many writers who are new to the business believe that they must use fancy formatting techniques in order to get noticed by agents and producers. So they add CAMERA ANGLES, clever DISSOLVES, arty MONTAGES, and so on.

I have a copy of the original BASIC INSTINCT spec script by Joe Eszterhas—the one he was paid $3 million for. There is not a single DISSOLVE, CUT TO, SERIES OF SHOTS, MONTAGE, INSERT, INTERCUT, or fancy technique in his entire 107-page script. Only scene headings, description, and dialogue—that's it. His focus is on telling a story through clear, lean, unencumbered writing.

Narrative description

A *narrative* is a story, and *description* is that which describes; thus, narrative description *describes the story*. Specifically, it describes the three elements of 1) *action*, 2) *setting and characters*, 3) and *sounds*. We'll break these three down to smaller units for purposes of discussion.

TECHNIQUES FOR WRITING EFFECTIVE DESCRIPTION

Narrative description is written in present tense because we view a film in present time. Double-space between paragraphs and do not indent.

Write lean

Keep your narrative description (and dialogue) on the lean side, providing only what is absolutely necessary to progress the story while emphasizing important actions and moments. Be clean and lean.

Limit your paragraphs to a maximum of four lines (not four sentences), although I would strive for paragraphs of one or two lines. Big blocks of black ink can make a reader black out.

Space twice after periods. Make dashes with a space, hyphen, hyphen, space.

As a general rule, allow one paragraph per beat of action or image. When a reader reads your paragraph, she should clearly "see" and "hear" what you describe. The result will be that she will "feel" what you want her to feel.

Beginning at [B] on page 119, you'll see a few things that I feel are necessary to set up in order for the sequence to work. First, my professor "looks" different from the stereotypical professor. Second, I establish that this scene is about script formatting. Finally, the professor has a leather pouch filled with candy mints. The pouch of mints is of tremendous importance to the story, so I take two lines to describe it.

I could have chosen to give the pouch a separate paragraph to give it more emphasis and to imply that the pouch deserves a separate camera shot.

Please notice that I describe very little in this classroom. I don't even describe how the professor dresses. In this scene, I don't need to. Generally, physical descriptions of locations and characters should be sparse. (Please see "Character Descriptions," which includes "Setting descriptions," beginning on page 151.) In fact, the only physical description I give of the classroom is the fact that there is a window by which Charlie sits. This is mentioned only because of its importance later as a transitional element. (See page 158 for more on transitions.)

Some visual images need just the briefest of descriptions. For example, I might describe an ordinary conference room as exactly that: "an ordinary conference room." The color of the walls and the number of seats may not be important. However, if, later in the scene, someone throws a TV at the discussion leader, I may describe the room as follows:

```
INT. CONFERENCE ROOM — DAY

A TV sits on a table in a corner.
```

Then again, there may be a lot that is unique about a different conference room that needs to be mentioned. Here's an example:

```
INT. CONFERENCE ROOM — DAY

About a dozen business people sit on leather sofas that form
a circle around a distinguished-looking woman dressed to the
nines. She smiles confidently.
```

Dramatize

If you're writing a dramatic scene, then dramatize it. If two principals are in a fist fight, don't just write *They fight*; describe the action. You don't need to choreograph every move, but you do need to *describe the action*.

Use short paragraphs, emphasizing specific images, actions, and emotions. As a general guideline, write one paragraph for each beat of action or visual image. What follows is a partial description of the key moment in a baseball game:

```
Duke sneers at the catcher. Taps the bat twice on the plate
and spits. A brown wad splatters on the plate.

The catcher refuses to notice. Keeps his eyes ahead.

Smiley steps off the rubber. Nervously works the rosin bag.
Wipes the sweat from his forehead with his arm.

Duke leans over the plate like he owns it. Allows himself a
self-satisfied grin.
```

Be choosy on your details

Unless important to the plot, incidental actions—such as *he lights her cigarette, she moves to the table, she stands up*—should be avoided. The actions in the above example—*tapping the plate, spitting*—would be incidental if this weren't the bottom of the ninth, two outs, score tied, and a three-two count.

If your character raises her cup of coffee to her lips, that's not important enough to describe . . . unless there is poison in the cup.

In any decision, err on the side of brevity. *Lean writing is appreciated and expected by Hollywood professionals.*

A key principle of spec writing is less is more. That means you should say as much as you can with as few words as you can.

Describe only what we see and hear

It is easy to slip and include information that cannot appear on the movie screen. For example, the following cannot appear on the movie screen, and, thus, should not be included in narrative description:

```
When she saw him, it reminded her of two years ago when they
first met.
```

Memories, thoughts, and realizations cannot visually appear on the movie screen unless you describe actions, facial expressions, or gestures that suggest them. As a general rule, only describe what the audience can actually see on the movie screen and hear on the soundtrack. (See "Describing what we see and creating mood" in Book IV.)

Use specific words and action words

Because a screenplay is written in present tense, it's easy to find yourself writing like this: John *is looking* at Mary. Suzy *is walking* past the cafe. Snake Koslowsky *is seated* on the couch. Replace those passive expressions with sentences written in present-tense active voice: John *looks* at Mary. Suzy *walks* past the cafe. Snake *sits* on the couch.

Now go one step further and create something even more active and concrete: John *gawks* at Mary, or John *gazes* at Mary. Suzy *scampers* down the sidewalk, or Suzy *sashays* down the sidewalk. Snake *coils* on the couch. Now the reader can more easily visualize the action and gain a greater sense of the character as well—and without the help of a single adverb. Use concrete verbs as characterization tools.

Concrete, specific nouns also help us "see." *Dinghy, rowboat, yacht,* and *pontoon* are more descriptive than *boat*. And no adjectives are needed. Instead of *He pulls out a gun,* write *He pulls out a Colt .45 automatic.* As a general rule, write short, crisp sentences.

Action should comment on character

Make sure your narrative description reveals something about character and about the story. For example, don't write

```
Charlie enters.
```

Instead, ask yourself *how* Charlie enters. Make it a *character thing* by being more *specific*. Let every action tell the reader (and the eventual audience) something about the character and/or the story. Here are two examples.

```
Charlie silently slithers in.

Charlie staggers in and, on his third try, kicks the door
shut.
```

Avoid redundancies

Steer clear of repetition in your narrative descriptions.

Redundant:

```
INT. CLASSROOM - DAY

Calcutta enters the classroom.
```

Correct:

```
INT. CLASSROOM - DAY

Calcutta enters.
```

Redundant:

```
EXT. OUTSIDE THE CLASSROOM - DAY
```

Correct:

```
EXT. CLASSROOM - DAY
```

Redundant:

```
He glares at her with anger.

                    STEVE
               (angrily)
     I feel like breaking your nose!!!!!
```

Correct:

```
He glares at her.

                    STEVE
     I feel like breaking your nose.
```

. . . And you might not need the glaring.

ACTION STACKING

For action sequences, the following style (called *action stacking*) may be used.

```
Duke sneers at the catcher.
Taps the bat twice on the plate.
Spits a brown wad that splatters on the plate.
Allows himself a self-satisfied grin.
```

If you decide to use it, keep in mind that the sentences must be concise and never over a line in length. Also, you should use the device fairly consistently throughout your screenplay. I worry about writers getting too caught up in stacking actions but losing their story focus. Additionally, most readers are used to seeing the traditional method of writing description. For those reasons, I don't recommend action stacking. However, I applaud the idea of concise sentences and brief paragraphs when writing action scenes.

[I] CHARACTER FIRST APPEARANCES

(Note: The reference code [I] and all other alpha codes refer back to examples in the sample script on pages 118-121.)

The name DR. FORMAT (at the first reference code [I] on page 119) is in CAPS because this is his first appearance in the screenplay. CHARLIE also appears in all-caps because it's the first time he appears in the story. So why wasn't "twenty students" capitalized? Because they weren't important enough to warrant drawing the reader's attention to them. In fact, do not CAP groups of people, just individuals.

When a character who is identified only by function or characteristic—BURLY MAN, DANCER #1, MUTANT—first appears in a script, then place that nomenclature in CAPS. When a character is mentioned for the first time in a speech, don't CAP the name. CAP the name only when that character actually appears in the story.

When a name in CAPS is followed by a possessive, the *s* is placed in lower case:

```
PENELOPE's scream shatters the silence.
```

As a general rule, name your characters at the moment they first appear in the screenplay. Doing that avoids confusion. It's difficult for a reader to keep track of a YOUNG MAN who, pages later, is called JOE. That's partly because someone referred to as YOUNG MAN is obviously not important to the story, or he would have a name. Make it easy on readers; name your characters (those that have names) when they first appear or very shortly thereafter.

At code [U] on page 119, we hear a woman's voice, but do not identify her until the next scene. Notice that I clearly connect DEAN ZELDA ZACK to the WOMAN'S VOICE.

CHARACTER DESCRIPTIONS

When a character first appears in the script, you have an opportunity to suggest something of his/her nature. In most cases we do not need to know the character's height, weight, hair color, or the fact that she looks exactly like Cher. Describe these specific physical characteristics only if they are critical to the plot. Do not give a driver's license description of your character and do not pin the name of a famous actor or actress on your character because it limits who can star in your screenplay. Your characters should not derive from other movies; they should be original.

Here is how my co-writer and I describe our lead in CELEBRITY WEDDING:

```
SAM BURNS sports a week's growth and unruly hair. Everything
about him, from his wrinkled suit to his careless manner,
suggests he doesn't give a damn about anything. In fact, Sam
would pass as a bum if it weren't for that hard, confident
look in his eye.
```

Yes, we take certain liberties here, but so can you. This is one of the few places where you can. Notice that Sam not only has certain clothes, but he carries an attitude. He's been somewhere before he got here—he's a human with emotions and a past.

Usually, it's important to include the character's age. Here is a description of a character in MY BEST FRIEND'S WEDDING:

```
This is DIGGER DOWNES, 36, kind eyes, an intellectual's
mouth, Saville Row's most unobtrusive and conservative
chalk-stripe suit. He's gay, but you wouldn't guess it.
Loyal and wise, and you might.
```

Notice that the physical description of Digger is qualitative. It characterizes him without forcing an actor to have a certain color hair, eyes, and build. And from SCREAM:

```
BILLY LOOMIS, a strapping boy of seventeen. He sports a
smile that could last for days.
```

Here's what *not* to write: *Jenny used to be a cocktail waitress and had an affair with Jane's husband just a year ago, although Jane doesn't know it yet.* You cannot write stuff like that because it cannot appear on the movie screen. How will the audience know all this? What you can do is say that Mark is Jenny's wife or that Jane is Jenny's sister—you can probably get away with that.

Here's my favorite character description from a client's screenplay:

```
She wears clothes that are too young for her, but gets away
with it.
```

The above, in effect, describes character. We understand something about that person. Here's a similar approach:

```
FRAN KOZLOWSKI, 29, enters the room. She's conspicuously
attractive -- like a house about to go on the market.
```

Be original in your character descriptions. Rather than "She was the most beautiful girl there," Shakespeare wrote, in *Romeo and Juliet*, she was "like a snowy dove trooping with crows."

Setting descriptions

As with your character descriptions, describe settings briefly to set mood or tone. Here's an example from one of my clients.

```
The room reeks of discount Tiparillos and stale pizza, as
four sleazy-looking Godfather wannabes play poker.

STANLEY BENENATI, 42 and looking about as good as you can in
a mauve polyester leisure suit, throws down his cards.
```

Do we really need any more detail than that to get the picture? And notice that any physical descriptions of the character or clothing serve to comment on the character (or nature) of the character.

VISUAL CHARACTERIZATION

It is often effective to give your character a visual identification such as Charlie's peanut butter and associated flies in the sample script. Where would the MEN IN BLACK (or THE MATRIX's Neo) be without their sunglasses? And don't NAPOLEON DYNAMITE's moon boots and half-opened eyes help make him unique?

CHARACTER NAMES

All of your major characters deserve names, as do your important minor characters. Characters with only one or two lines of dialogue *may* be given names, but usually *aren't* given names so that the reader knows not to focus on them.

When you give a character a name, especially in the first 20 or so pages, the reader believes that that character is important to remember. If you present too many characters too fast, the reader can be overwhelmed. For that reason, some minor characters and all characters with no speaking parts should be referred to in terms of their function or characteristics or both. For example, if you have three technicians who only appear in one scene, refer to them as GRUFF TECH, SEXY TECH, SHY GEEK, and so on.

Suppose you have six police officers speaking in a scene. You may choose to refer to them as OFFICER 1, OFFICER 2, OFFICER 3, and so on; but I don't recommend it. First, limit the number of speaking officers to one or two. If any of those six officers is an important character, try to give him most of the lines. If these officers are not important (have no lines, or just have one line, or only appear in one or two scenes), distinguish them in some visual way: MACHO COP, TOOTH-PICK, CHUBBY COP.

This makes them easier to visualize and signals to the reader that they are not particularly important.

What about unseen characters?
In the excerpt below, I use sound to communicate audibly that there is an unseen character lurking nearby. The audience won't know he or she is in the scene without the sound of the camera.

```
EXT. PUBLIC BUILDING - DAY

James Connors hurries up the cement stairs.

An unseen person clicks the shutter of a 35mm camera.
Another click. And again as James rushes into the building.
```

What if the character has more than one name?
See "Characters with two names" on pages 166-167.

[K] SIGNS, NEWS HEADLINES, BOOK TITLES, NOTES, AND LETTERS

At code [K] on page 119, I chose to write the words "CINEMA DEPT." in CAPS and to enclose them with quotation marks. I could have as easily not used CAPS while still using the quotation marks. That would also be proper. However, I wouldn't use italics or bold to set apart anything.

News headlines, nameplates, song titles, book titles, names of magazines, plaques, signs on doors, etc., are usually placed in CAPS with quotation marks. Sometimes the contents of notes, letters, or documents need to be shown. In those cases, you may want to use the INSERT. The INSERT is explained on pages 142-143.

[L] SOUNDS

You are not required to place sounds in CAPS. However, if you wish, you may do so. Some writers place only important sounds in CAPS. On page 119, I decided to place BUZZING in CAPS as a matter of preference. I may use CAPS or not, since both styles are correct. Do not use the archaic: SFX. BUZZING FLIES.

In the scene above, which takes place in a "public building," I did not place any sounds in CAPS. Of course, I could have, and that would be perfectly fine. Here's an example:

```
EXT. PUBLIC BUILDING - DAY

James Connors hurries up the cement stairs.

An unseen person CLICKS the shutter of a 35mm camera.
Another CLICK. And AGAIN as James rushes into the building.
```

MOS

Occasionally, characters speak silently, which is to say that we see their lips moving and they are obviously talking, but no sound is heard. Other times, a scene may play in complete silence. In such situations, indicate "without sound" with the term MOS. (The term *MOS* originated with German director Eric von Stroheim, who would tell his crew, "Ve'll shoot dis mid out sound." Thus, MOS stands for "mid out sound.") Here's an example of how to use the device:

```
The two lovers flirt MOS in the balcony.
```

You could just as easily (and perhaps more appropriately) write this as follows:

```
The two lovers flirt in the balcony. Their words cannot be
heard.
```

As you might guess, MOS is a useful device. However, don't use it just to use it. Use it only if you have a compelling dramatic reason.

[M] SPECIAL EFFECTS

A key moment in the sample script (code [M] on page 119) is Charlie catching a mint on his nose and barking like a seal. In the shoot, this may require a special effect. In the past, this may have been written FX. CHARLIE CATCHING A MINT ON HIS NOSE, but not now. (By the way, FX. and SPFX. both mean Special Effects; and SFX. means Sound Effects.) There is another possible special effect at [M] on page 120.

Don't use FX. or SPFX. Since special effects are costly, you don't need to advertise to the studio or producer how expensive your movie is going to be. Sell the script first. After the script is sold, a production person will go through your script and identify all the special effects. Besides, most special effects can be described without using technical terms. Here's another example:

```
Suddenly, the room turns green and the walls resemble
mirrors. Sue touches a wall and it is liquid, like mercury.
```

We don't need to type "FX." to signal that the above requires a special effect. The description is adequate for a spec script.

On rare occasion, you may want to MORPH from one image to another, or indicate that the action takes place in SLOW MOTION. Any such technical instructions should be placed in CAPS. (See "When to break the rules" in Book IV for an example of how to format time-lapse.)

SUPERS

SUPER is short for *superimpose*. Use this device anytime you need to superimpose some words on the screen. For example:

SUPER: "Five years later."

If you wish, you can place the superimposed words in CAPS:

SUPER: "FIVE YEARS LATER."

A third method indents the superimposed words. This is mainly used for long super-impositions; however, it's okay to use it for short superimpositions.

SUPER:

        "FIVE YEARS LATER."

Most SUPERs are used to orient the audience to time or place. Here's an example:

EXT. HOSPITAL - NIGHT

EMTs rush a patient out of an ambulance and into the hospital.

SUPER: "Bethesda Medical Hospital."

Scully's car comes to a stop. She steps out with her cellular.

              SCULLY
         (into cellular)
      Mulder? Are you there?

Please note that I followed the heading (or slug line) with a sentence of description. I want to first give the audience a visual image before presenting the SUPER that will appear over that image.

Avoid clever alternatives for the SUPER such as the following:

```
The words "BETHESDA MEDICAL HOSPITAL" spell out across the
lower left of the screen.
```

Although technically correct, the above could be seen as taking liberties. Let other professionals decide where the words will be superimposed.

Suppose you want to superimpose a quote on the screen before the movie begins. This would be the correct format:

```
BLACK SCREEN

SUPER: "Two can live as cheaply as one, but only half as
long."

FADE IN:
```

If the quote or text you want to superimpose is very long, you should indent it like dialogue and enclose it with quotation marks.

```
BLACK SCREEN

SUPER:

          "Two can live as cheaply as one,
          but only half as long."

FADE IN:
```

Scrolls

If you are scrolling words up the movie screen, as in all six STAR WARS episodes, you would simply use the word SCROLL instead of SUPER.

Words on TV

What do you do if a character is watching something on TV and words appear on the TV screen? Do you use a SUPER for those? No. Use the TV as a secondary scene heading and write something like the following.

```
Selma turns on the television.

ON THE TV

A city is engulfed in flames. The word "BAGHDAD" appears at
the bottom of the screen.

BACK TO SCENE
```

[N] TRANSITIONS

The SLAMMING of telephone receivers (at the top of page 120) is a transitional ploy. I am suggesting to the director that once Calcutta SLAMS her phone, that we should CUT immediately to the professor SLAMMING his phone. This situation could also be handled with the MATCH CUT, discussed next.

EDITING DIRECTIONS (SCENE TRANSITIONS)

If I wrote the transition described above to include the editing direction MATCH CUT, I would have written it as follows:

```
The dean CHORTLES. Calcutta smiles, then SLAMS the receiver.

                                              MATCH CUT:

INT. CLASSROOM - DAY

The professor SLAMS the phone receiver.
```

The MATCH CUT is used to match an object or image from one scene to the next. The above transition of Calcutta slamming her phone receiver to the professor slamming his is an example. However, an editing direction is not necessary here because the transition is obvious. Use the MATCH CUT when the *match* is not already obvious.

It is not usually necessary to indicate transitions (editing directions) in spec scripts. The use of CUT TO is seldom necessary. Obviously, one must CUT at the end of a scene, so why indicate it? Avoid such editing tools as the WIPE, IRIS, FLIP, and DISSOLVE.

Here's my rule-of-thumb: Use an editing direction when it is absolutely necessary for understanding the story, or when its use helps link two scenes in a way that creates humor or improves continuity.

The editing direction is placed flush to the right margin. As an alternative, you can place the left margin of the transition at six inches from the left edge of the paper.

CAMERA DIRECTIONS

Let's break current convention and rewrite this section (top of page 120) utilizing our vast arsenal of camera and editing directions. Note as you read the bad example below how the technical directions detract from the story and slow down the read for the reader. (Note: CU means CLOSE UP, and ECU means EXTREME CLOSE UP.)

What follows is an example of poor writing.

```
INT. CLASSROOM - NEAR SUNSET

CU PROFESSOR SLAMMING the receiver of his toy phone.

PULL BACK and BOOM to ESTABLISH classroom.

PROFESSOR'S POV: CAMERA PANS the class.

                                        DISSOLVE TO:

LOW ANGLE of the professor -- confident.

WIDE ANGLE of THE STUDENTS as they SIMMER with interest.

ZIP ZOOM TO ECU doorknob opening. PULL BACK TO REVEAL
Calcutta coming through the door. DOLLY WITH Calcutta's
SHUFFLING feet as she makes her way to her desk.

CLOSE ON the professor expounding.

SWIRLING SHOT of the professor in increasingly larger
concentric circles.
```

Please, I beg you, don't do this to your script! First, you may insult the director. Second, it breaks up the narrative flow and makes the script harder to read. Third, you take the chance of showing your ignorance. Fourth, professional readers are not pleased. So, go easy. Remember, the story's the thing. Concentrate on that. It's true that most shooting scripts (the scripts you buy to read) contain many such camera directions and technical devices. Keep in mind that these directions and devices were likely added *after* the script was sold to prepare it for the shoot.

Being fancy is chancy. There is an acceptable way to indicate all the camera directions your heart desires without using the technical terms. Simply be creative and write the script so that they're implied.

For example, at [N] on page 120, I use the word "hand" to imply a CLOSE UP or ANGLE of the phone SLAMMING. If Dr. Format "surveys" the class, that might imply a POV (Point of View) shot, but certainly it is a MEDIUM SHOT of some kind. The students SIMMERING with interest is a REACTION SHOT of the entire class or REACTION SHOTS of individual students. (See how I give the director a choice!) If it's tremendously important to the scene that Charlie react strongly, I will write that reaction shot in a separate paragraph, as follows:

```
Charlie is so excited that he leaps from his seat and
executes a flawless back-flip.
```

Although correct, avoid headings like: ANGLE ON CHARLIE, CLOSE ON CHARLIE, and ANOTHER ANGLE. You may decide to put the camera on Charlie in this way:

```
CHARLIE

leaps from his seat and executes a flawless back-flip.
```

The *spec* script's emphasis is on lean, visual writing. Your goal is to create images while avoiding the use of technical terms. Instead of CLOSE UP OF DARLENE'S TEAR, you write *A tear rolls down Darlene's cheek.* (It's obviously a CLOSE UP.)

In conclusion, use camera directions and editing directions sparingly, only when they are needed to clarify the action, move the story forward, or add significantly to the story's impact.

WE SEE and TO REVEAL

Some developing writers use the camera direction WE SEE. Another favorite is PULL BACK TO REVEAL or REVEALING. Avoid these terms, and don't place "We see" in CAPS if you do use it. Although correct, they are seldom the most interesting way to convey the action and details of the scene to your reader. Likewise, avoid "We move with," "We hear," and other first-person intrusions.

B.g. and f.g.

B.g. stands for *background* and f.g. stands for *foreground*. These terms may be used in your narrative description to clarify action (e.g., The T-Rex moves in the b.g.), but I recommend you use them sparingly. If you must put the T-Rex in the background, just write out the words: The T-Rex moves in the background. Or better yet:

```
Behind them lumbers the T-Rex.
```

[O] POV

Many writers use the POV ("point-of-view") device instead of writing creatively. Since the POV is a camera direction, you want to avoid it in your spec script. Sometimes the POV needs to be used for story reasons; that's the case with certain important scenes in FINDING NEVERLAND where it's crucial that we see the scene from a particular character's view. But how should you format a POV in a spec script?

You can probably get away with the following, although I discourage it:

```
JOJO'S POV - The killer advances toward him.
```

Instead, write this:

```
Jojo watches the killer advance toward him.
```

You're still directing the camera, even though you're not using camera directions. In RAIDERS OF THE LOST ARK, *What he sees:* is used in lieu of the POV.

The heading at code [D] on page 120 could have been written THE PROFESSOR'S POV, and that would be technically correct. Instead, I avoided the inclusion of a camera direction, but still made it clear (at code [O]) that the spinning room is seen from the professor's point of view (POV).

At the second code [G] on page 119, we see The Professor from Calcutta's point of view. This could have been written as Calcutta's POV, but that would interrupt the narrative flow.

Suppose you are writing a funeral scene and your character looks away to see something happening in the background. In a shooting script, that would be a POV shot. Here's the example in spec style:

```
Sharon looks up the

CEMETERY ROAD

where three teenagers break into her car.

                    RABBI (O.S.)
          The Lord giveth and the Lord
          taketh away.
```

PHANTOM POV

The Phantom POV is used when we don't know the identity of the character sneaking through the bushes toward your unaware hero. Just write: Someone (or something) pulls away tree branches and moves closer and closer to an unsuspecting Giselda.

Let's imagine a scene by a lake. Children are playing, and you have a compelling story reason to view this from underneath the water. Since EXT. and INT. refer to where the camera is, we could open with the camera at the lake shore, establishing the children on the shore. We could then cut to the camera underneath the lake.

```
EXT. LAKE SHORE — DAY

The children form a circle by the lake.

EXT. UNDERWATER — CONTINUOUS

While the others dance, Pam peers down into the lake.
```

Thus, Pam looks right down at the camera. Notice that we signaled that without having to use camera directions.

If you're thinking of the above scene in terms of a point-of-view situation, such as a monster watching the children from deep below the water's surface, just handle the second scene as follows:

```
EXT. UNDERWATER — CONTINUOUS

An unseen lake monster watches the dancing children. Pam
peers down into the lake.
```

MUSIC

Don't indicate music in your script unless it is essential to the progression of your story. Yes, if music is an integral part of your story—a movie about a rock singer, for example—then you may wish to indicate music in a general way:

```
A HEAVY-METAL RIFF rips through the silence.
```

Or . . .

```
Upbeat ROCK MUSIC plays.
```

Another way to indicate music generically is to describe the sound of it: The radio BLASTS. Keep in mind that since music is a SOUND, you can emphasize it by placing it in CAPS. Do not tell the composer where to begin the romantic background music.

A more professional approach is to intimate music indirectly by suggesting an emotional mood. You'll manage this through description, dialogue, and character. The director and composer will pick up on your *vibe*, and select or compose music that matches the emotion of the scene.

Regardless of whether you indicate music or not, the one thing you should *not* do is pick specific songs. Unless you own the rights to the songs, you are creating a no-win situation for yourself and a legal hurdle for anyone interested in buying the script.

MOVIE CLIPS

What's true for music is true for produced movies. You cannot use a clip from another movie unless you control the rights to that movie. In addition, do not base your screenplay on any work that you do not control the rights to. Do not write the sequel to SNOW WHITE unless you control the rights to SNOW WHITE. Just write an original screenplay.

Obviously, you may briefly refer to other movies in a character's dialogue if doing so moves the story forward or adds to character. For example, in SLEEPLESS IN SEATTLE, there are references to THE DIRTY DOZEN and AN AFFAIR TO REMEMBER. But don't write, "He turned on the TV and the sinking scene from TITANIC was showing." Doing that will give you a sinking feeling when your script is rejected.

[P] AUTHOR'S INTRUSION

In virtually every literary form, author's intrusion is unacceptable. In a screenplay, it is only permissible if it helps tell the story or clarifies something. However, don't overdo it and don't get cute. Don't interrupt the narrative flow of the story. When in doubt, stay out. At code [P] on page 121, I intrude with my sentence, "Can he do it?" I think I can probably get away with that.

Shane Black made "author's intrusion" hip. Here's just one example from page 91 of THE LAST BOY SCOUT: "Remember Jimmy's friend Henry, who we met briefly near the opening of the film? Of course you do, you're a highly paid reader or development executive."

Shane Black can get away with that; you and I can't.

In terms of foreshadowing, it's okay to remind us of something we saw earlier on, although I suggest that you not be as brazen about it as Shane Black is in the above citation. The following is acceptable.

```
Sheila hands the tiny cedar box to Gwen. This is the same
cedar box that Sheila received from her mother earlier.
```

Obviously, the information in that last sentence cannot appear on the silver screen, but it once did, and it is okay to remind your reader to keep him or her oriented.

Your personal style
There is a difference between intruding on the story and writing with your own personal flare. Author intrusion calls attention to itself; creative expression contributes to the reading experience. I loved reading ROMANCING THE STONE. The first line begins, "A size 16-EE boot kicks through the door. . . ." Notice that Diane Thomas's prose does not pull you out of the screenplay, nor does it call attention to the author. Instead, it enhances the reading experience. The script is a lot of fun to read. Your personal style has developed to some degree and will continue to develop naturally.

[Q] CONTINUED

In shooting scripts, when a scene does not conclude at the bottom of a given page, it is customary to double-space and type (CONTINUED) at the lower right (flushed right); and type CONTINUED: at the upper left (flushed left) of the next page, followed by two vertical spaces, after which the writing resumed. This is totally unnecessary in spec writing.

If you own software that writes CONTINUED automatically, I recommend that you disable that function. If you can't disable it, don't be overly concerned. Most agents and producers are aware that there is a lot of software out there these days that automatically inserts the CONTINUEDs.

WHEN TO USE CAPS

Let's summarize the use of CAPS.

You *must* use CAPS for the following:
1. Character first appearances.
2. Technical instructions, including camera directions, editing directions, the word SUPER, special effects, etc. These incidents should be rare.

You *may* use CAPS (if you wish) for the following:
1. Sounds.
2. The words on signs, book titles, news headlines, etc.
3. Superimposed words. For example: SUPER: "TWO YEARS LATER."

Concerning the words referred to in Numbers 2 and 3, make sure you place quotation marks around those words regardless of whether or not you type them in CAPS.

Remember, CAPS are hard to read and slow down a "read." That means you should not CAP anything else in your narrative description unless specifically requested by the person asking for your script. Do not use CAPS for props or other nouns that you want to emphasize. That's a shooting-script convention. If you must emphasize any words of narrative description, underscore them, but do so rarely. I would expect to see no more than one or two instances of this in any screenplay, and in most scripts, I would not expect any words of description to be underscored.

SPECIAL NOTES

Once every blue moon you get a creative idea that does not fit any known formatting guidelines. In these few cases, simply write a note in a separate paragraph. You may place the note in parenthesis if you'd like, although it's not necessary. Here's an example from one of my old scripts:

```
(Note: This scene is shot in BLACK AND WHITE. It should
appear old and scratched as if it originated from a 1950's
public information library. There are intentional JUMP
CUTS.)
```

Dialogue

The dialogue sections of a screenplay consist of three parts: 1) Character cue, 2) Actor's direction, 3) and Character's speech (the dialogue).

(Note: The reference code [R] below and all other alpha codes refer back to examples in the sample script on pages 118-121.)

[R] CHARACTER CUE

First is the character name or cue, sometimes called the *character caption* or *character slug*. It always appears in CAPS. A character should be referred to by exactly the same name throughout the screenplay. In the narrative description and dialogue speeches, you may use a variety names, but the character cue for a character should be the same throughout the script. (See "Character Names" on pages 153-154.)

Never leave a character cue alone at the bottom of a page. The entire dialogue block should appear intact. For the one exception, see "MORE" on page 171

CHARACTERS WITH TWO NAMES

What if a character changes his name from Tom to Harry? One solution is to refer to him as TOM/HARRY or TOM (HARRY) after the name change.

In the movie NORTH BY NORTHWEST, we have a case of mistaken identity, but the Cary Grant character is referred to by his true name in each character cue of the entire script. Whatever you decide, make sure you don't confuse the reader.

In stories that span a person's lifetime, you might refer to JOE BROWN and YOUNG JOE BROWN. That maintains the identity of the character while, at the same time, making clear the approximate age of the character.

What if a character speaks before we see her? What do you call her? You can refer to her in the character cue by her actual name if you wish, or you may handle the situation as follows:

```
                    FEMALE VOICE
          I want to tell you ...
```

Ed parts the curtain and sees BAMBI, a twenty-something bombshell with hair tumbling everywhere.

```
                    BAMBI
          ... how much I want you.
```

See another example at code [U] of the sample script.

ACTOR'S DIRECTION (WRYLIES)

Directly below the character name is the *actor's direction*, sometimes called *personal direction* or *parenthetical* or the *wryly*. The term *wryly* derives from the tendency in many beginning screenplays for characters to speak "wryly." Here's an example.

```
                    LEFTY
              (wryly)
          I've had my share of mondo
          babes.
```

Wrylies can provide useful and helpful tips to the reader, usually suggesting the *subtext* or attitude of the character. However, keep in mind that wrylies are optional and should be used in moderation. Avoid telling your actors how to act. In most cases, the context of the situation and the character's actions will speak for themselves. Only use wrylies when the subtext is not clear. If Chico says "I love you" in a sarcastic way, and we wouldn't guess that he is being sarcastic from the context, then use the wryly.

```
              CHICO
          (sarcastically)
      I love you.
```

On page 121, I use only one wryly, and you could argue for its omission on grounds that it is redundant—it is already evident by his action (moonwalking) that he is "the master" once again.

Generally, don't use wrylies to describe actions, unless those actions can be described in two or three lines, such as "tipping his hat" or "applying suntan lotion to her arms" and if the action is taken by the person speaking while he/she is speaking. Wrylies should not extend more than two inches from the left margin to the right margin. Wrylies always begin with a lower-case letter and never begin with the pronouns "he" or "she."

Describing brief actions in wrylies is not a bad tactic since some executives read dialogue only. A few well-placed wrylies can enhance the value and comprehension of a scene. I hasten to add that an executive seldom reads a script until a coverage is written by a reader (story analyst). Most professional readers read the entire script.

Don't describe one character's actions in the dialogue block of another character. The following would *not* be proper.

```
              SHORTY
      What do you mean?
          (Slim pulls a gun)
      Don't shoot.
```

The following would be much better form:

```
              SHORTY
      What do you mean?
```

Slim pulls a gun and points it at Shorty.

```
              SHORTY
      Don't shoot.
```

Don't end a dialogue block with a wryly, as with the following example:

```
              COQUETTE
      So why did you come here?
          (raising her lips)
```

Instead write:

```
                    COQUETTE
          So why ...
                    (raising her lips)
          ... did you come here?
```

Finally, use a wryly to indicate whom the character is speaking to when that is not otherwise clear.

```
                    MOE
                    (to Curly)
          Not you, ya knucklehead.
```

BEAT

Avoid using the word *beat* (a theatrical term indicating a pause). It's usually best not to instruct an actor when to pause. If you must indicate a pause, find a more descriptive word than *beat*. Instead, describe a small action, gesture, or facial expression that accomplishes the same purpose, but which also adds a characterization.

Let's examine the following.

```
                    JIM
          You know ...
                    (beat)
          ... I'll have to kill you.
```

The word "beat" does not tell us much. Is Jim confident or nervous? That could make a big difference in how the scene plays. Granted, the context will tell us something, but why not add a little characterization here while still implying the pause? Replace "beat" with something like "looking nervous," "nearly giddy," "with a smug grin," or "confidently."

Which of the following three examples creates more interest?

```
                    JANE
          Ed Darling, I want you to
          know...
                    (beat)
          ... how much I love you.

                    JANE
          Ed Darling, I want you to
          know ...
                    (eyes mist up)
          ... how much I love you.
```

```
                    JANE
          Ed Darling, I want you to
          know ...
                    (suddenly sneezing
                     on Ed)
          ... how much I love you.
```

None of the three examples will win any prizes, but certainly the first is the boring one. The second is dramatic. The third is funny (or disgusting). Here is the point: The word "beat" is the most colorless, lifeless term you can use to indicate a pause. Instead, use specific words that add to the story or help characterize your character. It's an un*beat*-able strategy.

SOLILOQUIES

Avoid characters talking to themselves. However, if you have a natural soliloquy or whispered comment, just write "aside" or "to self" as a wryly. Do not write "sotto" or "sotto voce." There's no reason to use Latin unless you are a priest or a music composer.

[S] CONTINUING AND CONT'D

On page 121, The Professor begins to speak, then stops, then continues. In fact, I interrupt his speech three times with narrative description (each continuation of his speech marked with code [S]). In the past, this would have been handled in one of two ways:

```
                    PROFESSOR
                  (continuing)
          But why, Calcutta? Why?
```

```
                    PROFESSOR (CONT'D)
          But why, Calcutta? Why?
```

The above devices are no longer used in spec scripts. Don't use either *continuing* or *CONT'D* or *cont'd*. If your software program is insistent about these devices and you cannot disable them, then just go with the flow. This is not a major issue.

MORE

When dialogue continues from the bottom of one page to the top of the next, you should type MORE (in parenthesis) below the dialogue, and then type "CONT'D" (in parenthesis) next to the character's cue at the top of the next page.

Here's the bottom of one page:

```
                 BUGSY
     I am at the bottom of the page, and
     I'm running out of room.
                 (MORE)
```

And then at the top of the next page:

```
              BUGSY (CONT'D)
     I'd like to continue my speech.
```

Most formatting software will do this for you. The word "cont'd" may appear in all lower-case letters if you prefer. Do not break to a new page in the middle of a sentence; end the sentence with a period before typing "MORE," as demonstrated above.

Ideally, your dialogue should be so lean that you don't have to use MORE at all. Just move the entire dialogue block to the top of the next page or cheat a little on your bottom margin to get that last line in at the bottom of the page. (Warning: Do not cheat on your left and top script margins and dialogue margins. We'll talk about cheating you can get away with in Book IV.)

[T] OFF SCREEN (O.S.) AND VOICE OVER (V.O.)

OFF SCREEN, at code [T] on page 121, indicates that Charlie is in the scene—he's at the location of the scene—but that he is not in the camera frame. We hear his voice, but do not see him on the screen. Why do I want Charlie OFF SCREEN? Because I want the camera to focus on The Professor, whose back is now to the class.

Now, if Charlie is not only off-screen but also out of the scene (not in the classroom), and The Professor HEARS his voice—say, in his mind—then this is a VOICE OVER as follows:

```
              CHARLIE (V.O.)
     You're done for, old man.
```

The voice trails off. The professor sees no one.

If Charlie is in the scene and hears his own voice in his head *and* his lips aren't moving, that's also a VOICE OVER.

```
Charlie looks worried. He nods in resignation.

                    CHARLIE (V.O.)
          I'm done for.
```

Narration of any kind is a VOICE OVER. In cases where a character is on screen and we hear his thoughts or he narrates his own story, use the VOICE OVER. In cases when the character is not on screen, but we hear his voice, use VOICE OVER. The VOICE OVER device was used extensively in AMERICAN BEAUTY. In that film, Lester (Kevin Spacey) narrates.

Narration example
Do you recall that train-accident flashback on pagse 139-140? Let's revise it for narration. In the scene below, Zep recalls an experience from his youth.

```
FLASHBACK - TRAIN TRACKS

David sees a train coming. In a surreal game of chicken, he
places himself on the tracks.

                    ZEP (V.O.)
          David always flirted with
          disaster ...

With the train nearly upon him, David tries to leap from the
tracks, but his foot catches on a rail tie.

He glances up at the unforgiving mass of steel.

                    ZEP (V.O.)
          ... Then one day, disaster
          responded.

The wheels of the train slice through his body.
```

We can learn three lessons from the above example.

1. Notice that I avoid repeating in dialogue what we already see visually. Whenever you use a voice-over in situations like this, let that voice-over dialogue add something that the visual does not already tell us. Don't just describe in your dialogue the same action. that you describe in your narrative.

Keep in mind that when you write narration, you take a chance. Most narration that professionals see in screenplays amounts to "obvious exposition" or unnecessary dialogue that simply repeats the action. Thus, professional readers have a natural bias against the use of a narrator. Narration should comment on the story, or add to it, in a meaningful way.

2. Do not write something as general as "The train ran over him." Present us with concrete, visual images that we can respond to emotionally or intellectually.

3. Start a new paragraph when you switch to a new visual image. Generally, a paragraph of narrative description should present one visual image or one beat of action. (This is a very general guideline.)

Beginning the scene before it begins
If we hear someone's voice at the end of the scene, but don't actually see them until the next scene, then we have a voice-over, as follows:

```
                TV REPORTER (V.O.)
          I am standing in front of the
          White House ...

EXT. WHITE HOUSE - CONTINUOUS

A huge crowd observes while the TV reporter points.

                TV REPORTER
          ... And, as you can see, it has
          been painted blue.
```

Incidentally, I used the ellipsis (see page 184) to show continuity in dialogue.

Voice-over in phone conversations
In phone conversations in which the person on the other line is *not* "in the scene" but we hear her voice, this would be a Voice Over. I've recently seen scripts where V.O. is not used in telephone conversations, and that's okay as long as the script is clear and not confusing. I'm not sure I'd be that brave. For more on telephone conversations, see pages 176-179.

CHARACTER'S SPEECH

The third part of dialogue is the speech itself, the words to be spoken. Because speech is indented, you do not use quotation marks or italics to indicate the spoken word. Avoid hyphenation and maintain a ragged right margin.

Each speech should be as brief as possible, and generally convey one thought. One or two sentences is plenty in most cases. Fragments are welcome. Avoid long speeches.

Write all numbers out except years: "I've told you twenty-five times now that I was born in 1950." Avoid using excessive exclamation points; they make a speech look like a want ad!!!

Write out all words. Do not abbreviate. Put quotation marks around anything that is quoted.

If you wish to emphasize a word, do not place it in CAPS, italics, or bold; instead, underscore it. Use this practice sparingly.

Acronyms

When a character spells a word, saying each letter individually, use hyphens or periods to separate the characters, as follows:

```
                    DELBERT
          That's Delbert. D-E-L-B-E-R-T.
```

Acronyms that are pronounced as words should be written without hyphens or periods. The following speech is correctly written. The letters F, B, and I are said individually; the acronyms MADD and UNICEF are pronounced as words.

```
                    DELBERT
          The woman from MADD was thought
          to be F.B.I. until the official saw
          her UNICEF badge.
```

When working with dialects and accents, sprinkle in bits of dialect and phonetically spelled words just to give us a taste of the accent or regional influence. Make sure the speeches are easy to read. The same holds true for characters who stutter; just give us a sense of his stuttering.

For information on dialogue punctuation, see pages 183-185. For information on where to set your tabs, see pages 126-127.

OVERLAPPING OR SIMULTANEOUS DIALOGUE

Here's the first of four ways to present two people speaking at the same time.

```
                    SAM AND JO
          Huh, what?
```

Or you can add a parenthetical to make it absolutely clear.

```
                    SAM AND JO
                (together)
          Huh, what?
```

Or replace the word "together" with "simultaneously."

Here's a third example that you can use when the two characters say the same thing at about the same time or when they say *different* things at about the same time.

```
                    SAM
          Huh, what?


                    JO
                (overlapping)
          Huh, what?
```

And finally . . .

```
              SAM           JO
          Huh, what?    Huh, what?
```

If you wish, you can have three or four characters speaking simultaneously. For another example of simultaneous dialogue and overlapping dialogue, see the comedy scene on pages 78-79.

[U] THE TELEPHONE VOICE

As mentioned a bit earlier, voices coming through telephones, walkie-talkies, radios, and similar devices are VOICE OVERS. Sometimes I see: *(on phone)* or *(amplified)* or the antiquated *(filtered)* typed adjacent to the name. In any case, the person speaking is obviously not in camera and not at the scene location. At code [U] on page 119, I use a VOICE OVER (V.O.) for clarity. For a discussion of VOICE OVER and OFF SCREEN, see pages 171-173.

Television
Treat the television set as a separate character. If there is a specific character who is on television, simply indicate as much in your description and type the character's name as the character caption or cue. If you want to be especially clear, add the following parenthetical: (on TV).

```
                    JOCK JIM (on TV)
          Hi, Mom. We're number one!
```

[V] TELEPHONE CONVERSATIONS

There are four methods for handling phone conversations.

Method 1

Use this method when the audience does not see or hear the other party. This is handled like any other speech.

```
                    MARY
          He said what?
                    (nodding her head)
          Well, thanks for letting me know.
```

Notice that I did not use the word "beat" to indicate a pause.

Method 2

The second situation is when the audience *hears* the other person, but does not *see* him or her. In that case, the dialogue of the person not seen is voiced-over.

```
                    MARY
          He said what?


                    JOHN (V.O.)
          He said you're as cute as a cuddle
          bunny.


                    MARY
          Well, thanks for letting me know.
```

Method 3A

The third situation is when the audience both hears and sees the two parties. In such cases, use the INTERCUT. You can handle it simply, as with the following example:

```
INTERCUT — DARIN'S CAR/SUZANNE'S KITCHEN
```

This would be followed by dialogue written like any other conversation. That's exactly what I do at code [V] on page 119.

Method 3B

Another method of using the INTERCUT, and perhaps the preferred method, is as follows:

```
INT. SUZANNE'S KITCHEN - NIGHT
```

Suzanne paces nervously, then punches numbers on her phone.

```
INT. DARIN'S CAR - SAME
```

Darin drives through the rain, looking depressed. His cell phone rings.

```
INTERCUT - TELEPHONE CONVERSATION

                    SUZANNE
          Come back.

                    DARIN
          What? Now?

                    SUZANNE
          Yes. Please.

                    DARIN
          Give me one good reason.

                    SUZANNE
          You forgot your casserole bowl.

                    DARIN
          I'll be right there.
```

The INTERCUT device gives the director complete freedom as to *when* to intercut between speakers. (He/she has complete freedom anyway, so why not be gracious?)

The reason you use this device is that otherwise you would have to write a master scene heading with each change of speaker. This can become laborious and interrupt the story flow. On the other hand, it may improve the story and give you more control over which character the camera is on at any point in the conversation.

Method 4

Let's rewrite the scene that begins at [H] on page 119 without the INTERCUT, using master scene headings.

```
EXT. CLASSROOM - DAY
```

The woman in the phone booth is CALCUTTA COTTER. With phone in hand, she turns toward the classroom window and frowns at what she sees -- the professor doing cartwheels down the aisle.

                    DEAN ZACK (VO)
         Make him pay, Calcutta ...

INT. DEAN'S OFFICE - DAY

The voice belongs to DEAN ZELDA ZACK, who stands at her
polished desk with a swagger stick tucked under her arm.

                    DEAN ZACK
         ... Make him pay.

INT. PHONE BOOTH - DAY

Calcutta's excitement is subdued by doubt.

                    CALCUTTA
         It'll work?

INT. DEAN'S OFFICE - DAY

Zack's confident smile reveals gold caps over her front
teeth.

                    DEAN ZACK
         Stumps him every time.

The swagger stick slashes the desk. The delirious dean
CHORTLES with satisfaction.

EXT. PHONE BOOTH - DAY

The CHORTLING is heard through the phone receiver. Calcutta
smiles, then SLAMS the receiver.

Now let's take another tack. Suppose you don't want the camera on Dean Zelda Zack,
nor do you want to hear the dear dean. In such a situation, you would use Method 1,
and the conversation would read something like this:

EXT. CLASSROOM - DAY

With phone in hand, CALCUTTA COTTER turns toward the
classroom window and frowns at what she sees -- the
professor doing cartwheels down the aisle.

                    CALCUTTA
         I'll make him pay, all right --
              (turns to phone)

```
You're sure it'll work?
          (nodding)
Beautiful.
```

Calcutta urges a smile, then slams the receiver.

This version also works well. The only thing we're missing is the identity of Calcutta's information source. It may serve the script better dramatically to withhold the name of this person. Ask yourself: What is the best way to move the story forward?

COMPUTER CONVERSATIONS

Let's discuss e-mail conversations. First of all, only words that are spoken should appear as dialogue. That is what dialogue is. However, if a person repeats out loud what she reads on the monitor, then you could write what she actually says as dialogue. Otherwise, you want to find a clear way to impart the contents that doesn't confuse the reader or slow down the read. Perhaps, you can create a variation of the INSERT by using ON THE MONITOR as a secondary scene heading.

Sid faces his computer monitor, then types on the keyboard.

ON THE MONITOR

Sid's words appear:

> "But Renee, they're tapping my phone conversations."

BACK TO SID

who waits for Renee's response.

ON THE MONITOR

Renee's response appears:

> "You're being silly, Sid."

Notice that the words that are typed are indented like dialogue and appear with quotation marks. You could also go to a shorthand version of the above by simply omitting the phrases "Sid's words appear" and "Renee's response appears." It goes without saying that you don't write something like SID'S POV - THE MONITOR.

SPEAKING IN FOREIGN LANGUAGES

In working with other languages, realize there is one general rule: Write your script in the language of the eventual reader so that he/she knows what is going on. In other words, avoid writing dialogue in a foreign language.

If a character speaks in French, do not write out the dialogue in French unless the eventual reader is French, or in the rare case that the meaning of the words doesn't matter. Simply write the lines as follows:

```
                    JEAN-MARC
                 (in French)
         I will pluck your head.
```

Instead of having your character speak in French, consider sprinkling his/her dialogue with French words to give us a French flavor. Then everyone knows what is being said.

```
                    JEAN-MARC
         Come with me, mon alouette.
```

Now, suppose your character absolutely, positively must speak in a foreign language. Your desire is for something realistic, such as the Italian spoken in THE GODFATHER. You have five options, depending on your specific purpose.

1. If it doesn't matter whether the audience understands the meaning of the foreign words, or if you believe the audience will be able to figure out the meaning of the words by their context, then just write them out in the foreign language. For example:

```
Tarzan shouts at the charging elephant.

                    TARZAN
         On-gow-ah!

The elephant turns and stampedes in the opposite direction.
```

Or write the words in English using a wryly to indicate what language the words will be spoken in, as follows:

```
                    PIERRE-LUC
                 (in French)
         Imbecile. Idiot. Retard.
```

2. If the characters speak in French throughout an entire scene, then make a clear statement in the narrative description that all the dialogue in the scene will be spoken in French; then, write the dialogue out in English so that the reader can understand it.

. . . But this begs the question: How will the *audience* know what is being said? They won't, unless they speak French. For that reason, this is seldom a viable option. If your character must speak in French *and* it's also important that the audience understand what is being said, then subtitles are the solution.

3. If you write a long scene in which French (or any other language) is spoken, and if you want English subtitles to appear on the movie screen while the character speaks in French, then include a special note in the narrative description, as follows:

```
NOTE: THE DIALOGUE IN THIS SCENE IS SPOKEN IN FRENCH AND IS
SUBTITLED IN ENGLISH.
```

Then, simply write the dialogue out in English. After the scene ends, write:

```
END OF SUBTITLES
```

4. Another option for using subtitles is to use a wryly.

```
                    MICHELLE
              (in French, with
              subtitles)
          I spit on your name. I spit on
          your mother's grave. I spit on
          your book.
```

```
The spittle flies.
```

5. There is one other option for using subtitles. Use this device only if the sound of the words in the foreign language is important; for example, in the case of this space visitor's language, the words have a humorous quality.

```
          ALIEN                     SUBTITLES
    Zoo-BEE, Woo-BEE.           You're cute.
```

My final advice is to choose English whenever possible and give us the sense of a foreign language by including a few foreign words and/or flavor of a foreign accent.

MUSIC LYRICS

There may be a rare instance where you'll need to include music lyrics in your script because a character sings them. First of all, never include lyrics from a song whose rights are not owned or controlled by you. It's a negative when a reader sees music lyrics from a popular song in a script. If you are creating a musical, or quoting a poem or song that is in the public domain, or even have a character who is singing nonsense for comedic effect, then you can write lyrics in two different ways. One is to write them as dialogue (since they are dialogue) in stanza form, just like a poem.

The lyrics quoted below are from an existing song; thus, the quotation marks.

```
                    McKAY
          "Well, you take the high road
          And I'll take the low road,
          And I'll be in Scotland before you."
```

An alternative is to use slashes, as follows.

```
                    McKAY
          "Well, you take the high road/and
          I'll take the low road/And I'll
          be in Scotland before you."
```

SOUNDS AS DIALOGUE

Only the spoken word should be written as dialogue. Human screams and dog barks are sounds, and are included in narrative description. Here are two examples.

```
Billy screams.
```

```
Sparky BARKS.
```

If a character reads someone's journal, those words should not be written as dialogue unless the audience hears them spoken. That could be done with a voice-over or the character reading the journal out loud.

MUTE DIALOGUE

What if you have a character who is mute and communicates by signing? Signing is not dialogue since words are not actually spoken. Of course, general audiences are not familiar with signing, so usually (in a film script) the mute person's meaning is communicated to the audience either orally or through subtitles. If the mute person speaks as he/she signs, then simply write the words he/she says as dialogue:

```
                MUTE PERSON
             (while signing)
       Did you understand what I said?
```

If the mute person is a major character, then indicate once in the narrative description that the mute person signs whenever he/she talks; that way, you won't need to include a parenthetical for each block of dialogue.

If the dialogue is written in subtitles across the screen, then write out the dialogue as in the example above, except write the parenthetical as follows: "while signing; in subtitles." An alternative method is to indicate in narrative description that the mute person signs and that the dialogue appears in subtitles.

As always in spec writing, your goal is to be as clear and unobtrusive as you can.

TELEPATHIC DIALOGUE

I think we have established that only dialogue is dialogue, but what do you do when people communicate telepathically?

The question to ask here is this: If there is an actual telepathic communication, how will the audience know what is being communicated? In other words, what does the audience see and hear in the movie theater? Whatever it is, that is what you must describe in your screenplay. If the audience hears words *without anyone's lips moving*, then clearly describe that and use a VOICE OVER for the words, although it's probably too hokey to use in a dramatic or serious work.

In STAR TREK, I have seen the empath simply state what she is *sensing* or *reading*. Thus, the audience knows what she is picking up.

[W] DIALOGUE PUNCTUATION

The use of the dash (--) and the ellipsis (. . .) has become very clouded in recent years. Usually, they are used to make dialogue look like . . . well -- er, dialogue.

There used to be very definite literary rules about these. Today they are often used interchangeably and you may use them anyway you like, as long as you are careful not to overuse them. However, understanding their actual use in terms of writing dialogue can be very helpful in presenting a consistent pattern in your written communication.

-- The dash indicates a sudden shift or break in thought, or to show emphasis. It is used when one character interrupts another, or shifts his thought, or a character is interrupted by a sound or an action, or a character speaks as if interrupted or with sudden emphasis.

The dash is created by typing a space, hyphen, hyphen, space -- like that.

... The ellipsis is used for continuity. A character will start speaking, then pause, and then continue. When a character stops, and then continues later, the ellipsis is used instead of the dash. When a character finishes another character's sentence, use an ellipsis.

The ellipsis is made by typing three periods followed by a space.

Here's an example of both the dash and the ellipsis.

```
EXT. BALCONY - EVENING

Coquette dabs her eyes with a handkerchief. Suddenly,
Vivi blunders through the French doors. Coquette turns
expectantly, then puts on an angry face.

                    COQUETTE
          Why did you come here?

                    VIVI
          I came here to --

                    COQUETTE
          I don't want to know why you came
          here ...

He moves earnestly toward her. She softens.

                    COQUETTE
          So why ...
               (raising her lips)
          ... did you ... come here?

Vivi's lips are now just a silly millimeter from hers.

                    VIVI
          I came here to ...
```

His gaze fades into a blank stare, then stupefaction.

          COQUETTE
   You have forgotten --

            VIVI
      (recovering)
   But one kiss and I will remember
   why I came here.

He lays one on her, then looks joyously into her confused face.

            VIVI
   I came here to kiss my
   Coquette. You.

For another example of dialogue punctuation, see the comedy scene on pages 77-79.

How to format TV scripts

This section builds on information in the previous sections of this book. Sample scenes of a sitcom spec script can be found on pages 192-193.

TV MOVIES

A teleplay for a TV movie (called *long form* or *MOW* for "Movie-of-the-Week") is normally seven acts and about 100-105 pages for a 93-minute TV movie slated for a two-hour time slot. If you write such a teleplay, I recommend you use standard spec screenplay format as discussed in the previous section. That way, you can avoid the pain of delineating acts and pacing the story's major turning points for commercial breaks. Besides, your MOW could actually become a feature movie in the selling process. Just write it as a feature screenplay—this is perfectly acceptable to virtually all MOW production companies. Once your teleplay is sold, then you can convert it into the seven-act format preferred by the production company.

There are standard act lengths for most MOWs.

Act 1:	18-23 pages
Act 2:	12-15 pages
Act 3:	12-15 pages
Act 4:	9-12 pages
Act 5:	9-12 pages
Act 6:	9-12 pages
Act 7:	9-12 pages

As you might guess from your reading in Book I, you need a strong cliffhanger, twist, or turning point at the end of Act 1. That's also true for Act 3. Acts 2 through 5 correspond to the second act of a standard screenplay. Thus, Acts 6 and 7 are your resolution.

As mentioned before, use standard spec screenplay format. At the end of each act, you will break to a new page and center the act number at the top of that page (ACT ONE, ACT TWO, and so forth). From the act designation, double- or triple-space and write the next scene. It's as simple as that.

Acts should end on dramatic moments. Acts 1 and 3 should end on particularly strong twists, cliffhangers, or dramatic moments to keep people from switching channels at the first commercial break and at the "end of first hour" break.

PILOTS

It is nearly impossible for novices to break into television with a new series pilot or miniseries. If you have a hot idea that you believe in, write the pilot as a TV movie (using standard spec screenplay format) and market it as a feature script or TV movie. That way, it will be easier to get it read. If it truly is a great series idea, the agent or producer reading it will see that potential.

DRAMATIC SERIES

If you want to write an episode for a one-hour series—whether a dramatic series like CSI, or one more humorous like ALLY MCBEAL—you will still use standard spec screenplay form (as used with feature scripts). You do not need to indicate scenes; however, you must designate the four acts, teaser, and tag.

Teaser
This is the brief (about one minute or so) initial section establishing the show. Seldom do you find an episodic series anymore that doesn't open with some kind of teaser. However, it is seldom indicated as a TEASER in the script. Most scripts simply FADE IN just like a feature screenplay.

The four acts
After the teaser, break to a new page and center ACT ONE at the top of the page, triple-space, and write out the scenes just as you would in a feature screenplay, using standard spec screenplay format.

Many production companies also request that you add END OF ACT ONE at the end of the act (just triple-space and center END OF ACT ONE), after which you break to a new page to the second act, and so on. Some shows, like the STAR TREK series, have five acts. After each act, break to a new page.

Tag
The tag, often called the epilogue, is the brief (about one minute or so, and often less) ending section that ties up loose ends. In some shows, this is "scenes from next week's episode." Usually, the epilogue or tag is identified as such at the top of the page.

Title page and script length
Your script will be about 54 pages in length.

The title page for any episodic TV show, regardless of length, is similar to that of a feature script, except that the title of the episode is included along with the title of the series. Here is an example from an imaginary series entitled L.A. SCRIPT DOCTORS.

L.A. SCRIPT DOCTORS

"THE PERSPICACIOUS PROFESSOR"

The titles of the series and episodes may also be underscored if you wish. Also, you can space twice (as I did) or three times between the series title and the episode title.

It may be worthwhile to acquire a script from the series itself as a guide to writing style, number of acts, how acts are labeled, and formatting quirks (keeping in mind that you are writing a spec script, not a shooting script, and that you will avoid camera angles and editing directions in your script.) Also, try to get a copy of the show's bible (see page 353).

SITUATION COMEDY

Situation comedy (sitcoms) utilizes a mutant variation of standard spec-screenplay format because sitcoms are essentially dialogue-driven stageplays with just one or two sets. Due to the special format, several pages of explanations plus an example follow.

If you want to write for a specific TV show, obtain a copy of one of their scripts, since each show varies slightly in formatting style, as you will see in the explanations that follow. Keep in mind that scripts you purchase are shooting scripts and not spec scripts, but it always helps to become familiar with the writing style of a given show. Sitcoms are either taped or shot on film, which is one reason for variations in formatting style. As suggested for the dramatic series, try to get the show's bible as well (see page 353).

A half-hour sitcom script is about 40-50 pages, but can be longer depending on the show. This differs from standard spec screenplay form, which is about a page per minute of screen time.

The title page for a sitcom script is handled in the same way as a dramatic series script. See example above for L.A. SCRIPT DOCTORS.

A sitcom is simpler than a screenplay, both in structure and content. Comparing the screenplay scene on page 119 to the sitcom scenes on pages 192-193 should prove instructive. What follows applies to sitcom scripts only.

The cast list and sets list

Although these two lists appear in shooting scripts, you will *not* include them in your spec script. They are *not* required. If you are writing a shooting script, the cast list will include any actors already assigned to the series. Usually, the characters appearing every week are listed first, followed by any guest characters. The sets are listed in three categories: exteriors, interiors, and stock shots.

Typeface, margins, and tabs

Like all other scripts, sitcoms are written in Courier 12-point. Margins for sitcom scripts are at 1½ inches on the left, one inch on the right, and one inch at the top and bottom. Tabs from the left margin are 10 spaces for dialogue (although some scripts indent more) and an additional 12-14 spaces to the character cue (character's name).

Page numbering

Page numbers are typed at the top right corner of each page and are usually followed by a period. Some shows ask you to indicate parenthetically the act and scene numbers just below the page number. That is what I did in my example (pages 192-193). Some shows, such as *Frasier*, ask you to indicate only the letter of the scene below the page number (without indicating the act number). Other shows only require a page number at the top right corner of each page.

Acts and scenes

Sitcoms consist of a teaser, two acts, and a tag. The first act ends on a major turning point, followed by a commercial. Acts are designated in CAPS and (for example, ACT ONE) and are centered at the top of the page in the same manner as a dramatic series. If you wish, you may also underscore them. At the end of the act, break with END OF ACT ONE, centered two or three spaces below the end of the act.

A teaser is often not included in a spec script, but when it is, it is designated as a TEASER. A tag is designated as the final scene in ACT TWO, or as a TAG, or not included at all. Again, it depends on the sitcom series you are writing for.

In sitcoms, scenes are designated with letters: Scene A, Scene B, and so on. Sometimes the word "scene" appears in CAPS: SCENE A, SCENE B, and so on. Often, you see just the letter, without the word "scene": A, B, and so on.

Please note the sample scenes on pages 192-193. Each time you change to a new scene, you break to a new page, come down about a third or a half of the page, and then center your scene designation and place it in CAPS.

On page 193, we have a new scene. Naturally, if this were a continuation of the previous scene, I would have continued the scene at the top of the page.

End scenes with a CUT TO: or FADE OUT, neither of which must be underscored.

Occasionally, you see a script that includes the designation for an act along with each new scene change, as follows:

ACT ONE
Scene D

Only do this if the particular sitcom you are writing for requires it.

Headings

Each scene begins with a master scene heading—indicating exterior or interior camera position, location, and day or night—written in CAPS and underscored, as follows:

INT. SMALL CLASSROOM - DAY

In a few scripts, the characters in the scene are included parenthetically, as follows:

INT. JERRY'S APARTMENT - DAY
(Jerry, Kramer, Elaine)

In either case, you will double-space to description.

Description

Narrative description always appears in CAPS and is single-spaced. Because a sitcom is really a TV play, the emphasis is on dialogue rather than on action, so there will be comparatively less narrative description and more dialogue in a sitcom than in a motion picture screenplay.

Entrances, exits, and transitions

In situation comedy, there are very few changes in location (sometimes none). To keep the read from bogging down, and because sitcoms are really stageplays written for television, all entrances and exits of characters are underscored. This includes a character movement from place to place within a scene. For example:

ELLEN STEPS OUT OF THE CLOSET AND INTO THE LIVING ROOM

Or

<u>ROZ ENTERS FRASIER'S BOOTH</u>

Or

BART <u>CROSSES</u> INTO THE KITCHEN

All first appearances of characters are underscored. Furthermore, at the beginning of each scene, after the heading, establish which characters are in the scene. Do this with the first sentence of narrative description. Note my example on pages 192 and 193.

Transitions (editing directions) are underscored.

Sounds
Sounds no longer need to be underscored. However, on occasion, there may be a particularly important sound that you want to emphasize. In such cases, double-space and write the sound out as follows:

<u>SOUND: DOORBELL RINGS</u>

Special effects are handled in exactly the same way.

<u>FX: NUCLEAR EXPLOSION</u>

It's hard to imagine much need for a special effect in a sitcom script.

Dialogue
Because there is such an emphasis on the dialogue in television comedy, it is double-spaced for ease of reading. Actor's instructions (wrylies) are used more freely than in a screenplay, and are usually placed within the dialogue block itself. (Sometimes they are brought to the left margin, but they are always enclosed in parenthesis.)

Here's one of my favorite lines from a SEINFELD script. (George pretends he is a marine biologist to impress Holly. Suddenly they come upon a beached whale and a crowd.)

                    HOLLY
          (BLURTS) Stop! Everyone, this
          is one of the world's foremost
          marine biologists. (WITH PRIDE)
          This ... is George Costanza.

AS ALL EYES TURN TO GEORGE, A MAN WITH A VIDEOCAMERA BEGINS
CAPTURING THE MOMENT FOR POSTERITY.

ACT ONE

Scene A

FADE IN:

INT. SMALL CLASSROOM - DAY

About <u>8 STUDENTS</u> AWAIT <u>THE PROFESSOR</u>, WHO <u>ENTERS</u> WITH EXCITEMENT. OVER HIS SHOULDER IS A STRAP SUPPORTING A "SEA WORLD"-TYPE LEATHER POUCH, ONLY THIS ONE IS FILLED WITH CANDY MINTS INSTEAD OF FISH.

<u>CHARLIE</u> RAISES HIS HAND.

                    CHARLIE

      Hey, Mr. Professor, how do you

      handle phone calls in a script?

                  PROFESSOR

      (SCINTILLATING) A most excellent

      question.

HE TOSSES THE GRATEFUL BOY A CANDY MINT. CHARLIE CATCHES IT IN HIS MOUTH AND SMILES BROADLY.

                    <u>FADE OUT.</u>

Scene B

<u>INT. DEAN'S OFFICE - DAY</u>

<u>CALCUTTA COTTER</u> SPEAKS WITH <u>DEAN ZELDA ZACK</u>.

CALCUTTA

... And then the professor gives

everyone a candy -- all except me.

DEAN ZACK SLAPS HER SWAGGER STICK ACROSS HER POLISHED DESK.

DEAN ZACK

Make him pay, Calcutta, make him

pay. (PACING) Now do exactly

what I told you. It stumps him

every time.

CALCUTTA <u>EXITS</u>.

DEAN ZACK

Now, Mr. Professor, let's see you

get out of this one.

DEAN ZACK LAUGHS INSANELY.

<u>FADE OUT</u>.

Glossary of terms not discussed elsewhere

ANGLE - Directs the camera to a particular person or object. The character's name itself could be written as a heading in CAPS and serve the same purpose. Angles (or SHOTS) can be wide, low, tight, close, high, bird's eye, etc.

AD LIB - This instructs the actors to fill in the dialogue with incidental lines.

ANAMORPHIC LENS - A lens used to shoot a wide-screen film; also, to project it onto the screen.

CRANE SHOT - A moving shot from a camera on a lift.

DISSOLVE - An editing direction where one scene "melts" into another, the former fading out while the latter fades in.

DOLLY or **TRUCK** - Picture this as a camera on wheels. Variations abound: CAMERA IN, PULL BACK TO REVEAL, TRUCK WITH, CAMERA PUSHES IN, etc.

FADE OUT - The image fades to black. This editing direction appears two spaces below the last line, flush right.

FREEZE FRAME - The image freezes on the screen and becomes a still shot. Often used with END CREDITS.

MOS - Without sound. Originated with German director Eric von Stroheim, who would tell his crew, "Ve'll shoot dis mid out sound." Use this to describe action that appears without sound. Occasionally characters will speak MOS in the b.g.

O.C. - OFF CAMERA, a term now used only in television.

OVER THE SHOULDER - Shooting over someone's shoulder from behind.

PAN - A stationary camera pivots back and forth or up and down (TILT).

PINKS - From the expression *fix it in the pinks*. Revisions of shooting scripts are usually done on colored paper.

REVERSE SHOT - When we're looking over Vivi's shoulder to Coquette, then reverse to look over Coquette's shoulder to Vivi.

SHOCK CUT - A sudden cut from one scene to another. (Also SMASH CUT.)

SLOW MOTION and **SPEEDED-UP MOTION** - You know what these are.

SPLIT SCREEN - The picture is divided into two (or more) sections.

STOCK SHOT - A film sequence previously shot and stored at a film library.

SUBLIM - A shot lasting a fraction of a second.

SUPER - A superimposition—one image (usually words) overlaid on another.

WIPE - An editing direction where one image moves another out of frame.

ZIP PAN - A super-fast PAN, creating a blurred image and a sense of quick movement.

ZOOM - A stationary camera with a zoom lens enlarges or diminishes the image.

Formatting index

WRITING & REVISING YOUR BREAKTHROUGH SCRIPT

BOOK IV

A Script Consultant's View

The spec script—your key to breaking in

When a writer breaks into Hollywood, it's with a *spec script*. When a writer is paid millions of dollars, it's for a *spec script*. Although *shooting scripts* abound and can be easily purchased, *spec scripts* are difficult to find and little is written specifically about them. And yet, agents and producers alike are searching for the right *spec script* that convinces them you are the next great screenwriter.

Virtually every script you purchase from script services or find in screenwriting books is a *shooting script*. And yet, you must write a *spec script* to break in. (The differences between the two are explained in Book III.)

A SPEC WRITING COURSE

The main purpose of Book IV is to demonstrate effective spec writing. A secondary purpose is to reinforce principles taught elsewhere in *The Bible*. In this book, we will look at scenes from several of my clients' scripts and revise them into the current spec writing style. You will be encouraged to write your own revision before viewing my suggested revision. Each example will present new writing problems and provide new insights, from the elementary to the complex.

I will also analyze excerpts from three of my scripts that have made a difference in my career, and will conclude with a line-by-line analysis of the first ten pages of a screenplay.

AVOID THIS COMMON TRAP

Many writers make the crucial mistake of assuming that they understand spec format and spec writing. For that reason, some make glaring errors in their scripts that could have been avoided. Because the information in this book on spec writing builds on the foundation laid in Book III, I strongly urge you to read (not skim) Book III if you haven't already. *You will find a great deal of direction concerning spec writing, including examples of dialogue, description, and the effective use of headings (slug lines).*

Key principles and exercises in revising scenes

DIRECTING THE CAMERA WITHOUT USING CAMERA DIRECTIONS

What follows are the opening scenes in a writer's screenplay.

```
EXT. HIGHWAY 27 - DAY - AERIAL VIEW

WE SEE the lush Florida countryside until we FIND our
subject, a dark green van.

SLOW ZOOM IN ON VAN

VIEW ON VAN - MOVING

Two characters shout at each other while the CAMERA MOVES
beside the van until we see the child/protagonist looking
out the window at us.

INT. VAN - PAT, SALLY AND ALEX

Everyone is quiet.
```

Try your hand at revising the above sequence. Make any assumptions you wish about the characters, the story, and the vehicle. Naturally, you'll want to use correct spec screenplay format. Once you have written your revision, read my analysis and revision below.

Obviously, there can be many "correct" responses and many revisions that would work beautifully depending on your dramatic goals. Before showing my revision, let me comment on the above sequence.

First of all, I would not call the original scene a riveting "reading experience." Notice in the original scene that the focus is on *how* the story is told, not on the story itself. What is going on in the van? We don't know. Who are the two characters shouting at each other? Are they parents, kidnappers, siblings? We're not sure. Why is the child looking out the window? What is his or her facial expression? Is the child's name Pat, Sally, or Alex? We don't know because the writer is too involved *directing* his movie and choosing which technical directions to use.

Of course, we don't need the answers to each of these questions. Not everything needs to be revealed at once. But we need to know more than is currently being communicated.

Let's try to improve on the original without sacrificing much in terms of the "feel" that the writer wanted to communicate.

EXT. FLORIDA - DAY

From the Atlantic shore, the lush countryside extends for miles. Below, a black two-lane highway meanders through the Spring growth. A green van scoots down the highway.

EXT. VAN - CONTINUOUS

The van rumbles along. Inside, two twenty-something parents, RALPH and SALLY shout at each other, although their words cannot be heard.

INT. VAN - CONTINUOUS

Ralph shoots an angry look to the back where ANGIE, age 6, leans away from him and stares out the window at the beautiful trees and shrubs whizzing by.

EXT. VAN WINDOW - CONTINOUS

The child is motionless, sad, trapped. One little hand presses against the glass.

INT. VAN - CONTINUOUS

The parents are silent now -- gathering steam before their next eruption.

In the revision, I have *suggested* almost everything the original writer wanted, but my focus is on the story and the characters, not on fancy ways to tell the story.

In addition, I *imply* a POV shot of the child staring at the trees and shrubs. If desired, I could even describe the reflection of trees on the window glass (without using technical terms).

I identify the child's sex by giving her a name that is definitely a female name. I also changed the father's name.

I direct the camera (without using a camera direction) to a CLOSE UP of the child at the window. In effect, I am directing the reader's eye more than I am directing the camera. And I do that for a *story* reason. I want the reader to know that the child is the most important character in the scene, and that maybe she is the central character, or protagonist, of the screenplay; and I want the reader (and the movie audience) to emotionally identify with the child's situation. That's the reason for Ralph's look at Angie. It implies that the child may be the subject of the parents' shouts.

I end the scene with a promise of things to come. I am trying to create some interest in what happens next while revealing the emotions of the parents.

In summary, my advice is to focus on story and character; and, while you are at it, use clear, specific language.

• • • • •

Let me make one small formatting point on the above revision. I could have written my second paragraph as follows:

```
The van rumbles along. Inside, two twenty-something parents,
RALPH and SALLY, shout at each other MOS.
```

As discussed in Book III, MOS means "without sound." For more on the origin of this term, see the glossary at the end of that book.

EVERY SCENE SHOULD HAVE A SPECIFIC PURPOSE

Here is a short scene that needs a little help. The three children—Jamie, age 14; Billy, age 10; and Sissy, age 6—stand over the grave of their alcoholic father (Larry). They're on their own now, and it has been established earlier that Jamie has been taking care of the family anyway. How would you revise it?

```
EXT. COUNTY CEMETERY - DUSK

A soft wind rustles the hair on three darkly dressed figures
standing over an unmarked grave. Eyes fixed on freshly
covered ground. Everyone there who ever cared about Larry or
his family. Jamie, Billy, and Sissy stand alone.

                    JAMIE
          We used the last of our savings to put Dad
          here. (pause) There's not much left.

Her conversation is with herself.

                    JAMIE
          I guess we'll have to rely on ourselves.
          (ironically) We've always had to anyway.
          Not much different now.

She regains some composure.

                    JAMIE
               (thinking softly)
          Gotta get some dough. Fast.
          There isn't much time.

She doesn't even have the luxury to allow herself to mourn
for more than a few minutes. It's on to the next crisis to
solve. She has been -- and now certainly is -- the only one
to find the answers to all their worries.

                    BILLY
          We gonna be split up now!
```

Have you written your revision? Okay, let's take a close look at the original again. In terms of formatting, the dialogue lines for Jamie's first two speeches are too wide (more than 3½ inches wide) and the wrylies are not written correctly. You caught that immediately.

What is the purpose of the scene? That's a good question to ask of any scene you write. Every scene should have at least one specific purpose.

In this case, the purpose is apparently to show Jamie as the new head of household and to show Billy as worried about being abandoned—which, of course, adds to Jamie's burden. In your revision, you want to make sure the scene focuses on that aloneness and that burden (now it's us against the world).

The dialogue is too on the nose. Jamie is saying precisely what she is thinking and feeling. What's worse, her combined lines represent a soliloquy—a must to avoid. How can we improve the dialogue?

Because it is already obvious that they are alone in the world, she does not have to come out and say it. Just them standing alone around the grave would *show* it without her having to *tell* us.

The exposition about the savings being gone might be worth keeping because it adds to the opposition. But let the line come in response to something Billy says or does.

Jamie's last line about needing "some dough" is already implied in the exposition about the savings, so her third speech can be omitted as well.

What does the last wryly, "thinking softly," mean? First of all, how can you think softly? And how can you say a line by thinking softly? So the wryly makes no sense.

The first paragraph of narrative opens with a soft wind. Why do we need the wind? I don't see why, as this is written now, but since the whole world is against these kids, let the whole world come at them like the wind. That might help dramatize their situation. In my revision, I'm going to use a cold wind (not a soft wind) to subtly represent the opposition in this scene. And I'm going to end my revision with Jamie accepting the challenge of that wind. I think that will help move the story forward a little better.

The last two lines of the first paragraph are confusing. Who is everyone? I assume the writer means that the three kids are the only people in the world who cared about Larry. You cannot afford to confuse your reader with general or vague language.

In the third paragraph, Jamie regains some composure. When did she lose it?

The fourth paragraph is an "author intrusion." The writer is including things that cannot appear on the screen. You cannot *tell* us this stuff, you've got to *show* us through action, sound, and images; or reveal it in dialogue.

Once you have written your revision of the above scene, take a look at mine. Remember, there is no one correct way to revise this scene. I'm hoping your version is better than mine.

Here's my revision.

```
EXT. COUNTY CEMETERY - NIGHT

Jamie, Billy, and Sissy huddle over a fresh, unmarked grave.
Alone. A cold wind tangles their hair.

Billy peers up at Jamie, looking forlorn.

Jamie stifles a sob. Speaks to no one in particular.

                    JAMIE
          Didn't leave us with even a dime.

                    BILLY
               (chin quivering)
          You gonna go away now -- huh?

Jamie pulls Billy close. The three gently embrace.

The wind picks up, but Jamie slowly lifts her countenance
against it.
```

COMMON DIALOGUE PROBLEMS

Overwritten dialogue
Here's one beat of dialogue.

```
                    KASPER
          We've been over this. This is our
          home. It's where we met, fell in
          love, got married.

                    LIZ
          I realize that we have history here.
          I loved this city once. But I don't
          feel safe anymore. The world's a
          different place.
```

Liz's speech above is overwritten. The first sentence is repetitive of what Kasper just said. The rest is implied by one simple thing that she could say:

```
                    LIZ
          ... But I don't feel safe anymore.
```

Notice how much more powerful that one line is when it stands alone.

Here's another example of an overwritten speech:

>   SCOTT
>   I'd be willing to give it a decent
>   shot. At least that sick bastard
>   would be out of my life entirely.
>   He would stop sending me Christmas
>   cards. Sick prick acts like he's
>   my father.

And here's the revision:

>   SCOTT
>   I'll give it a shot. At least that
>   sick bastard would stop sending me
>   Christmas cards.

These are not really revision, but easy edits. They only require a little focus and a desire to write lean dialogue.

Not writing for subtext
In the following example, the first sentence says it all, and the second line states the subtext, which, of course, should not be stated. Here's the flawed speech:

>   YOUNG ROBERT
>   Daddy, are we almost done?
>   Remember, the game is at two and we
>   have to be there early to lime the
>   field.

Not only does the above speech state the subtext, it unnaturally forces exposition into the speech. Since the first line implies the second, the second is not needed.

>   YOUNG ROBERT
>   Daddy, are we almost done?

Here's an example of the same problem.

>   COOPER
>   I should have studied harder in
>   high school. I think I made a
>   mistake.

Since the first line implies the second, omit the second, and you allow the subtext to remain below (sub) the speech (text). Remember, the subtext is the unstated, underlying meaning of the text.

```
                    COOPER
          I should have studied harder in
          high school.
```

Speaking too often in complete sentences

Let's look at a longer example of an overwritten speech. Try your hand at revising the following speech before reading my comments below.

```
                    MORGAN
          Have you experienced a lot of violence
          on the job?

                    COOPER
          Not too much, but definitely enough.
          Plus things have been crazy here
          over the last couple of years.

                    MORGAN
          So you couldn't stand it anymore?

                    COOPER
          It was all right. I like my job.
          It was certainly not boring, but my
          wife couldn't stand it. After nine-
          eleven, she didn't sleep much.
```

Please notice that Morgan and Cooper are mainly speaking in complete sentences. It doesn't sound like natural conversation. The revision below contains fragments of speech.

```
                    MORGAN
          Seen a lot of action?

                    SANDERS
          Plenty.

                    MORGAN
          Couldn't stand it anymore, huh?

                    SANDERS
          Wife couldn't.
```

As you know, the above is not the only correct way to revise the exchange. It may be that Cooper is a talker who uses colorful and original phraseology. If that's the case, write on. I loved listening to the long-winded Professor G. H. Dorr (Tom Hanks) in THE LADYKILLERS. That's mainly because his character speaks with original phrases and a vocabulary unique to him, rather than delivering derivative or boring speeches.

Overwritten wrylies

There is a growing school of thought that suggests writing actions as parentheticals. If an action can be described in three or four words and seems to accompany the speech, then I think that's fine.

                         TEX
                 (tipping his hat)
         Pleased to meet you, ma'am.

However, don't go overboard with this. I consider the following an abuse of parentheticals (sometimes called *actor's direction* or *wrylies*).

                         JACK
                 (grabing Jill by the
                 hand)
         Could sure use some water, my
         dear.
                 (a beat; starts up
                 the hill)

                         JILL
                 (snatching the bucket
                 out of his hand)
         Sounds like a good idea, Jack.
                 (swings bucket around
                 and around as they
                 near the well)

I'm not seeing a major problem with the parentheticals that precede each of the two speeches. However, you should not end a dialogue block with a parenthetical. A dialogue block should conclude with dialogue—the speech. Finally, the speeches are rather stiff. Here's my revision.

Jack shows Jill his empty bucket.

                         JACK
             Water?

Jill snatches the bucket.

                         JILL
             Race ya.

She swings the bucket around as they gallop to the well.

CHOOSING THE RIGHT DETAILS

What follows are the first two paragraphs of a screenplay written by one of my clients before she became a client. Rather than overwritten dialogue, we have overwritten description. The following big blocks of black ink are guaranteed to discourage any reader. Let's see if we can't whittle them down a little while being more specific in describing images and actions. Here's the original.

```
EXT. TRAIN - DAY

We see the skyline of New York from a train. Painted on the
side of it are words that say, Brooklyn Railroad. It's going
very fast and has a gray look to it.

INT. TRAIN - DAY

Inside the train are all kinds of commuters. They are from
every age and ethnic group and they fill the train car
clean up. They are all headed to work in New York City, as
can be plainly seen from their working clothes. A bunch of
them cannot find seats and must stand. One of them is SALLY
STANWICK, who has piercing blue eyes and long, flowing locks
of blonde hair. She is in her mid-twenties and is wearing a
silk blouse with a pink sweater over it and a plain black
cotton skirt. She senses someone behind her and turns to see
a young man giving her the eye and smiling at her in a very
peculiar way.
```

Let's critique the first paragraph. To start with, let's avoid writing "We see" and describe the scene in a more interesting way. The second sentence contains the pronoun "it," which could refer to the train or to the skyline of New York. It is unclear. Be specific.

Because no paragraph of narrative description should exceed four lines in length, the second paragraph represents a major violation. We need to condense it or break it up.

Why must this woman's eyes be blue and her hair blonde? Unless essential to the plot, get rid of specific physical descriptions. Describing her attire is a good idea, but would be better if that attire commented on her character.

The writer uses too many words to describe the group and its ethnic diversity.

Finally, what does the writer mean when the man smiles "in a very peculiar way"? That's too general. How does the reader visualize it? Be specific.

Our revision should include only what is essential to move the story forward; and since this is an opening scene, it needs to establish a mood, atmosphere, or something about the nature of this story.

As you know from reading Book III, each paragraph of narrative description should, ideally, present one beat of action or one main image. This is not a hard-fast rule, just a guideline. Let's adhere to that guideline in this revision.

Without using camera directions, let's open with a shot of the train in the foreground and Manhattan in the background. In fact, let's handle this in four brief paragraphs.

1. Our first image will be of the train, establishing departure location and destination (with the train in the foreground and Manhattan in the background).

2. Our second image (and second paragraph) will be of the people in the train car.

3. Our third paragraph will describe Sally and her action.

4. Our fourth will describe the second character.

We will omit Sally's eye and hair color to keep casting options open. The specifics of her clothes are irrelevant, so let's omit them, unless you can describe her in something that comments on her character. I think I'm going to give her a simple cotton dress—this is an uncomplicated young woman.

Let's also make sure that the young man's smile says something about him—I think I'm going to use his smile as an action. And let's use a strong, active verb, like *assaults*.

Finally, let's make sure that our narrative description is as "lean and clean" as possible and makes the reader ask, "What happens next?"

```
FADE IN:

A speeding silver train races down the tracks toward
Manhattan. A sign on the train reads: "BROOKLYN RAILROAD."

INT. TRAIN - DAY

Working professionals crowd the train car. Some stand.

Among them is SALLY STANWICK, 25, pretty in a simple cotton
dress. She turns abruptly, sensing someone's stares.

A young man in a suit assaults her with a smug smile.
```

REVEALING EMOTION

When evaluating scripts, I often find myself writing something like the following: *Insert a character reaction or small action here, or describe a facial expression or gesture, to give the reader a better sense of what your character is thinking or feeling.*

These little "reactions" or "actions" can be as simple as the following:

```
He squeezes her hand.

Anita looks frustrated.

Her face relaxes into an expression of mixed gratitude and
relief.
```

These details invite us into the character's inner life and help the reader to more easily sympathize with the character.

Let your reader in
What follows is an excerpt from my screenplay HEMINGWAY'S TWIN (written with Lucille deView). Marcelline Hemingway Sanford is about age 40, and Lila is her college-aged summer help.

```
                    LILA
        It must have been wonderful to
        get engaged here.

                    MARCELLINE
        Yes. But Walloon can break your
        heart, too.

                    LILA
        I can't think about love. My writing.

                    MARCELLINE
        Of course.

                    LILA
        Mrs. Sanford, could you talk to your
        mother about ... everything?

                    MARCELLINE
        Yes. I could. Why?

                    LILA
        'Cause I need my mother -- my real
```

```
             mother. I need her and I'm angry
             with her for leaving. Imagine being
             angry at your dead mother.
```

The key moment, of course, is the revelation about Lila's mother, so let's dramatize it. What little details would you add to invite the reader into Lila's heart? In the revision that follows, I will not change any of the dialogue, just add three bits of action.

```
                    LILA
             It must have been wonderful to
             get engaged here.

                    MARCELLINE
             Yes. But Walloon can break your
             heart, too.

                    LILA
             I can't think about love. My writing.

                    MARCELLINE
             Of course.
```

Lila leans forward, face to face with Marcelline.

```
                    LILA
             Mrs. Sanford, could you talk to your
             mother about ... everything?

                    MARCELLINE
             Yes. I could. Why?
```

Lila looks away a moment, trying to contain her secret.

```
                    LILA
             'Cause I need my mother -- my real
             mother. I need her and I'm angry
             with her for leaving. Imagine being
             angry at your dead mother.
```

Lila's chin quivers -- perhaps from the chill, perhaps from the longing.

Your character's experience is your reader's experience
Let's look at another example.

In the scene excerpt that follows, the patient is the central character. How would you revise the scene to get the reader (and the audience) more involved with him?

INT. TRAUMA ROOM — NIGHT

The flight crew enters with a man C-spine/stabilized on a
backboard.

The TRAUMA RESIDENT, appearing like he just got out of bed,
is stationed at the head of the table. The other trauma team
members assume their positions to do their tasks.

The patient is transferred from the backboard to the trauma
table.

The flight nurse commands attention. She fires her report.

> FLIGHT NURSE
> (announcing loudly)
> We have a thirty-nine-year-old male
> involved in a single car rollover.
> He was extricated from the vehicle.
> No allergies. No significant history.
> His Glascow Comma Scale is 15.PERLA
> at three millimeters. He complains of
> pain, nine out of ten, in his mid-back
> and has no feeling or movement in his
> lower extremities. All other assessment
> is negative. I gave him a half liter
> of LR in flight and twenty milligrams of
> Decadron IV. He has received no pain
> medication yet. Any questions?

> FLIGHT PARAMEDIC
> Oh, by the way, this man is a Vandy
> resident in OB. His name is Brad
> Malone.

By the way, the word "Vandy" is short for Vanderbilt Hospital. The scene takes place
in Vanderbilt Hospital. Good luck with your revision.

There are two main points I want to make about the above excerpt. First, the focus is
on medical procedure, not on the central character. In fact, the writer is so focused on
the medical aspects of the scene that she refers to Brad as "patient" in the narrative
description. It reads more like a case study than a drama.

Second, the Flight Nurse's speech contains too much medical jargon. Just give us a flavor.

One goal that we have as screenwriters is to get the reader and audience to feel emotion.
People come to movies to feel emotions vicariously through the characters. Readers want

to be emotionally affected by what they read. Thus, our task becomes to get our audience involved with our characters. With that in mind, here is one possible revision.

INT. TRAUMA ROOM — NIGHT

The flight crew enters with Brad strapped to a backboard.

The TRAUMA RESIDENT, appearing like he just got out of bed, is stationed at the head of the table. Trauma team members quickly gather around Brad.

The FLIGHT NURSE fires off her report.

              FLIGHT NURSE
     We have a thirty-nine-year-old male ...

Brad takes a gulp of air, responding to the pain, as he is transferred from the backboard to the trauma table.

              FLIGHT NURSE
     ... involved in a single-car rollover.
     No allergies. No significant history ...

Brad holds a trembling finger to his head, trying to control the pain enough to hear.

              FLIGHT NURSE (O.S.)
     He complains of pain, nine out of ten,
     in his mid-back and has no feeling or
     movement in his lower extremities. He
     has received no pain medication yet.

Brad looks helplessly up at the impassive faces of the professionals surrounding him.

              FLIGHT PARAMEDIC (O.S.)
     Oh, by the way, this man is a Vandy
     resident in OB. Brad Malone.

In my revision, I keep the focus on Brad and on his situation. I include dialogue that highlights Brad's situation and pain. I include a POV shot of Brad looking up at the medical professionals. The word "impassive" helps the audience sense Brad's aloneness in this scene. Notice that most of the dialogue is spoken off-screen (O.S.), so that the camera can be on Brad. That helps the reader and audience better identify with Brad, and it gives potential actors something to act. Finally, I removed the unnecessary wryly "announcing loudly."

DESCRIBING WHAT WE *SEE* AND CREATING MOOD

One of the biggest problems I see in scripts that I evaluate is narrative that describes realizations, thoughts, feelings, and memories. These cannot appear on the silver screen. Only write what the audience sees on the movie screen and hears on the soundtrack. That's it. The following examples are all incorrect.

```
When Susan saw his face, she remembered the first pizza she
ever ate.
```

```
Pablo stopped walking toward her. He was thinking about how
much he wanted her, but also how much his mother hated her.
He was at a stalemate.
```

```
James felt awful.
```

```
Sigourney knew that this was the last time she would ever
see home again.
```

In each of the above examples, I ask, *How will this appear on the screen?* How will the audience know, for example, that Susan is recalling a pizza, or what Sigourney "knew"?

Let's review these examples one by one and decide how to revise them.

In Susan's case, you could describe his face, FLASHBACK to Susan's pizza, then describe her shuddering and turning away. You see, you can describe only that which we actually see to convey your story.

In Pablo's case, I think you will have to write some dialogue to convey his indecision, or you might write an earlier scene where he joyfully tells his mother that he is in love, and she expresses her hatred for the girl. Then you could cut to him walking toward his beloved, stopping, looking confused and unsure.

With James, describe his facial expression or a gesture that will convey that he feels awful. What do we *see*? *See* is the key word. "James felt awful" is not a visual image. Instead, how about something like this:

```
James drops his forehead into his hand, then gazes up with a
guilty look on his face.
```

As with James, you may want to describe Sigourney's facial expression or a gesture. Here's one possible description:

```
Sigourney gazes at the homestead as if memorizing every
detail.
```

For whom the bell tolls

What follows is a paragraph of overwritten description that I'd like you to revise.

```
Matthew's wife, ELLEN, a pretty woman in her twenties, with
red hair, is sitting at a sewing machine making a baby
quilt. There is lots of evidence of the room being made
into a nursery. She HEARS the rain, gets up and goes to the
window. It's evident she's in the early states of pregnancy.
As she looks out to sea, she HEARS the local church bell
RING, signaling that a boat has been lost. She closes her
eyes.
```

First of all, the scene exceeds the four-line limit. No paragraph of narrative should exceed four lines in length, and even that can be too long.

In the second place, you have two visual images here. The first is the image of the Ellen in the room. The second is Ellen's looking out to sea and hearing a church bell. Thus, we already know there should be two paragraphs. Since the ringing of the bell is so important, that deserves its own paragraph anyway.

Third, let's only include what's essential in the description. Ellen's hair color is probably irrelevant, so we can omit that.

Fourth, in terms of readability, we should eliminate the present progressive expression "is sitting" and use an active verb like "sits." As you will see below, the writer used the active verb "sews" in her revision.

And fifth, the audience can't know what the ringing of the church bell means because that "meaning" (it's a signal that a boat has been lost) cannot appear on the movie screen; thus, we cannot mention the meaning here. It's probably going to have to come out in action and/or dialogue later.

My client made the following revision, based on my evaluation.

```
Matthew's wife, ELLEN, 26 and pregnant, sews a baby quilt.
An unpainted crib sits nearby.

Hearing a driving rain, she hurries to the window and gazes
out to sea. The church bell rings. She closes her eyes in
pain, her hand clutching her blouse.
```

In her first paragraph of her revision, my client provides specific evidence that suggests the room is being made into a nursery.

In the second paragraph, she chooses details that will help create a *mood* and also give a sense of what the ringing of the church bell means. She uses the "driving rain," the specific verbs "hurries" and "clutches," and the emotional reaction "closes her eyes in pain." The mood created will suggest possible music to the composer.

WHEN THE WRITING IS TOO VAGUE

Sometimes, the narrative description is general, and specific details need to be added.

EXT. THE CAMPUS — SERIES OF SHOTS

We see Marie going to her classes, studying, and eating.

Not only is the excerpt formatted incorrectly, but it also doesn't tell us much. What follows is the screenwriter's revision based on my evaluation.

MONTAGE — MARIE ON CAMPUS

-- Marie steps into a science class and nearly walks into a skeleton. Students laugh, including Sam.

-- She hands the professor a paper with a confident smile.

-- She savors her lunch salad. She smiles comfortably at Sam, who chows down on a hamburger and fries.

CHARACTER MOTIVATION IN A SCENE

Virtually every scene should feature a character with an intention, goal, desire, need, or problem. There should also be some opposition to the central character's actions toward that goal or intention. This creates conflict. The conflict will escalate if the central character continues to be thwarted in his efforts. The character will be forced to act more strongly until an outcome is determined.

This simple scene is from THE SECRET OF QUESTION MARK CAVE, a comedy written for children more than a decade ago. It became a sample script that I never sold but which found me work. The children are about ten years of age. Just prior to the scene, the Red Hat Bandit was about to harm the children, who discovered his hide-out. They defended themselves with wood swords, tree limbs, and rocks to render the Red Hat Bandit unconscious. Here is how the scene breaks down dramatically:

Stinky wants to control the group, be the leader, prove he's smarter than the rest. Everyone calls him Stinky because he likes to "cut the cheese." He even woke up his sleeping uncle once that way (established in Act 1).

Ralph's primary emotion in this scene is curiosity, which leads him to challenge Stinky. Stinky asserts that the bandit is dead, but Ralph is not so sure. So the primary conflict in this scene is between Ralph and Stinky. Both are motivated in their intentions. Note the differences in their speaking styles.

Glodina's primary emotion is fear. She fuels a secondary conflict with the three boys (the Magnificent Three) because she wants to leave and they don't. Her desire to leave creates a little suspense—we suspect something bad could happen if they stick around too long. In fact, Glodina's line "Let's go then before he wakes up" foreshadows the end of the scene.

Seebee is a big fan of ZOMBIE BUSTERS, a TV show where zombies suck the brains out of their victims (again, established earlier in the screenplay). Although Seebee is the central character of the movie, he is only a minor character in this scene. His purpose is to plant the seed that the bandit might be a zombie. The crisis question in the scene is this: "Is the Red Hat Bandit dead?"

This scene accomplishes many things. It serves as a bridge between two action sequences. It plays up the innocence of the children. It moves the story forward—the bandit is more strongly motivated now. After this scene, there is no doubt in the children's minds that he is going to kill them if he can catch them. Plus, we want to know what happens next.

Finally, look at all the white space! The description is sparse, dialogue speeches are short, and the wrylies are useful.

EXT. QUESTION MARK CAVE - DAY

The Magnificent Three plus Glodina stand in a circle gaping at the fallen bandit. They cling to their weapons -- just in case.

> GLODINA
> Is he dead?

> RALPH
> Nah, dead people stick their tongues out. Like that.

Ralph demonstrates the death tongue.

> GLODINA
> Let's go then before he wakes up.

> STINKY
> Don't worry, he's dead.

> RALPH
> Maybe his tongue don't stick out cuz he swallowed it.

> SEEBEE
> If he's dead, we have to go to jail for killing him.

> STINKY
> Heck no. Self-defense.

> RALPH
> Yeah, he was going to kill us. Now he's a stiff. Wait a minute, is he stiff? Dead people are stiff. That'll prove it.

> STINKY
> Why don't you grab him and see?

Ralph is reluctant to touch the "corpse."

> RALPH
> He looks kinda stiff.

> GLODINA
> You guys, let's go.

                         RALPH
          Wait a minute, aren't dead people blue?

                         STINKY
          I say he's dead!

                         RALPH
          He looks kinda blue.

                         SEEBEE
          He looks just like the zombies in
          Zombie Busters.

                         RALPH
                    (a victorious smile)
          How can he be a zombie if he's dead?

                         SEEBEE
          They are dead, but then they blink
          their eyes open and they suck
          everyone's brains out.

Seebee makes convincing SUCKING SOUNDS. Glodina shivers.

The children shuffle in for a better look at the bandit.

                         RALPH
          Wait a minute, I heard dead people
          kept their eyes open.

                         STINKY
                    (the last straw)
          I'll prove he's dead.

He squats over the robber's face and FARTS.

The Red Hat Bandit's eyes blink open. He grimaces at the
pungent odor.

                         RALPH
          A zombie! He'll suck our brains
          out.

The children panic and tear down the trail.

The bandit, angry and groggy, chases after them.

                         RALPH
                    (to Stinky)
          See, I told you he wasn't dead.

SHOW IS BETTER THAN TELL

Here is one last scene to evaluate and revise. Good luck.

INT. HELEN'S HOUSE - NIGHT

Helen has torn herself away from her students' papers and is watching Marilyn pace.

>   HELEN
> Yes ... then what?

>   MARILYN
> Then they asked me to sing. It was
> the love song. I belted out the
> solo part without a single problem.
> I was inspired! Then Antonio
> joined me on the duet and ... and

She shudders like a chill just ran up her spine.

>   MARILYN
>   (continuing;
>   melodramatically)
> the angels wept!

>   HELEN
> That's perfect! Then you got the
> part! It's what you've always
> wanted! I'm so happy for you!

>   MARILYN
>   (cuts her off)
> It's not going to happen. They
> said they'd get back to me.

>   HELEN
> What? Why? I don't get it. You
> said ...

>   MARILYN
> I said I did a superb job in the
> audition. That isn't enough on
> stage. They don't like the way
> I look.

Marilyn drops, dejected, onto the couch.

                    HELEN
          How do you know that?

                    MARILYN
          After the reading and singing,
          they whispered among themselves
          for a few minutes. Then they
          had me walk back and forth across
          the stage a few times. Then they
          had Antonio stand next to me.

She stands back up again and resumes pacing and gesturing.

                    MARILYN
                  (continuing)
          Then they had me walk back and
          forth with Antonio. Then they
          had Antonio put his arms around me.
          Then they said, "Thank you very
          much, we'll be in touch."

                    HELEN
          Well, that doesn't necessarily mean ...

                    MARILYN
          Yes it does. Believe me, I've seen
          it a bunch of times.

She slows her pace and becomes thoughtful. She looks a
little depressed as she walks over and picks up her coat.

                    MARILYN
                  (continuing)
          You know it isn't fair. I'm
          just not sure whether to give up, or
          cry, or just go to Baskin-Robbins.

                    HELEN
          Well, whatever you do, don't just
          give up. You have an amazing
          talent. Sooner or later, that will
          win out.

                    MARILYN
          I hope so. Good night, hon. Don't
          forget we're going to the mall
          tomorrow after school.

Okay, now take a moment to analyze what you've read and revise it into something more interesting.

• • • • •

Here are my thoughts: The dialogue is quite ordinary with the only action being Marilyn's pacing. And Marilyn's experience is overwritten: First she sang; then Antonio joined her in song; then they (whoever *they* are) said, "We'll get back to you"; then they whispered; then they had her walk back and forth; then they had Antonio stand next to her; then they had her walk back and forth with Antonio; then they had Antonio put his arms around her; and finally they thanked her. That list could be easily condensed, as could the dialogue. There is also too much repetition of the phrase "then they." And both characters speak the same way.

My first impulse is to take Marilyn's experience and *show* it to the reader, then MATCH CUT from Marilyn's pacing on the stage to her pacing in Helen's room as she finishes telling Helen the story. Just doing that will give the scene more movement.

In terms of the relationship between Marilyn and Helen, Helen is in the position of nurturing a whiner. Let's revise this so that Marilyn comes off as more sympathetic (not so much of a whiner). Let's allow Marilyn to decide to not give up. And let's give Helen more personality and wit. After all, she's a teacher and knows how to motivate people.

Just doing those things already mentioned will help the dialogue, but we can also tighten it up and render it less "on the nose."

A scene should end on a strong moment. Let's open with a song and close with a song, demonstrating that Marilyn will not give up. And maybe the teacher can give Marilyn an "A," since she's already grading papers. We'll do that indirectly, of course.

Now let's take a look at some of the specifics of my revision. We see an empty theater as Marilyn sings. The next image is of Marilyn, which creates a contrast—she's not great looking, but near the angels in her singing. The third image is of two young men, the opposition characters in this scene. Incidentally, even the opposition will recognize her voice, so the reader can be confident that this woman has some talent.

But then the opposition humiliates her. This creates sympathy for her. This moves us into our transition, which we accomplish by putting the camera on Marilyn's face and changing the location. This is easy to do since she is pacing in both places.

Then we have our moment between the two women. We set up Helen with the red pencil so she can use it at the end of the scene. And instead of Helen saying the expected, she tries a more original approach, creating a little conflict in the process.

The laughter relieves the tension and sets up the serious moment. Again, we have a contrast. And we get Marilyn to indicate that she won't quit trying without her actually saying any words. Instead, she sings.

• • • • •

Okay, here's my revision, just one of many ways to approach this material.

```
INT. THEATER - NIGHT

A lovely female voice sings a love song. Her music fills the
empty theater.

The voice is Marilyn's, looking chubby in her leotards. But
her face is angelic -- she is one with her music.

Antonio, slick black hair and tank top, joins her in a duet.

A young turk with a clipboard steps onto the stage.

                    TURK
          Okay, okay. Enough!
               (circling the couple)
          You'll make the angels weep.
          Beautiful, Marilyn, beautiful.

Marilyn smiles gratefully.

When he signals Antonio away, Marilyn glances offstage at
her image in a mirror. She touches her stomach and frowns.

                    TURK
          Gimme a strut. Back and forth.

Marilyn walks across stage, then back.

The young turk studies her. Antonio steps over to him and
whispers something. Looks doubtful.

Marilyn's eyes fill with tears as she paces.

INT. HELEN'S LIVING ROOM — NIGHT

Marilyn paces while Helen listens from her couch. Homework
papers cover the coffee table. Helen fiddles with a red
pencil.
```

                    MARILYN
        ... That's when he said he'd get
        back to me.

                    HELEN
        Well that doesn't necessarily mean --

                    MARILYN
        Yes it does. I've seen it.
            (shaking her head)
        They don't like my looks. That's
        what it is. Always what it is.

                    HELEN
        Well, your voice survived.

                    MARILYN
        The question is ... will I?

                    HELEN
        You can always get a tummy tuck.

Marilyn is indignant until she sees Helen's warm smile. Then
her tension releases into sudden laughter. Helen joins in
the laughter.

                    HELEN
        You were made to sing, honey, like
        a big, fat, beautiful bird.

Helen stands and the two briefly embrace.

                    HELEN
        So why don't you fly out of here
        and let me grade some papers, huh?

Marilyn mouths a "thank you." She steps out the door. And
starts singing the love song.

Helen smiles. Writes a big, fat "A" on one of the papers.

When to break formatting rules

As you know, the rules can be bent and broken. But when? Two conditions must be present. Let's express these conditions as questions.

- Will breaking the rule improve the reading experience? The answer to this question should be "yes."

- Will breaking the rules call attention to the broken rule and create a negative impression? The answer to this question should be "no."

If you have little experience writing, your responses to those questions will necessarily be based on your subjective evaluation. As your experience grows, your assessments will become more objective. You'll have a better feel for what you can get away with.

SLUGGING IT OUT WITH SLUG LINES

Here is an excerpt from my screenplay A WINDOW IN TIME.

```
EXT. TEMPLE RUINS - DAY

Abu nods gratefully to the Man in Khakis, then rushes to

THE TEMPLE BASE

where a small hole has been cut into the foundation. The Man
in Khakis leads Abu into the blackness.

INSIDE THE CATACOMBS

Abu and the Man in Khakis crawl on all fours toward the
torch light ahead, and finally into
```

```
A LARGE CIRCULAR CHAMBER

where torches illuminate the stoic faces of a dozen workers
standing back against the single, circular wall.
```

In the above scene, I break a rule about headings (slug lines). The scene starts outside (EXT.) the temple ruins, then goes inside (INT.). That's a change that requires a new scene heading as follows: INT. CATACOMBS – DAY.

I probably get away without creating a new master scene heading. My purpose is to make the scene flow better. In addition, I don't see where someone would become confused. I also don't think the peccadillo would concern a reader.

So—yes!—you can bend or break the rules, but be careful not to get *too* creative. You never want to lose or confuse a reader. Your goal is a clear, unencumbered flow of images, sounds, and actions.

CHARACTERS AS LOCATIONS

Technically, characters cannot be used as scene locations because they aren't places. However, this rule is bent all the time, often with good effect. Suppose you want to focus on two characters in an intense scene. Instead of the common ANGLE ON MONA or CLOSE ON MONA, you simply write:

```
MONA

removes a gun from her purse and points it at

FAHID

who stops cold in his tracks. He looks at her in surprise.
```

Now you are using characters as locations, and the story flows easily without being encumbered by camera directions. In such a situation, be careful not to describe something happening some distance away. As long as the camera is on Fahid, you cannot describe anything or anyone except Fahid. If you want to next show Fahid and Mona together in the same shot, you will need to create a new heading.

Can you ever include a camera direction in a screenplay? Of course you can. But do it rarely and only when you have a good story reason or character reason to do so.

A PROBLEM WITH TIME LAPSE

Throughout Books III and IV, I have emphasized the importance of avoiding technical intrusions. We're going to break that rule here.

Here's a description of a formatting problem as described by my client:

> I want to show a time lapse from day to night for a story reason. A character, Jimmy, parks a Chevy automobile next to a building; someone is locked in the trunk (established in an earlier scene). I want to focus on the Chevy while everything around it changes. Jimmy will stand by the car and then disappear. The sequence will end in a light rain for the next scene.

How would you format that?

I suggested she use a format similar to the MONTAGE for the time lapse. Here's the result:

```
TIME LAPSE

The Chevy stays in the same place as everything around it
changes.

-- Jimmy disappears.

-- The day evolves into night as lights go on, then out, in
the building behind the car.

-- Two teenagers gather around the Chevy, then disappear.

-- A light rain drizzles.

EXT. STREET - MORNING

The only sound is the rain on the Chevy. And then the usual
sounds of morning become apparent.
```

CHEATING

If your script is a little too long after all of your excellent revision work and editing, there are little ways you can cheat.

Margins

First of all, do *not* cheat on dialogue margins. Speeches should not extend more that 3.5 inches across the page. Do *not* cheat on your regular left margin; that should always be at 1.5 inches from the left edge of the paper. Do *not* cheat on the top margin of the page either. The trained eyes that will read your script will readily spot these cheats.

Since the right margin can be anywhere between .5 inches and 1.25 inches, you may set it anywhere within that range. Consider changing the bottom margin from 1 inch to .9 or .8 inches so that you can add another line. However, let me add a word of caution to that suggestion: Some studios and large production companies automatically convert scripts into a "uniform format." This assures them that they are always looking at the same format with each script they get. Of course, in order to do that, they would need an electronic copy of your script.

Line spacing

You may be able to cheat a little on your line spacing. If you are using a word processor like Microsoft Word, adjust your line spacing so that your page holds about 54 or 55 lines, which is standard. (Visit the "Bible Updates" page of www.keepwriting.com for the latest information.)

You might be able to make that adjustment with other software programs as well. Most software programs give you about 53-57 lines per page. If you are not getting 54-55 lines, adjust your line spacing so that you do. More than 55 lines per page could look too cramped and may be spotted.

Note: I am not including the page number or the space after the page number in my line counts above.

Orphans

Another trick that saves space is shortening paragraphs where the final line contains only one word (referred to as an "orphan"). Thus, if your paragraph contains two lines plus one or two words on the third line, condense the paragraph to two lines.

The same is true of dialogue. If you have just a single line of dialogue that carries over to another page or a few words of description that carries over to the next page, find a way to move those to the previous page or condense the dialogue or description.

Often, being forced to revise long paragraphs and speeches results in a cleaner, better-written version. I've been able to lose a half-dozen pages in a script just be *tightening up* dialogue and description.

Wrylies

I mentioned in Book III that you can write action in your wrylies (*actor's direction* or *parentheticals*) if that action can be described in no more than two or three lines. As I've said before, think of the rules as guidelines. There may be an instance where a long wryly of four lines works just fine, and saves some space by avoiding breaking to a new paragraph to write action and then double-spacing to write more dialogue.

Naturally, any cheating you do will only be done after the screenplay has been revised and is ready to show. There's no sense in making nitpicky corrections until the script is polished.

Finally, always use 12-point Courier or 12-point Courier New.

REACHING THE READER

Keep in mind that your primary audience is the reader of your script (not the movie-goers), and that he/she is weary of reading scripts.

As you have probably gleaned from our earlier discussions, one of the key principles of spec writing is to avoid using the camera directions that you would normally find in a shooting script. Direct the camera without using camera directions. That involves using specific language in creating visual images in the mind of the reader.

Obviously, if you write *A tear forms in her eye,* that's a CLOSE UP. You don't have to use the camera direction to clarify that. Just let the story flow like a river. That river will flow if you use visual, clear, and concrete language that directs the eye and touches the heart.

The first ten pages

What follows are the first ten pages of my action/time-travel/romance, A WINDOW IN TIME, along with a complete line-by-line analysis of those pages. This script was slated for a network movie, but low ratings for other time-travel shows and movies at that time nixed the production. I include this excerpt in response to the many clients and students who have asked for an example of a successful *spec script*. In my analysis, I will tell you my reasons for writing this the way I did. I hope that discussing my rationale will be helpful. In many cases, you may think of a better way to present the same story information. Wonderful! It means you are thinking and learning, and becoming the next great screenwriter.

What are the general strengths and weaknesses of these pages? Overall, the structure is good and the pacing is fast. Characterization and dialogue could be stronger. The writing is generally clear and easy to follow.

Since A WINDOW IN TIME is primarily an action-adventure story, there are many paragraphs describing the action. One of my challenges is to keep those paragraphs as short as possible while still conveying dramatic action. Although four-line paragraphs are acceptable, I make sure that only one paragraph in these ten pages exceeds three lines.

In today's competitive market, something must happen by page 10. The reader needs to feel that she is into the story by that point. She must want to read more. You will be the judge if these pages accomplish that.

The first scene is not an action scene and is 2½ pages long. It would be better to open with action. In fact, a previous draft opened with the scene now found on page 5, but I finally settled on opening with this scene to establish the hero and set up his world. Also, this scene motivates or grounds succeeding scenes, allowing me to create a pace that accelerates to the turning point on page 10.

Note: For ease of reading, the analysis for each page of script will appear directly to the left of each page of script.

Before you begin, you might consider reading first the page of script, and then my analysis of it. Another approach would be to read the entire ten pages first, and then come back and read the analysis.

Typically, you FADE IN on page 1, but you cannot fade in on a black screen. My opening is meant to be thematic. The first thing we see is a window that lets in light, and this story is about a window in time that lets in the light of the future, the light of self-knowledge, and the light of love. I'm hoping to create a small sense of mystery right here at the beginning.

Jake is described simply as a NASA employee. That's all that needs to be said here because this entire scene comments on Jake. Mark is described as Jake's "best buddy."

Because so many scenes take place in this room and involve this house, I feel that I must take pains to describe it. So we establish that this room is on the second floor and that there is an orange grove in the backyard. The orange grove along with the NASA cap implies that we're in Florida. Also, the grove is where we'll hide a helicopter later.

We'll soon learn that this is Jake's hide-out, not his residence, and that he's showing it to his best-friend Mark for the first time. Why? Because he needs Mark to prepare a sales presentation for him. Now if we try to reveal all of this in one line of dialogue, it will come off as boring exposition. So we provide our first clue with Mark's first line; obviously, Jake owns a condo. (Incidentally, that first line also indicates that they are in mid-conversation.) And then Jake explains, "No mail-man, no sales-man, no meter-man." The subtext is: *This is my secret hide-out.* The second clue.

Then Mark helps establish something of Jake's private life. Later, we learn that he's not afraid of anything but women. Mark, of course, is probably a skirt-chaser. Mark's line, "I can set you up," is a setup line for the last scene of the movie, when he says, "I told you I'd set you up." The slug in the arm replaces the lifeless words "a beat" that I originally used.

I debated over the two paragraphs describing the desk lamp, drafting table, blueprint tubes, and tiny laptop jacked into a computer. But I decided to keep them because Jake is an aeronautic engineer and computer whiz who loves miniatures. Besides, he uses the laptop later. The one line you could omit is, "It [the arching desk lamp] hovers over a drafting table like a flying saucer." I'm shooting for mood, here, and genre. Technically, this is a science-fiction love story against the background of high adventure.

Jake then declares his love. First we have the declaration, then we show the reader what he loves: His design of a new kind of helicopter. He asks Mark to help him sell it, so now the reader understands the situation before turning the page. *An aeronautic engineer wants his marketing buddy to help him sell his secret helicopter plans, so he brings him to his hide-out.*

A BLACK SCREEN

Footfalls of two men ECHO across a wood floor. CLICK -- someone
releases a latch and KICKS open a window shutter, then the other.

INT. UPPER ROOM - DAY

Bold beams of sunlight burst through a large window.

JAKE DEKKER, wearing a NASA ball cap, and his best buddy MARK are
bathed in wide shaft of white sunlight.

Mark gazes out the second-story window to the back lawn and beyond
to a grove of orange trees, then up to a blue sky.

                    MARK
          Beats the hell out of your condo.

The room's walls are covered with posters of military flying craft
of all kinds. Miniatures hang by string from the ceiling.

                    JAKE
          No one knows about it. It's in
          my uncle's name, in Georgia. Got
          a generator downstairs. No mail-
          man, no sales-man, no meter-man ...

                    MARK
          ... And no wo-man.

                    JAKE
          I value my privacy.

                    MARK
          If you saw the babe I just met,
          Jake, you'd go public.
                    (slugs him in the arm)
          I can set ya up, ya know.

Jake crosses the room and twists the knob of an arching desk lamp.
It hovers over a drafting table like a flying saucer. Large metal
blueprint tubes lie beside the desk.

On the desk is a tiny laptop jacked into a nearby computer.

                    JAKE
          My only true love. And you're
          going to help me sell it.

His only true love is on the drafting table: The design of a black
and angular helicopter. Mark sighs in amazement as he turns page
after page of blueprint designs.

Jake's first line on page 2 exists to lend authenticity to the story (the materials described are used in stealth bombers).

Mark doesn't care, so he interrupts. Apparently, he heard something at work that he shouldn't have about Jake's design. He's sheepish about it and feels he has to explain himself to Jake. This short interchange helps establish Mark's employer as NASA or the military. We also get a hint of Mark's dark side. He "hears rumors" he isn't supposed to hear. He interrupts his friend who is describing his "only true love" and (on page 1) he (Mark) is chasing the babes. And at the bottom of the page, Mark's last line reveals that of all the uses the little miniature could be put to, he'd use it to spy on women at the beach. These little hints do not add up to much now, but they help make Mark believable when he betrays his friend later. We're setting up foils: Jake is straight and serious; Mark is loose and shallow. We're doing this with dialogue that also reveals exposition. This may not be immediately obvious to the reader; but it lays the groundwork so that these characters will seem believable and consistent in later scenes.

A loud whack scares Mark. Why do I do this? I want to scare the audience and Mark both. I want to create a sense of unpredictability. I want to show Jake as calm and Mark as skittish. I want to emphasize Mark's little indiscretion. And I need to distract Mark so that Jake can grab a hand remote. Note that I describe the gadget in detail as clearly as I can so that you, the reader, can see it in your head and recognize it in later scenes. This is necessary exposition. The reason I invented this little miniature was because in my first draft the two characters only talked about what the eventual helicopter would look like. I decided I needed a way to *show* people. Finally, this is another example of Jake working with miniatures.

The helicopter is described as behaving like a hummingbird. I settled on that to make it easy for the reader to visualize. Later, I call it the Hummingbird MG-11.

The next thing Jake does is to describe his "new concept." Dramatic characters tend to stick to a single train of thought and an intention. Jake's intention in this scene is to get Mark to help him sell this helicopter design to top brass. At the top of this page, Jake begins to describe the helicopter in order to carry out that intention, but Mark interrupts him, providing subtle opposition. Now Jake must do something to get Mark's attention, so he shows Mark the miniature and then continues describing it as "small, quick," etc., and what it's purpose is: "For rescue."

And Jake has not forgotten Mark's question (Mark's first line on this page). He answers it by telling Mark that the military has already rejected it. And he tells him why. I think it's important to explain why the military would reject this, because when we see it, we really like it. Why would they reject it? Because it's not big enough. And that seems realistic.

Mark has not lost his train of thought either. He's supposed to sell the designs and so he tells Jake that the miniature is his best selling tool. The subtext is *Show them that.*

                    JAKE
          The outside will be made of
          kevlar, carbon fiber, and --

                    MARK
          -- Didn't you just present some-
          thing like this to top brass?
                    (sheepishly)
          I heard -- A rumor going 'round.

A loud whack from behind scares Mark. Jake grins. The wind has
blown the shutter against the wall.

While Mark re-opens the shutter, Jake covertly grabs a small hand
remote. It has a short antenna, a control knob, and a tiny TV
monitor on its face. Jake pushes a button and moves the knob.

A miniature helicopter darts up to Mark's face like a hummingbird, and hovers. He jumps back in fright, waving his hands.

                    MARK
          Hell, Jake....

                    JAKE
          A new concept, Mark. Small, quick.
          Can slip anywhere. For rescue.

Jake smiles proudly, then frowns as he answers Mark's question.

                    JAKE
          Yeah, NASA, the military -- they
          rejected it. Don't think it's
          do-able. Besides, they want the
          big-gun ships. Fire power.

                    MARK
                    (pointing at helicopter)
          Hell, Jake, that's the centerpiece
          of your sales promo right there.

Jake signals Mark over. Mark gazes into the tiny TV monitor. As the
helicopter flits about, Mark views different parts of the room in
the tiny monitor. He chuckles, his face aglow.

                    MARK
          A TV camera. Boy, could I get an
          eyeful at the beach.

Mark almost pants. Jake manipulates the knob and the tiny chopper
scoots away and bolts out the window.

From the previous page, the chopper bolts out the window for four reasons: 1) to demonstrate its abilities, 2) to demonstrate Jake's intelligence, 3) to establish it as a lifeline that is used later, and 4) to establish more about Jake's house, one of our main sets. I called up a client in Florida and asked him what grows in Miami. His answer is in the first paragraph. (That's research.) That first paragraph (the longest paragraph in the screenplay) fully orients us to the general setting (a suburb of Miami) and Jake's hideaway. Also, Jake—the secretive engineer not interested in women—drives a jeep. That adds just a bit of dimension to his character.

More exposition: The chopper is silent and cannot be detected on radar. Then the fascinating little miniature darts into the sky, allowing us to cut from blue sky to blue sky. This is a match cut, a smooth transition from our first scene to our second scene. Why is Jake's last line spoken off-screen? Because we want the camera to be on the blue sky so that we can match-cut to the blue sky of the next scene.

Jake's last line is interesting. He's describing the helicopter, but what's the subtext? Well, *Jake* likes to be free and quick. It comments on his self-image.

There is a lot of exposition in this first scene (technically, three scenes in the first 2½ pages). I'm betting that the interest created by the situation, the characters (using dialogue that would be natural for that situation because they have an apparent motivation for saying what they say), the hide-out, and the cute little helicopter makes the exposition interesting; in other words, we want to learn all this stuff. Now let's double-space to a new master scene and cut to an immediate payoff in the next eight paragraphs:

1. We see the sky and the ocean.

2. A one-sentence paragraph focuses on one image: A superimposition telling us this is the Bermuda Triangle. This will create some anticipation. After all, the Bermuda Triangle has a reputation.

3. and 4. Nothing but sound. Clearly, what is happening is not normal.

5. The helicopter bolts from the blue. Yes, I consciously used the cliché.

6. "It is upon us, silent and swift." I'm breaking a rule with the word "us" (author intrusion), but I believe it is worth it. Here's what this really says: *This helicopter suddenly fills the movie screen and flies right into the camera.*

7. The next paragraph allows us to see exactly what this looks like. It is absolutely clear that this looks like the miniature but is *real*. Muting the WHOP-WHOP of the rotors reinforces the point that this helicopter is unusually silent.

8. A new character is introduced—Kendall. I'm hoping these first three pages have already got you hooked.

3

EXT. JAKE'S HOUSE

The tiny chopper flies over the Norfolk pine, coconut palms, and philodendron of the Florida countryside, then over the dirt road leading past the front of the two-story house. Jake's jeep is in the driveway. Miami sits like a jewel in the far distance.

Suddenly, the tiny model flits around the house and through the back window.

INT. UPPER ROOM

Jake maneuvers the remote knob and suddenly Mark is gazing at himself in the monitor. He lifts his head and the chopper is an inch from his nose -- silent. It orbits his head twice.

                    JAKE
          Silent. Invisible to radar ...

It darts out the window and disappears into the blue sky.

                    JAKE (O.S.)
          ... And as free and quick as a
          hummingbird.

EXT. ATLANTIC OCEAN, SOUTH FLORIDA - DAY

A clear, blue sky vaults over a calm, blue ocean. The only sound is the natural movement of the waves.

SUPER: "THE BERMUDA TRIANGLE."

Then: A low RUMBLE, similar to distant thunder. Strange. Unworldly. Slowly crescendos into a sharp, deafening CLAP ...

... Cutting abruptly to a mysterious silence, and at that moment, filling the vacuum ...

... A black helicopter bolts from the blue, as if suddenly emerging from a long invisible tunnel.

It is upon us, silent and swift.

Small, angular, and futuristic. It looks exactly like Jake's miniature model -- only this chopper is real. Strangely, the WHOP-WHOP of the rotors is muted.

INSIDE THE HELICOPTER

KENDALL's nervous hands work the instruments.

A grid appears on the windshield instead of on some computer screen, adding to the futuristic quality of the helicopter. We also establish an empty seat—that's a setup for a later payoff.

The second paragraph and weak "throwaway" line of dialogue demonstrate that she is having difficulty flying this thing. She is not a Navy flyer, not an expert. The blood-stained clothes indicate that something happened just before the movie began. That something is the backstory. We won't learn what happened until about page 70. But it prompts several questions: Is she escaping? Did she kill someone? Where did she come from? Why is she here?

The Egyptian symbol-of-life earrings are the first clues (not yet obvious, of course) that Kendall is an Egyptologist and that she brings life and light to our hero, Jake. (Yes, she came through a window in time, and—yes—she is the love interest.)

At this point, while writing the third draft, I wondered if I needed to make this chopper seem "more real" while also showing off its futuristic capabilities. At the same time, I had a problem of creating a way to get our hero into the hands of Wardle (we'll meet her later). The United States Coast Guard came to the rescue. The addition of the Coast Guard Officer solved both problems, as you shall see. I have found in revision work that when the solution to one problem also solves another, you are probably on the right course.

In this little scene, our Coast Guard Officer demonstrates that the helicopter is invisible to radar. The reader will recall Jake's words, "Silent, invisible to radar." We have now *shown* that, which begs the question: Do you need Jake's words? To be honest, that is a good question. We might have an opportunity to shorten that first scene.

Meanwhile, back in the helicopter, we re-establish the backstory with Kendall's tears. In addition, we add a touch of authenticity to the story with the Collective Pitch Lever. I knew nothing about helicopters until I conducted my research.

A word about the blood and tears: When finally produced, the movie version may be much different, depending on a variety of factors. Nevertheless, the director will note the blood and tears, and conclude, "She is distraught—something has happened." And he will make sure that that concept comes across in his version of the story. The purpose of the spec script is to communicate the story—make the reader see, hear, laugh, and cry (feel)—not plan the shoot. We only hope other professionals will have the good sense to see the story the way we writers do. Right?

4

A grid appears on her windshield. The seat next to her is empty.

On the far horizon an island jumps into view as the chopper suddenly drops. She is frantic, distraught.

                    KENDALL (O.S.)
          Where's that button?

She sighs in relief, and brushes her hair back behind black sunglasses that contrast silver Egyptian symbol-of-life earrings.

Her futuristic clothes are blood-stained.

Below, the sparkling, blue ocean glides silently by.

EXT./INT. COAST GUARD CUTTER - DAY

A COAST GUARD OFFICER spots the erratic movements of the silent helicopter. Dumbfounded, he races to the radar room.

                    COAST GUARD OFFICER
          How fast is it going?

INT. RADAR ROOM

The Coast Guard Officer rushes to the radar screen. He looks in vain for a blip.

                    COAST GUARD OFFICER
          Where is it? Where is it?

The TECHNICIAN looks at him like he's crazy.

                    TECHNICIAN
          Where's what?

EXT. RADAR ROOM/DECK

The officer hurries through the door and searches the sky. He sees nothing.

INT. HELICOPTER - DAY

Just a few feet below, Florida Bay streaks past at amazing speed.

Kendall lifts her sunglasses slightly, wipes away tears.

She pulls up on the Collective Pitch Lever and suddenly she is a half mile above the water. The southern coast of Florida ascends on the horizon.

Miami appears to be the destination, and who lives in a suburb of Miami? Jake Dekker. Good. Cut.

There's not a word of dialogue on this page. Makes me shiver. It would be nice to break this up in some way and create some white space.

We now move to our third major sequence in this screenplay. This setting is so different from the others that we need to take two or three lines to establish it. In my first draft, I described this site at length. I even described the sun pouring through a window high in the temple. The light was blood red. It was a gorgeous description, teeming with thematic elements. I could almost hear the orchestra. However, it wasn't necessary for moving the story forward, and I didn't need it for mood since that is established inside the temple. The appearance of the temple is irrelevant. So my wonderful description is gone now. (A moment of silence please.)

We are in a circular room. If that is not entirely clear, you might suggest a master scene heading that says INT. CIRCULAR ROOM. The torches and the black headdresses add a bit of mystery and mood to the scene.

To complete the scene description, we describe what is at the center of the circle—a pyramid. The four statues mean that this little pyramid is important. In fact, this entire build-up is meant to establish the importance of the "Eye of Ra." Why is it so important? We don't know now, but later we learn (remember, Kendall is an Egyptologist) that the Eye of Ra (Eye of God) can see you through time. This object is also important to the bad guys, because they want to start a New World Order. Look at a dollar bill and you will find on it an "all-seeing eye" at the top of a pyramid with some Latin words below that mean "New Order of the Ages." Of course, I cannot say that in narrative description because it cannot appear on the screen. Instead, it must come out later, through action (narrative description) and dialogue. All I can do here is establish the importance of the object and bring in more information later. Don't tell your reader everything at once. Withhold information, but take care to never confuse your reader in the process.

(Incidentally, any hope of re-selling this screenplay was lost with the release of NATIONAL TREASURE and THE DA VINCI CODE.)

One of the bad guys has disguised herself as a worker. I refer to her as a thief. I hide from the reader the fact that this character is a woman by avoiding the use of pronouns. I also establish the woman's method of operation: a knife under her sleeve. What's the payoff for not identifying the thief? Later in the story, we see a woman, Cherise Joulet, flick a knife into her hand and suddenly we know she is the thief—but our hero does not. This creates suspense because the reader is in a superior position.

Okay. We cannot go any longer without coming back to our central character, Jake. This is one reason I went with Jake's hide-out scene first. So much is going on, I feel that we must establish the hero first so that we know who he is immediately.

5

Soon we are over the Everglades, with Miami on the far horizon.

FROM THE EVERGLADES

The chopper whisks off into the distance. Silently.

EXT. EGYPTIAN DESERT - DAY

The ruins of an ancient Egyptian temple lie partially submerged in the desert earth, obviously part of an archaeological dig.

SUPER: "NEAR LUXOR, EGYPT."

At the temple base, a man-sized hole has been blasted through.

INT. TEMPLE - DAY

Torches illuminate the figures of a dozen motionless workers, all wearing black headdresses obscuring their faces and heads. They stand back against the single, circular wall.

At the center sits a four-foot marble pyramid, protected by four Egyptian statues.

A goateed SHEIK carefully touches the hieroglyphics on the wall, then gestures to the marble pyramid.

Quickly, several workers pry the heavy marble pyramid from its foundation and push it over. It CRASHES to one side. Silence.

There, at the center spot, stands the "EYE OF RA" -- a dark, metallic pyramid only six inches tall. Embedded into the top section of each of the four sides is a purple glowing crystal.

The sheik's eyes water -- awestruck. The workers are stunned. What is this tiny pyramid? The sheik carefully picks it up -- almost expecting a jolt -- and examines it with wonder.

A THIEF, disguised as a worker, strides up to the sheik. A knife flicks into the thief's hand from under the sleeve, and quickly slashes the sheik's throat.

The other hand snatches the Eye of Ra.

A worker attacks the thief, but is repelled by a swift kick to the face. A flash of the knife severs another worker's windpipe.

Instantly, the thief dashes through a door frame and escapes.

Sandy Beach is another important location because it becomes a romantic spot later on. Before we see Jake and his boy scouts, however, I have a little fun with perspective. We see a rocket, then realize it's a miniature. I do it to re-emphasize that this is one of Jake's miniatures (that later becomes a lifeline) and to change the mood from the serious one in the preceding death scene. That's my rationalization.

I hope you've been noticing that each scene has a main story purpose. It's not there just to establish character or mood or location; it's mainly there to *move the story forward*. From here on out, you will see more of the cause-and-effect relationship that should exist between scenes, how one thing leads to another. This is called scene motivation.

The primary purpose of this scene is to get Jake into the hands of Wardle (to be introduced later). What motivates that? You will see as you read the remaining pages. The portion of the scene that appears on this page has another purpose as well—to establish Jake as a good guy. Wait a minute! Didn't I just say don't have a scene just to establish character or mood? Yes, but the entire scene itself does more than just establish character, as you'll see on script page 7. In addition, the boy scouts play a small role later on, so we need to establish their existence.

(Keep in mind that guidelines exist to be broken on occasion. And sometimes, just establishing character can move the story forward, especially in character-driven scripts.)

Anyway, Jake is a good guy because he is a boy scout leader. So what? Big deal. We need a *personal* touch here. Yes, his ability to relate to the boys by having a sense of humor, providing a rocket (which is believable because Jake works at NASA), and eliciting their participation is nice; but what moves people is one person relating to one other person. That's why Sport is here. (Notice that I don't use a POV shot when Jake spots Sport.) Jake is sensitive, perceptive, kind, and encouraging to a kid who has been rejected by the others. Jake makes him feel important without embarrassing him.

In review, the scene as a whole (pages 6-7) exists for the following reasons:
1. To get Jake into the hands of Wardle
2. To establish the existence of the boy scouts
3. To show Jake as a good guy who's not isolated from the community.

In terms of pacing, this section on page 6 acts as a buffer. We just experienced some serious action in Egypt and are about to have storm clouds blow in on page 7. We could use something light and fun here. That's a fourth purpose.

Why is Mark in this scene? To more clearly establish him as Jake's best friend. Obviously, these two see each other a lot. It also gives Mark some dimension. He's apparently a good guy at heart. You see, we planted the seeds of his dark side earlier. Now we show his good side. When the dark side reappears, it will be surprising, but believable.

6

EXT. A SANDY BEACH - DAY

The blue sky meets a beautiful secluded beach at the horizon.

From ground level, the USA X-1 rocket towers upward, ready to blast off. When the gargantuan head of a boy moves into frame, we realize that the rocket is actually a miniature.

The boy is a normal-sized BOY SCOUT. He lies prone on the sand next to Jake -- in Levis and NASA cap -- who examines the rocket.

Jake jumps up. Holds a megaphone to his mouth. Faces north.

                    JAKE
          Attention. Clear the launch area.
               (facing south now)
          Please clear the launch area.

Mark and about a dozen boy scouts of various ethnic groups and races join Jake. These are all inner-city kids. One of the scouts makes emergency-siren sounds for effect.

Jake spots a small boy (SPORT), who stands apart from the others, looking dejected. In fact, the other boys ignore him.

Jake walks over to the boy and squats down, sees his dejection.

                    JAKE
          Hey Sport, I need someone with a
          strong voice for the count down.
          How about it?

Jake hands him the megaphone and a comforting smile. Sport returns the smile. Jake leads Sport to a spot on the sand.

At the same time, Jake nods to Mark who nods to a TALL SCOUT. The tall scout -- intense with anticipation -- holds a remote control in his hand. The remaining scouts stand back with Mark.

Jake winks at an expectant Sport.

                    SPORT
          Ten-nine-eight-seven-six-five-four-
          three-two-one-zero-Blastoff!

The tall scout pushes a big, red button -- FFUSSSH! -- the rocket blasts off.

They watch the stage-2 rocket separate and drop to earth while the X-1 continues upward. Finally, it explodes over the ocean.

Speaking of surprise, instead of letting this fun moment play out, we interrupt it with a plot twist. In a previous draft, this scene played out for another page with the boys having fun. In fact, one boy goes out into the ocean to catch the parachute and Jake rescues him like a BAYWATCH stud. Then Jake goes home and gets a phone call from Wardle. Do you see how this current version is more dramatic? Plus, we lose a couple of pages we didn't need. Also, the surprise of the big Chinook helicopter interrupting all of the fun creates suspense, just like the slam of the window shutter on page 2.

The transition is abrupt. The scouts cheer and watch the parachute descend. We expect to see the parachute land. Suddenly, the chopper is upon them. Jake, of course, is focused on the boys. I try to create a sense of chaos here with the sudden appearance of the Chinook—the boys running scared, their caps flying off, Mark looking confused, and so on. It's a dramatic moment, so I dramatize it. After all, this chopper will take Jake to Wardle and, as a result, Jake's life will suddenly be in chaos. There's something about that subliminal link that creates a sense of unity.

The dialogue, which in a prior draft went on for an entire page, is just two lines. Jake first speaks with an action, holding his arms out. I believe the uniformed airman refusing to answer Jake's question speaks more eloquently than something like, "Someone wants to see you." Why say that and break the suspense? Keep the audience wondering: Now what's going to happen?

In a way, the Chinook is Wardle, so I try to link the scene of the Chinook with the scene of Wardle. We match-cut from slamming door to slamming door (without using a CUT TO or MATCH CUT) to link the scenes.

I could waste space by showing Mark and the boys reacting to Jake's disappearance. I don't because Mark and the boys are minor characters. Let's keep the story moving.

Note the description of Wardle. When you describe your character, do so in a way that reflects on her character and who she is. Wardle is an ambitious no-nonsense soldier.

The Coast Guard Officer links the plot of Kendall's helicopter to Jake's plot. The Egyptian plotline links to the bad guys after page 10. That means that although Wardle is a powerful opposition character to Jake, she is not the main opposition. Nor is Cherise Joulet, the woman with the knife, although she becomes a powerful opposition to Jake. It's the man who hired Cherise. And even Kendall, who becomes the love interest, will be at odds with Jake for a while. Why all the opposition? Because opposition creates conflict, and conflict is drama. And adversity is good for revealing character and motivating characters to grow.

As you can see by the Coast Guard Officer's reaction, Wardle is formidable. We're taking the opportunity with this next scene to build up Wardle and make her powerful while, at the same time, revealing more important exposition without being boring.

7

The scouts CHEER when a parachute opens and the small capsule flutters downward.

Without warning, a huge Chinook helicopter -- loud and ominous -- descends. Two boys fall on their backs in fear.

The tiny rocket capsule falls to the sand, but no one notices.

A few boys run scared. Jake grabs them.

> JAKE
> Whoa! Take it easy. She's one of
> ours. Isn't she pretty?

Caps fly off, but the boys calm down as the Chinook lands on the sand. Mark looks confused, shaken -- what's this about? Jake shrugs.

Two uniformed airmen approach the group. Jake steps forward. Holds his arms out asking for an explanation.

> UNIFORM
> Jake Dekker?

Dekker calmly nods. They escort him to the chopper.

> JAKE
> What's going on?

The silent airmen usher Jake into the chopper and SLAM the door.

INT. HALLWAY - DAY

A metal door SLAMS shut and ECHOES.

J. C. WARDLE, a sexless woman with an ambitious stride, snatches a paper from the hand of PALMER, her muscular male aide.

Palmer opens a conference room door for Wardle.

INT. CONFERENCE ROOM - CONTINUOUS

The Coast Guard Officer, alone in the room, stands at attention. He doesn't know whether to salute Wardle or shake her hand.

> WARDLE
> Sit down.

He sits. Palmer opens his notebook and prepares to take notes.

The scene on script pages 7-10 can be divided into two dramatic segments. The first is with the Coast Guard Officer; the second is with Jake Dekker. It gives the reader someone to compare Jake to since both must deal with the same woman. It will help define character.

Wardle is intimidating, tough, and caffeinated; she carries around a coffee cup. Palmer is silent and misses nothing. He keeps a note pad and methodically takes notes. These little props say something about each character and give the reader something visual to identify with the character.

Wardle's intention in this scene is to get information. The Coast Guard Officer's goal is to give her the information she wants so he can get out of there. Since they have the same objective, you would think that this scene would be devoid of conflict, but Wardle's manner creates conflict and dramatic tension. Let's examine the dialogue.

Wardle's first line affirms her superiority and threatens the officer at the same time. It also provides exposition to the reader: She's a Pentagon official.

Wardle's next line is innocent enough, but she challenges him with her eyes and wins.

Wardle's third line cuts him off in mid-sentence.

Wardle's fourth line asks him to qualify what he just said. She is calm; he is a mess, afraid of getting into trouble. She's clearly in control. (Incidentally, the officer is right about helicopters being unable to fly at the speed of sound—a result of my research and an example of exposition dropped in at a dramatic moment.)

Wardle's fifth line (on page 9) tells him what to think.

Creating conflict is fun. It makes this encounter more interesting and presents a standard by which Jake will be measured when he comes up against Wardle. We will worry for Jake from the moment he first steps into the room with her. So the dramatic tension here creates suspense later. In fact, if this encounter between Wardle and the Coast Guard Officer works dramatically, then the reader is setup like a pigeon for the slammer on pages 9 and 10.

After this dialogue exchange, we foreshadow Wardle's upcoming encounter with Dekker. She pauses (at the bottom of page 8) and exchanges knowing glances with her aide, who hands her a top-secret file. Top secret? Must be important. And then we see Jake's helicopter. In the paragraph that follows, we learn that it is called the Hummingbird MG-11.

The officer is relieved to see the drawing, meaning that this drawing matches what the officer saw. This drawing matches Kendall's helicopter. He is so relieved that he smiles as if he has won, but Wardle quickly erases his smile on the next page.

8

Wardle slumps into her chair, takes a sip of coffee, and eyes the officer like he's the fly and she's the spider.

> WARDLE
> I just flew in from the Pentagon, so this better be good.

> COAST GUARD OFFICER
> Yes ma'am.

> WARDLE
> You sighted an unusual-looking helicopter.

Her glare is steady, forcing him to glance down at his notes.

> COAST GUARD OFFICER
> Yes ma'am, at twenty-five degrees, six minutes latitude and --

> WARDLE
> -- I have your report. Just tell me about the craft.

> COAST GUARD OFFICER
> Well, it was black. Had strange angles.
> (with erratic gestures)
> Very fast and it made no sound.

> WARDLE
> (after a sip of coffee)
> How fast?

> COAST GUARD OFFICER
> Well, no chopper can go the speed of sound, but this one was close. Yeah.
> (fidgeting)
> And it didn't appear on radar. I checked. I followed procedures.

Wardle and Palmer exchange knowing glances. He hands her a file stamped "Defense Department -- Top Secret." From the file, she removes a computer-generated drawing of a helicopter.

She slides it over to the Coast Guard Officer. It roughly matches the black helicopter the officer saw. The caption underneath says, "HUMMINGBIRD MG-11."

The officer looks, and immediately a smile of vindication spreads across his face.

Why would Wardle say that the helicopter does not exist? The subtext is *Keep your mouth shut. I don't want this to become public.* Why? We're not sure yet. This creates interest in what's about to happen. And it motivates a future scene.

In terms of character dynamics, she's telling the officer what to think and warning him at the same time. She then orders him out. In a moment of near-comic relief, the Coast Guard Officer runs away from her.

In this script, I try to provide information to my reader piecemeal. We saw the top-secret file on page 8, but did not reveal the name on the file until now.

So now we see Jake's name on the file. It is so important that I use the INSERT to focus the camera on the file. Wardle's command to "send in Dekker" is off-screen (O.S.), meaning that the camera stays on the file while Wardle says her line.

Note that no introductions are made and there is no chitchat or small talk. We just get into the scene. (Incidental dialogue can be added during the shoot.)

After Wardle's line, it would be proper and correct to write BACK TO SCENE to indicate that we are no longer looking at the file. The reason I don't use BACK TO SCENE is to save space. I justify doing that because the prose is clear—it's just a one-line INSERT. No one will be confused.

Throughout this script, Jake has been presented as calm and steady. Now is the moment to test that. The suspense is there because the audience is in a superior position. We know what Wardle knows about the helicopter and Jake doesn't. We know how tough she was on the officer and Jake doesn't. We know that she is a formidable foe.

She asks him if the chopper design is his. We know it is because we saw it in the first scene. In fact, he told Mark that the military had rejected the design and that he wanted to create a presentation for selling it. Jake's response confirms that. He's telling the truth. The ball is in Wardle's court.

Wardle delivers. She simply restates what she knows to get his reaction. Jake is on trial. The ball is now in his court. Palmer's stoic presence adds additional pressure. (Don't be afraid to run your character through the ringer.)

Jake states the truth as he understands it. After all, he is a scout.

                    COAST GUARD OFFICER
          That's it. That's the one.

He breathes heavily, his brow covered with sweat.

                    WARDLE
          Now listen carefully. That helicopter
          does not exist. You never saw it.

The officer nods. Wardle reinforces it with an insincere smile.

                    WARDLE
          Get out of here.

The Coast Guard Officer nearly runs out.

Wardle catches Palmer's attention. His eyes drop to the top-secret
file. She BUZZES the intercom.

INSERT THE FILE HEADING, which reads: "DEKKER, JAKE."

                    WARDLE (O.S.)
          Send in Dekker.

She sips her coffee as Jake Dekker steps in and sits down.

                    WARDLE
          Is this your work?

Wardle tosses the computer-generated drawing of the Hummingbird MG-
11 on the table. She drinks the last of her coffee.

                    JAKE
          Yes, I submitted the design to Bates.
          He rejected it.

                    WARDLE
          The Coast Guard spotted this less
          than fifty miles from here. In the
          air.

She waits. Jake is stunned, but calm.

Palmer -- face of stone -- nods to himself, making mental notes.

                    JAKE
          Impossible.

She brings in new information about other people seeing the helicopter. Her tapping the helicopter drawing with her finger is an unimportant, incidental action. I justify leaving it because the scene is a key scene and I want to dramatize it. But I could easily drop it to save space if necessary.

Wardle's second line is a challenging question, but Jake is equal to it. He confronts her by telling her directly that it didn't get into the sky. He's a reasonable man and explains why. The ball is back in Wardle's court.

Wardle uses his words against him. Because it was in the sky and he can't afford it, someone must have paid him. The conflict escalates. And now we're beginning to see Wardle's point of view. It's generally good policy to give each of your characters a different view of the facts. And we'll continue to see (after page 10) how she views things differently from Jake. In this particular case, Jake has not seen the facts yet, but *we* have, and Wardle sees this situation differently from us. The result is to create more sympathy for Jake and less for Wardle.

What's the purpose for Jake's action of glancing at Palmer and running his hand through his hair? It is to show his emotion. We need to know what he is feeling, and his action communicates his frustration to the reader. Do not cut off your characters emotionally from the reader. (Note the style of the writing in the second paragraph. Many screenwriters omit the repetition of pronouns; it's a style popularized by Shane Black.)

Jake responds with "NASA"—that's who he works for. I do not instruct the actor how to say this line. It could be a sarcastic answer. A question mark after "NASA" might suggest more of a smart-aleck attitude. There are many ways to go here and I don't give in to the temptation of telling the actor how to say this.

The exchange of power between the two crescendoes to the moment when Wardle stands up and challenges Jake with her eyes. But unlike the Coast Guard Officer, Jake does not flinch.

Next comes the Catalyst of the movie, the event that upsets the equilibrium of Jake's life. There's even a deadline on it, which creates pressure and suspense. How can Jake accomplish this? He doesn't even know where "the bird" is, or even that it exists. We've laid a lot on the shoulders of our hero. Hopefully, the reader wants to read more.

In a previous draft, I ended the scene differently. But the producer I was working with dismissed it because it sounded "too much like Mel Gibson." He felt that Jake should be "shaken" at the end of the interview to emphasize the enormous burden he was under. In the end, I agreed with the producer, but you can read that previous version on page 254. Which do you prefer?

Finally, Jake staggers out. That final paragraph is simply an assessment of Jake's emotional state, so that the reader can identify emotionally with him.

                    WARDLE
          Later, two civilians in separate
          incidents. Thought it was aliens.

She taps the helicopter drawing with her finger.

                    WARDLE
          So how did this ... get into the sky?

                    JAKE
          It didn't. It would take millions of
          dollars to manufacture a prototype.

                    WARDLE
          Exactly. So who you working for?

Jake is mystified. Casts a glance Palmer's way for an explanation.
Runs a frustrated hand through his hair.

                    JAKE
          ... NASA.

                    WARDLE
          Not anymore. You're terminated,
          Dekker, and I'm considering
          prosecution.

                    JAKE
          The charge?

                    WARDLE
          Espionage.

                    JAKE
          You think I sold the plans to a
          foreign government?

Wardle stands slowly, glares down at Jake, but he doesn't flinch.

                    WARDLE
          The helicopter is out there. If
          you're connected with it, you're
          going down. Unless you come clean.

Jake's eyes narrow.

                    WARDLE
          I want that bird. And I want it in
          twenty-four hours. That is all.

Jake -- violated, confused -- staggers out.

Here's the fifth-draft ending of the scene on page 10:

```
                    JAKE
          What I've done on my own time
          belongs to me.
```

His finger comes down hard on the table. Palmer notes it.
Dekker's eyes shift to Palmer and:

WHACK! Wardle slams her empty coffee mug on the table.
Palmer is so startled that he drops his notebook, but Jake
doesn't flinch.

```
                    WARDLE
          Now you listen up, Dekker, if you're
          freelancing I swear I'll break you.
          I want that bird. And I want it in
          twenty-four hours.
```

Jake slowly stands. A monolith.

```
                    JAKE
          You ought to switch to decaf. It's
          easier on your nerves.
```

And after a friendly nod, he exits.

• • • • •

Don't be misled by my analysis into thinking you need to be analytical when *writing*.
However, you do want to use your reasoning powers in *evaluating* what you've written. And you don't need to emulate my writing style. A more gifted writer could do a
better job of presenting the same material.

Finally, when all is said and done, the real test of your first ten pages is this: Does the
reader want to know what happens next? If you want to know what happens next to
Jake and Kendall, then I have succeeded.

HOW TO SELL YOUR SCRIPT

BOOK V

A Marketing Plan

Five steps to selling your work

Congratulations! You, the next great screenwriter, have written a stunning script! You have reached a major milestone. Reward yourself with positive self-talk and a bowl of ice cream.

There are five general steps you should take before you begin to market your screenplay. These steps will be covered in the next five chapters of this book. Additional chapters build on and supplement those first five chapters.

1. Protect your work. Before you send your screenplay out to anyone, make sure it is protected and ready to show.

2. Prepare your screenplay for market. You have a completed screenplay, but is it a "showcase" screenplay? Will it attract a buyer? In this section, we will explore the value of writing groups, script consultants, and conduct an analysis of the marketability of your screenplay.

3. Assemble your selling tools. Before you begin selling, you want to forge the marketing tools that will make a difference in today's markets. Don't step into the marketplace empty-handed and empty-headed.

4. Create your strategic marketing plan. In any business, it is important to have a plan of attack. The same is true in the movie business. You not only want to be professional, you want to be effective. You want to nail a deal.

5. Implement the plan.

The remaining chapters in this book focus mainly on specific aspects of implementing your plan, such as getting an agent, selling without an agent, and penetrating alternative and smaller markets. They also provide instruction on developing certain key selling tools that were described in the third chapter, such as query letters and treatments. Many areas are touched on more than once. That's because, in this book, I present information in layers. Before you reach the end, you should have a complete picture.

Note: Nothing in this or any other book of The Screenwriter's Bible *should be construed as legal advice. That can only be provided by an attorney.*

1. Protect your work

In Hollywood, no script is sacred. Don't worry, there are ways to protect yourself and your creative offspring. There are ways to protect your rights.

KEEP RECORDS

First, be organized. Life can get very complicated, so write things down. Keep a journal of meetings you have and record what was discussed (see pages 288-289.) Keep a log of phone calls, queries, and script submissions. You'll need these if any legal concerns should arise. You'll also use these records to follow up on contacts and create future strategies for selling your work.

If there's ever any question in your mind that there might be a legal problem, consult an entertainment attorney. You may even want an attorney to review any contracts you're offered, particularly if the offerer is not signatory to the Writers Guild of America.

COPYRIGHT

Keep in mind that there are certain things you cannot protect: ideas, historical facts, plots, titles, phrases, and anything not written down. Here's what you can protect: Your original expression of an idea or plot; in other words, your original, spec script is the only thing you can protect.

There are several ways to protect your spec screenplay. Under the current copyright law, you own the copyright to your work even as you write it. You don't even need to use the copyright symbol. To create a public record of your script, however, you may wish to *register* your copyright with the U.S. Copyright Office in Washington, D.C. It's a simple, painless, and inexpensive procedure. Just contact the Copyright Office in Washington, D.C. Once done, you must display the copyright notice on your script. That notice will look something like this: © 2006 David R. Trottier or Copyright 2006 David R. Trottier. If you register your copyright with the U.S. Copyright Office, ensure international protection by adding the phrase: All Rights Reserved.

My personal observation is that most working writers do not register their scripts with the copyright office, presumably because the eventual producer will own the copyright to the completed film, and thus to the script. That doesn't mean that *you* shouldn't. Registering your copyright gives you the best protection available. Throughout my career, I have not registered the copyright of my scripts; however, when I sold my most recent script, my attorney advised me to register my copyright at that time.

Registering one's copyright and displaying the copyright notice on the script's title page is no longer seen as something done by paranoid writers. And even though the date of the copyright notice "dates" the script, many writers are now registering their copyright. In fact, I've heard more than one entertainment attorney say that screenwriters should register their copyright once they begin circulating their script.

THE WGA

The purpose of WGA registration is to establish yourself as the creator of your original work. Most writers register their scripts with the Writers Guild of America. All of my scripts are registered with the WGA. Although WGA registration creates valid evidence that can be used in court, it does not provide as many legal remedies as registering your copyright with the U.S. Copyright Office will.

The Writers Guild maintains two offices. One is in Los Angeles; the other is in New York. The Mississippi River serves as a boundary between the jurisdictions of the east and west guild offices.

To register your script with the WGA, simply send your screenplay, treatment, or synopsis to them with $20 ($22 for the Writers Guild, east) and they will hold the copy for five years (WGA, west) or ten years (WGA, east). It can be retrieved at any time thereafter. When the registration period has expired, you may renew your registration. You may register your script more than once. Some writers like to register their first draft as well as their final polish. You should register a treatment or synopsis if you are going to present it to others, or if you're going to delay the writing of your script.

The Writers Guild provides many additional services to writers. You do not need to belong to the Guild to benefit from their services, or to register your script.

WGA services include the following:

- Registration of your script, treatment, or synopsis for a period of five or ten years. You may renew your registration after that.

- Pre-negotiated contracts if you sign with a producer or studio that is signatory to the Guild or acquire an agent who is signatory to the Guild.

- Arbitration if a dispute arises regarding credits or for other grievances, such as non-payment or slow payment of contracted writing fees.

- A list of agencies that are signatory to the Guild. The cost is nominal. Visit their website at www.wga.org or www.wgae.org.

- A library where you can go and read scripts.

- Information as to who represents a particular writer. This could help in your search for an agent.

Again, you need not be a member to use these services. You may join the Guild once you have the required number of credits. For more information, contact the appropriate office. Refer to Book VI for addresses and phone numbers.

OTHER MEANS OF PROTECTION

Another way to protect your work is to have several people read it so that they can testify that you wrote it. Keep records of meetings and phone conversations.

Still another method is the Poor Man's Copyright. Put the script in an envelope, seal it, and send it via *registered mail* to yourself. Don't open it; keep it for the lawsuit later. Although this works in principle, I doubt it would protect you in actual fact, which is why I always just pay the small fee and register my work with the Guild.

An additional protection

Perhaps your best protection is the completed script itself. If you pitch an idea to a producer that she likes, she'll ask for your script. Why would she steal the idea and pay a working writer $250,000 to execute your idea when she can pay you $50,000 to $100,000 for a script that already exists?

WRITING PARTNERSHIPS

If you collaborate with another writer, first make sure that your goals for the project are in harmony and that you basically get along with each other. Do you bring different skills to the table that will benefit the project? My co-writer on several scripts, Greg Alt, once wrote me, "Dave, you flesh it out, and then I'll add the wit, charm, and humor." Well, you need to define your roles in more specific terms. Also, expect a certain amount of clashing and decide in advance how you will resolve conflict.

Before you do any writing, be sure to have a written agreement, especially if your co-writer is your best friend or a relative. Often, loved ones expect the other to cut them a lot of slack. The agreement should cover these points.

- Exactly what each will contribute in terms of time and content.
- Who gets top writing credit.
- What happens if someone drops out or doesn't perform.

If your co-writer does not want to sign a contract, then that's a red flag. Just tell that person that this is a normal part of business. You want to be serious about your writing career. You are a writer, not a hobbyist.

As mentioned in Book III, when two or more writers work together on a project, their names are joined by an ampersand, not the word "and," as follows:

```
                   Written by

      Herman Cappuccino and Mocha Smith
```

When you see the word "and" used on writing credits, it means that the people whose names are joined by that "and" did not work together.

2. Prepare your script for market

There are several markets for scripts, and we will discuss them all. But before you even think of approaching the marketplace, you want to get your ducks in a row. I have watched with sadness the many writers who have broken their hearts by approaching the market prematurely. Don't let your passion or the prospect of dollar signs obscure your vision!

Make sure the writing is done before the selling begins. Do not contact producers and agents until you are prepared. Be sure that your script is finished, evaluated, and registered—and your marketing plan is written—*before* you mail that first query or make that first call. I cannot overemphasize this. I get calls all the time from clients and students who sadly confess that they entered the market prematurely. I worked with one client on a query letter that brought in over 20 requests for the script. The problem was, his script needed a polish. It wasn't ready yet, and the opportunity was lost.

YOUR CALLING CARD

To break into this business, you need at least one showcase script (preferably two or more) that is proof of your writing ability. If you want to write for television, you will need one feature script and at least one sample television script.

This showcase script (or scripts) should be registered with the Copyright Office or Writers Guild, formatted correctly, and should be complete in every way. Never submit a work in progress. Realize that your script is a prospectus asking for a $10-$30 million investment or more. That is why it must be good.

Since Tinsel Town is into appearances, it is essential that your script look as good as it possibly can. Obviously, you will want to follow the conventions you read about in Books III and IV, including the avoidance of camera directions and other technical intrusions that, as previously explained, are part of the *shooting* script rather than the *spec* script.

Make sure you understand spec writing. Some conventions have recently changed. I don't know how many times writers have sent me their script for evaluation after it has been rejected all over town, and I find formatting errors, obvious writing mistakes, and easy-to-fix problems that might have made a difference. Again, please be sure to carefully read, and frequently refer to, Books III and IV; they are your friends.

To further guide you in preparing a professional-looking script, refer to the "17 Commandments" on page 124. Many of the points seem nitpicky. They are, and for good reason. The poor souls who must read dozens of scripts every week are looking for any excuse to eliminate scripts from their reading stack. Abiding by their simple rules is an easy way to make a good impression.

Of course, appearance isn't everything, and correct format alone will not save you. Remember what you learned in the previous books—your script must tell an interesting story. It must be well-crafted. There can be no references to the thoughts and feelings of characters such as *When John saw Mary, it reminded him of the first time they met.* Don't write anything that cannot appear on the screen. You are limited in your writing to what can be *seen*, and what can be *heard*. That's it.

Make sure your script is ready. Ask yourself the questions in Book II. When I present seminars, about 80% of the questions I'm asked has to do with selling the script. I often find these people coming back months later a little beat up, but a little wiser. They want to make sure their next script is well-written before they try to sell it. You must write it before you sell it.

Your spec script should provide a smooth *read*. Your description should focus on images and actions; your dialogue should be crisp and allow for subtext. The writing in general should be concise, specific, and clear.

Before submitting your script, you may wish to get feedback. One place for that is through a writers' group. I recommend writers' groups of about seven to ten writers who meet regularly and read each other's work. You will get worthwhile feedback and the advice will be free.

WRITERS' GROUPS

Writing can be a lonely job. A writers' group may be just the place to turn for comfort, support, and feedback.

Where to find writers' groups
Writers' groups are everywhere if you know where to look. Here are six general areas to begin your search:

1. Attend writers' conferences, workshops, and writing classes. Network with fellow writers and ask them if they know of any writers' groups.

2. Read the classified ads of writing publications. Many groups and individuals advertise in the classifieds, seeking to form or continue a group. Some established groups, like The Scriptwriters Network in Los Angeles, have special requirements.

3. For a fee, you may join large, professional organizations such as The Scriptwriters Network (already mentioned), the National Writers Association, or the Wisconsin Screenwriters Forum (see listings in Book VI). I have created a place at my website (www.keepwriting.com) for writers' groups and organizations. Look there or advertise (free) your writers' group.

4. Call your state film commissioner or county film board (if one exists) about possible writers' groups in your area.

5. Other places where writers might hang out include film festivals, movie clubs, bookstores, websites, and universities with adult education programs.

6. Don't forget to approach non-writing friends and acquaintances who might know writers who belong to groups.

If your search for a writers' group proves fruitless, there's only one thing left to do—start your own group.

Ten ways to find writers to start a group
You know now where writers can be found. Here are ways to gather them into a group.

1. Network with them at conferences, expos, seminars, and workshops. Trade phone numbers. One writer recently used this simple, proven method to create a group composed of participants of my seminar and Michael Hauge's.

2. Ask the instructor or seminar leader to put your name and phone number on the board because you'd like to start a writers' group. That way interested writers can call you. Ask me to post your writers' group at my website (www.keepwriting.com).

3. Post a notice on bulletin boards and classrooms at conferences, asking people to sign up. You can pick these lists up later.

4. Distribute flyers to classmates or fellow conference-goers. You can even go out on a limb and announce the first meeting in the flyer.

5. Network in screenwriting organizations such as Scriptwriters Network and Independent Film Project (IFP).

6. Place a "Writers Wanted" classified ad in scriptwriting newsletters and magazines (see Book VI for a list of periodicals).

7. Send a letter of invitation to college or adult-education classes, announcing the date of your meeting.

8. Connect with writers at bookstore events.

9. Try bulletin boards and blogs (web logs similar to bulletin boards), virtual writers' groups, chat sessions, and roundtables featured in online computer services.

10. Surf the web. Start a website. Consider an online writers' group that meets in a chat room or via a messenger service.

How to keep the group going
While you're forming the group, you will want to create some rules or guidelines at the same time. Here are some things to keep in mind.

1. Include writers who are at basically the same level. One group might consist of people who are just getting started. Another group might set up a requirement of one completed screenplay.

2. Keep the group small. Five people may be enough. Seven is an ideal size. If you start with twelve to fifteen people, you'll likely end up with the magnificent seven who are dedicated.

3. Make it a participative group. You may need a facilitator to head the group, but make sure everyone has an equal say in making rules. You might even rotate responsibilities, such as making reminder calls and assigning refreshments, so that no one is unduly burdened and everyone is involved.

4. Find a place to meet. This will probably be someone's house. It might be easier to use the same location continuously, but some groups like to rotate. Many libraries, some savings-and-loan associations, and other businesses have "community rooms" that are without cost for noncommercial use. You qualify if admittance to your group is free.

5. Have a regular meeting time, such as the first Tuesday of every month, or every Wednesday at 7:30. Get people into a routine.

6. Decide on the purposes of the group. For example, here is the stated purpose of a group of my students: "To provide each member with the feedback he or she needs to forward his or her screenwriting career. Group members share screenwriting knowledge and provide friendly, constructive critiques of each other's script, treatment, or outline. Members also exchange screenwriting books, magazines, tapes, and their experiences finding agents and marketing scripts."

Some groups focus on one or two writers per session. Some groups require members to send the work to others in advance of the meetings. It's often profitable to read scenes aloud at the meeting itself and evaluate them on the spot, or discuss writing ideas and specific writing problems.

7. Make sure critiquing sessions do not turn into slugfests. Writers should avoid a defensive posture. Listen carefully, avoid speaking, take the advice seriously, but remember that you are the writer of *your* script. Criticism should be given constructively. Members should avoid speaking in absolutes, but instead offer their opinions, reactions, observations, and suggestions.

8. Each member should agree to a code of silence. Everything discussed or read is confidential. If people are concerned about theft, suggest that all work be registered before it is distributed. You can even ask people to sign a nondisclosure agreement. Don't get too paranoid about theft. It does happen, but your car may be stolen at the grocery store, too, but that doesn't stop you from shopping.

How to creatively maintain your group
After a while, a motivating routine can degenerate into a fatiguing rut. Because all members of the group are *creative*, this problem can be solved by being creative. Here are some ideas to get you started.

- Organize a script-swap night

- Read a script, then view the movie together

- Sponsor a contest, or challenge another group to a contest

- Invite a working writer to address the group.

- Compile a collection of query letters or rejection letters

- Have special awards when a writer passes a milestone

- Set aside a night just for pitching practice; rotate the roles of writer and producer/executive

When groups get too large, create specialized areas such as the "Comedy Writers" or the "Sci-Fi Chapter" or "Advanced Writers." You can have a short, large meeting for everyone, and then break into the specialized groups.

In the best writers' groups and organizations, a feeling of camaraderie develops, enabling each writer to root for the other's success. It's an upward spiral of positive energy that revitalizes each writer. This is the fuel each writer needs to keep writing.

SCRIPT CONSULTANTS

Some writers seek out professional readers for a *coverage*. A coverage is what a reader (actual job title is *story analyst*) writes for the agents, producers, and executives who hire her. A coverage usually consists of a two-page synopsis, a brief analysis of the screenplay, and a recommendation. The cost to writers for such a coverage is about $100 or more. You can read a sample coverage on pages 336-340.

More extensive than a coverage is a detailed evaluation provided by professional *script consultants* like myself. That's going to cost you more, but a professional, independent option may be worth it. Check the listings in Book VI under "Script Consultants and Teachers."

Another way to get feedback is to ask your spouse and friends to read your script. It's free, but may not be entirely objective. Feedback from a writer's group might prove more valuable. A few writers' contests (see Book VI) provide feedback. If you get comments from more than one reader, look for patterns in those comments.

Once you know that the script is ready (and you may not need a consultant to know that), it's time to forge effective writing tools in preparation for your market entrance.

3. Assemble your selling tools

TEN KEY SELLING TOOLS

Before you try to sell your script, you need a complete set of marketing tools. Assemble these *before* creating your marketing plan and making your move. Many of the tools listed below are discussed in depth later in this book, but I thought you'd want to see them all in one place so that you can begin to accumulate them at this step in the selling process.

1. A showcase script
You need a great script (preferably two or more) that is proof of your writing ability and can be used as a calling card. If you want to break into television, you will need one feature script and at least one sample television script.

2. A provocative pitch hook
As mentioned, this will consist of a logline, one-sentence concept, or premise statement that you can insert into a query letter, use over the phone, or pitch in person. Everything in Hollywood is sold on its premise.

3. A compelling story summary
This will be one or two paragraphs in length and can be used in your query or as part of your pitch. This summary and your pitch hook comprise a two-minute pitch and will also be used in your query letter. We will discuss pitching in depth in a later chapter

A variation of this is the one-page synopsis that can be handed off or left behind at meetings. This is a *pitch on paper* (POP), and will open with your logline, hook, or concept, and then the story summary—all on one page.

4. A captivating query letter

Never send a script out unannounced. A query must precede it, and this query must convince the producer, executive, agent, director, or actor to request your script. A query letter (or *pitch letter*) is a one-page pitch. It contains the pitch hook, story summary, genre, and your qualifications (if impressive). It's your main weapon in your battle to break through the clutter and get your script read. I have devoted a later chapter to this key topic.

5. A scintillating synopsis

A synopsis is a one- or two-page story summary written in present tense, double-spaced, using a conservative 12-point font (Times Roman, Arial, Helvetica, Courier, etc.). It can be attached to a query letter (if requested by the executive), directed to producers or talent (actors, directors), or delivered in an oral pitch (over the phone or in person). Synopses and treatments (discussed below) are more often requested by producers than by agents. In either case, the request for your script or for your synopsis or treatment comes as a result of your query letter or oral pitch.

When you send a synopsis to an agent or producer, include a cover letter that contains the main concept, title, genre, and your qualifications (much like a query letter would but minus the story summary). Some writers simply attach a copy of the original query to their cover letter as a reminder of what the excitement's about. Many producers prefer seeing a synopsis or treatment before reading the script.

6. A tantalizing treatment

This is essentially a 3-8 page synopsis or story summary. Like the synopsis, it is a written pitch. Usually, 3-4 pages is about right. Treatments and synopses are sometimes requested in response to your query. A synopsis or treatment might be requested before the script. Most often, they are not requested at all.

IMPORTANT: The terms *synopsis* and *treatment* are often used synonymously. Both are written summaries. However, sometimes the term *treatment* is used to refer to a story summary used as a marketing tool (regardless of length), while the term *synopsis* might refer to an informational document, such as the synopsis that's included with a coverage. Both are written in present tense. On rare occasion, someone might use the term *outline* when they mean *treatment*. Don't confuse an *outline* used in this sense with the more detailed scene-by-scene *step outline*. Generally, an *outline* of any kind refers to a list of scenes.

I'll discuss the writing of treatments and synopses in a separate chapter.

7. A convincing telephone script

You need this next to your phone when you call anyone about your screenplay or TV script, or they call you. Don't be like a client of mine who was called back on a query and who blanked out on the phone. After six seconds of silence, the agent hung up. Quickly, she called me and I told her to call the agent immediately and explain that she had a cold and had lapsed into a coughing spell. Fortunately, her explanation was satisfactory.

The key element of your telephone script is your hook and summary (Numbers 2 and 3 above). You will carry a copy when you go to places where you might meet producers, agents, or other film people. You might meet them at conferences, expos, or a particular social event. It's better to improvise off notes than to read. It's even better to deliver your pitch without any notes at all. Also, prepare pitches of other scripts you've written or want to write and have them handy in case you're asked the golden question: "What else have you done?"

A telephone script is what all professional telemarketers use. It tells you what to say if the person on the other line says yes, no, or makes a particular excuse or objection. Here's just one possible example:

> "I'm [name]. I'm a screenwriter with a [name genre, such as action/ romantic comedy] that I think might be right down your alley. May I send it to you?"

> (What's it about?) [Here you will pitch it, leading with a headline, logline, premise, or concept; then, if you feel encouraged, moving into the story summary.]

> (I'm sorry, we're developing our own projects.) "Great. Would you like to read this with an eye toward a possible assignment? I'd love to hear what you're doing [or] I loved NAZIS IN SPACE [or whatever his/her last production was]. [Here you are identifying your script as a mere sample of your work. You hope it will lead to a meeting and a writing assignment. You're not looking to sell the script itself.]

> (Do you have an agent?) "Actually, I'm making a decision between several agents, so I'm shopping the script now rather than letting it gather dust." [Or] "I'm looking right now. If you have any suggestions, I'd be delighted to hear them."

> (We can't accept a script without an agent.) "Why don't I send it with a release?" [The release is a legal document discussed at the bottom of page 341.]

> (I'm sorry, we're not interested.) "Fine. Tell me, is there someone you know who might be interested in this material?" [You might just get a referral here.]

Keep in mind that you may need to "sell" the assistant first before reaching the party you want. Be professional with all parties that you deal with. Don't engage in "small talk" on the phone. Get to your point immediately.

8. A ready list of resources

You'll find plenty of resources in Book VI and also at www.keepwriting.com. Review these carefully and consider how you can use these resources. Subscribe to publications and network with other writers and industry types. Search the Internet. Join blogs. (Blog is short for "web log." Think of blogs as web journals or bulletin boards.) Read other books as a supplement to *The Bible.*

9. An inventory of salient strengths

Build on your strengths when you present yourself and your work. Strengths might include your script's genre and market appeal. In fact, you might envision how your move might be sold to the public through ads and one-sheets (movie posters). Your personal strengths might include your willingness to do assignments, your devotion to a writing career, the fact that you've written a half dozen scripts, and so on. Fill your mind with positives.

In addition, list possible objections you might encounter and how you will overcome those.

10. A positive attitude

Success in the marketplace requires a certain mindset. You want to be professional in your dealings with others. Be confident without being arrogant; be wily without being devious. It's easy to be intimidated by these "glamorous" people, but in reality they are no different from you, except that they have a different job.

Today's screenwriter needs to be enthusiastic and pleasantly persistent. I've seen very talented writers fall by the wayside, and mediocre writers make it because they were persistent. Usually the marketing process takes time. You must be committed.

People want to work with writers they can "work with." This is you if you can stand back from your work and be objective about it. It's difficult taking criticism, particularly mindless criticism, but being defensive will work against you whether you are right or wrong. At the same time, you must believe in your work and be excited about it. After all, if you don't believe in it, who will?

Confidence, conviction, and initiative are pluses. Arrogance, doubt, and passivity are minuses.

Don't count on hitting a home run on the first pitch. You are probably not going to get a million dollars for your first spec script, although it has happened. Allow yourself to be realistic without being negative. Be prepared to walk this road one step at a time without appearing too hungry along the way. Someday, you may find what prolific producer Lynda Obst (SLEEPLESS IN SEATTLE, HOW TO LOSE A GUY IN 10 DAYS) calls "a place at the table."

The Eleventh Tool

Create a Strategic Marketing Plan, and get into the habit of using the Weekly Action Plan, both to be discussed later.

4. Create your strategic marketing plan

The movie business is a *business*. To succeed in business, you need to successfully market your product and your service. Your product is your script. And your service is your ability to write. Marketing is not a matter of mass-mailing a query letter and hoping you win the jackpot. And it's not throwing scripts and ideas against the wall to see which ones stick.

Today's market is more closed to outsiders and more competitive than in years past. You need a refined approach, a laser-like focus. You need a strategic marketing plan in which you determine your target market, create marketing strategies that will help you achieve your sales objectives, and position yourself in the market.

You will likely get many ideas while reading through this section, including the worksheets. Write them down as you get them. Once done, read the entire Book V, and then return to the worksheets.

PRINCIPLES

First, let's review a few basic marketing principles that affect all of your marketing efforts.

Two key marketing concepts are segmentation and differentiation. *Segmentation* is identifying the market segments that seem best for your script. *Differentiation* is how you differentiate yourself from other writers competing for that same market segment.

Differentiation has to do both with your product—your script, story, concept—and with your marketing approach. What gives you that competitive edge?

Purpose, audience, strategy

In any persuasive presentation in any business arena, there are three planning steps: purpose, audience, and strategy. First, identify your purpose, then understand your audience (your market), and finally create strategies to reach that audience (market). These steps sound simple enough, but few people apply them.

Purpose has to do with what *you* want to accomplish, what you want to sell. It derives from your point of view. The audience is whom you want to influence. Once you understand your audience—your market—then you know what they need to hear.

In my earlier years, I was a marketing executive. I have since become a writer/producer, script consultant, and seminar leader. But I still do a little marketing consulting and even teach an occasional college-level marketing course. I can't tell you how many business people I've given the following speech to: "You cannot say what you want to say; you have to say what they want to hear. They don't care how much your family sacrificed to build your business, they just want to know if the product works." So strategy comes from the point of view of your audience.

Here's an example. You want a raise. That's your purpose. Your audience is your boss. And most people's strategy is to state all the reasons they deserve the raise (using a lot of sentences that begin with "I"). A better strategy is to come from the boss's point of view: "Boss, here is how *you* will benefit. . . ." So strategy is involved with communicating the benefits to your audience. But your purpose should be specific, too. You don't want "a raise," you want a 10% increase over the next two years. There is power in specifics, and the more specific you can be with your purpose, audience, and strategy, the better off you will be.

Your purpose is to sell your script or get a writing assignment. Actually, that's a little vague. You need to identify a *specific individual* you want to sell your script to. Once that's done, you need to understand that person and his or her company. What is their buying history? What are they looking for now? Do they prefer query letters or phone calls? Who is *their* market? In the final analysis, they don't care if you're starving. They don't care that you've been writing scripts for five years. They want to know if *your* ideas can be used to reach *their* market. Or, they want to know if you are the writer who can execute *their* ideas into a script.

Your strategy—therefore—*derives* from their needs. What do *they* need to see in a query to interest them in *your* script? How will they benefit from what you have to offer?

This same principle applies to meetings. What is your goal for the meeting? Who are you pitching to? What approach is most likely to succeed with this particular person? We'll discuss how to gather all this marketing information later.

Features and benefits

In any sales situation, the "informed" salesperson presents features and benefits. *Features* constitute the logical argument; *benefits* are emotional. This ballpoint pen in my hand now features a retractable point. The benefit to you is you don't get ink in your purse or pocket.

Some time ago, I was trying to sell my car and an engineer dropped by. I thought this person would be most interested in specific facts about my car. But his reactions were all negative. During the test drive, however, I turned on the radio. And he said, "Whoa, what's that?"

I thought to myself, "It's your emotional hot button and I am about to push it as a strategy in presenting an emotional argument (or benefit) for buying the car." Here's how the conversation went. I said, "What kind of music do you like?" He liked classical, so I dropped in a tape and said, "Imagine yourself driving through the Irvine hills. Just you, the road, and Mozart." Well, he bought a car stereo with a car attached.

In any situation, try to think in terms of how the producer or agent will benefit, and what turns them on emotionally. For example, in a pitching situation, if there are merchandising opportunities that naturally flow from your story, mention them. If your story presents a role that an "A" actor would be interested in, that's a feature that provides an emotional benefit to the producer. Be sure to stress the benefit: "With 'A' talent attached, you know the financing will not be a problem. It's a go."

The "short attention span" obstacle

No one needs to tell you that concept is king in Hollywood. Concept also sells in other industries. Marketers need a handle that buyers can hang on to. In the case of my book, *The Screenwriter's Bible*, the handle or concept is: Six books in one. Everything you need under one cover (how-to text, workbook, formatter, spec writing guide, marketing plan, and resource directory—all included).

Agents, producers, and executives have too much to read. That's why it is crucial to find the right concept, those few words in your query or pitch that drive the message home. Be able to tell your story, or present a story hook, in 25 words or less. (Refer back to "The low-down on high concept" in Book I.)

But concept is nothing without conviction. Your enthusiasm and conviction about your project are probably your most important assets. The voice of conviction is what sells the concept. Enthusiasm is contagious.

MARKETING RESEARCH

When you sit down and write a script, you cannot know what the market will be when the script is finally completed. You can't outguess the market. Yes, there are some genres and structures that seem perennial favorites. For example, action stories, romantic comedies (date movies), and thrillers are usually in demand. But you don't know specifically what will sell, even though some trends last for years.

However, a study of the market can help you avoid problems. For example, if you are writing a social drama, don't write it for a huge budget. Why? Because it's not likely to become a big-screen movie; it's more likely to become a TV Movie-of-the-Week.

It will also help you if you create a role that an "A" actor will covet. Usually this means that the story revolves around an original character with a great character arc, and that most of the scenes are about that character. In particular, there should be emotional scenes of high drama. Ideally, you want to write a script with a strong growth arc that demands some emotional range. Stars drive this business.

Although there are many production companies looking for character studies, most want scripts strong on story with a role that will attract a star. I'm sorry to report that more top male stars than female stars can get movies made, but that is changing, and scripts for female leads are purchased all the time. Lists of "A" talent can be found in special issues of *The Hollywood Reporter, Premiere,* and elsewhere.

On the other hand, you may have a small, independent market or avant-garde niche in mind. Perfect. Now ask yourself what kind of screenplay will likely meet the needs of that market. We will address specific markets later.

It is true that you want to be aware of your market before you write, but write the story you have passion to write. In other words, forget about the market once you start writing your script. Remember, you cannot predict the market one year from now. You can only make informed choices.

What to do with all of those scripts

From one perspective, you need only three things to break in: connections, concepts, and scripts. As time goes by, and you begin stockpiling unsold scripts, you will want to use wisdom in managing your business.

First of all, don't send a script immediately after you finish it. Let it sit and ferment. Some of its problems may solve themselves in your head. New ideas may come. Some problems that you didn't know existed may show themselves. On the other hand, don't rewrite it to death. Another reason to let your script lay idle a month or so is to let your emotions cool. Now you can be objective. In the meantime, you can prepare your ten marketing tools and create your marketing plan.

If a movie similar to your script is about to be released, wait and see how that movie does. If it succeeds, send your script out immediately. If it fails, wait about a year before sending your script out. If a script similar to your script was sold recently, start marketing yours. If the word goes out that a producer wants an ecological Western, and you have one in inventory but waited until the market was ready for it, now you're in a position to cash in. Your patience, restraint, and common sense have paid off.

Where to go for information about markets
Read the trades. *Variety* (which leans a bit more toward features) and the *Hollywood Reporter* (which leans a bit to the world of television) are worthwhile business publications. Weekly editions are also available. They tell you what sold, who sold it, who bought it, when it will be shot, what the logline is, etc.

Both of these publications list films in development and films in production. You will find special focus sections on specific market segments. And there's marketing information on all the players, including the independents. You will even find ads for seminars and scripts.

For example, say you want to sell to Showtime. Would it be worthwhile to know that half their financing (as of this writing) comes from foreign sources? That means your project needs to appeal to the foreign market. Now you might say, "Well, that's what I have an agent for." And you're absolutely right. But whether you have an agent or not, understanding the market at some level will help you in pitches, meetings, phone calls, and in planning your next script—for that matter, in planning your career.

There are many other industry publications. *Premiere* provides a power list once a year. *Hollywood Scriptwriter* provides interviews with successful writers and other articles. *Entertainment Weekly* is a good general movie periodical. *Scr(i)pt* is an excellent magazine filled with articles about writing and selling for a variety of markets, including mainstream. *Creative Screenwriting* is also good. If you subscribe to nothing else, subscribe to two or three of the above publications.

There are numerous directories, such as the *Hollywood Creative Directory*. These are listed in Book VI. New resource tools, screenwriting websites, and directories pop up all the time. Industry guidebooks (like this one!) often have accompanying websites that offer supplementary and updated information. See the "Bible Updates" and "Hot Links" pages at www.keepwriting.com for supplements to this volume. One of the links you will find is the Internet Movie Database, an excellent source of industry information. You'll find other links to information about script sales.

Attend workshops, expos, conferences, and seminars, and meet the people there. Don't overlook film festivals, such as the Sundance Film Festival.

Writer's organizations such as Women in Film and the Scriptwriters Network in Studio City can provide information and support. Some organizations publish newsletters. Just a local screenwriters' group can be helpful because you can network with other writers who may have information to share. Meet people. Ask questions. It might even help you to join non-writing industry organizations.

CREATING YOUR PERSONAL STRATEGIC MARKETING PLAN

Beginning on the next page, you will find a number of worksheets to help you create a marketing plan and focus your marketing strategies. You have my permission to photocopy the worksheets for your own personal use. Before completing them, however, I recommend that you read this entire book. Each worksheet is described below.

The Project Plan
The first worksheet is entitled "Project Plan." Let's start there first. Your project is the script you wish to sell. After you identify your target market, complete the remainder of the Project Plan (four pages) and focus on more specific possibilities.

Ask yourself, Where do you see your project playing? Is it a SIMPSONS-type project? If so, who are potential producers of such projects? Is it a summer blockbuster movie? Who produces summer blockbusters? Or who wants to? Is it a teenage horror movie?

Don't ignore the smaller cable markets, reality programming, infomercials, direct-to-DVD, and so on. I call these Hollywood's back door. If you live outside of California, investigate local production companies. What's happening in your own region? Start somewhere small and work your way to glory.

And don't think you must have an agent to succeed. Most first scripts are sold without an agent. Marketing centers on filling needs. If your script fills a need, then your task is to get the script to the person who can benefit from it. This involves understanding your prospective buyer in order to create an effective strategy; it also entails recognizing obstacles and seeking ways to overcome them.

So be honest in your assessment. Where does your project belong and why? Who produces for that venue? Choose *producers* who have worked on projects similar to your proposed movie. List individual names, not production companies.

Text continues on page 290

Project Plan

Title _____

Genre/description _____

TARGET MARKET

What is the best market for your script?

☐ Feature screenplay   ☐ Network MOW   ☐ Cable movie

☐ TV series (1 hour)   ☐ Sitcom (network)   ☐ Sitcom (cable)

☐ New technology (interactive, CD-ROM, etc.)   ☐ Animation

☐ Reality programming   ☐ Direct-to-DVD (feature)   ☐ Infomercial

☐ Other _____

More specifically, what is the best venue for your project? (This question asks you to look realistically at the market. Where would you find a similar project? A blockbuster summer release? A Fox network weekend one-hour TV series? A woman-in-jeopardy movie for the USA Network?)

_____
_____
_____
_____
_____
_____

List producers or production companies that produce for this target market.

_____
_____
_____
_____
_____

If appropriate for your market, list potential talent that could be interested by this project. This means that the actor or actress sees a role in your script that will further their career.

_____

_____

_____

_____

_____

_____

List potential directors, if appropriate, for your project.

_____

_____

_____

_____

_____

_____

If finding an agent or manager will help you sell this project (and it probably will, although you can sell to some markets without an agent), then list potential agents here (list specific individuals, not agencies).

_____

_____

_____

_____

_____

_____

_____

_____

MAKING CONTACTS

Who in the film business has read your work and responded favorably?

_____

_____

_____

_____

_____

Who do you know in the business (not listed above) who might refer you to someone else or otherwise be helpful? (These people do not have to be in high places.)

_____

_____

_____

_____

_____

List any friends, relatives, acquaintances, business associates who might have industry contacts. (The premise here is that everyone knows someone who knows someone who works in Hollywood. Spend some time with this.)

_____

_____

_____

_____

_____

_____

_____

_____

_____

List places you can go to network. These can be writers' groups, professional organizations, social gatherings, clubs, festivals, seminars.

_____

_____

_____

_____

_____

_____

_____

List other marketing research sources (i.e., "the trades," directories, etc.)

_____

_____

_____

_____

_____

_____

_____

List other marketing ideas that might be right for your script, such as contests.

_____

_____

_____

_____

_____

_____

_____

POSITIONING STRATEGIES

Important note: Positioning has to do with creating perceptions in the prospect's mind. The worksheets that follow will provide more detail and support for your marketing strategies and project plan.

How is your project similar to other successful projects in the medium you have chosen? _____

_____

_____

How is your project original? What fresh twists does it add? _____

_____

_____

Draw a picture of a movie poster or a newspaper ad for your script.

Include the ad copy. How will your story or idea be sold?

_____ A script that can be sold in a brief pitch by you to an agent, by an agent to a producer, and/or by a producer to a studio. Is it a commercial project?

_____ A role that an "A" actor or actress will covet.

_____ A story that is visual, active, and fresh, that doesn't rework other movies.

_____ An ending that is emotionally satisfying.

_____ A character (and characters) that is believable and interesting.

_____ A script that is not too similar to a recent failure.

_____ A script that has something in common with successes within the past five years. This could be a new twist on a past, successful idea.

_____ A script that is in correct spec format, and that reads easily.

_____ A one-sentence concept, hook, premise, or logline that says, "This is a movie. Buy me!"

_____ The ten marketing tools developed, including a concise, hard-hitting query letter.

_____ The resulting budget is about right for the specific market you have chosen. (Don't be concerned with budget for mainstream, studio movies.)

What personal pluses do you bring to the table?

_____ Enthusiasm—Do you have the "voice of conviction"? Are you confidence without being arrogant?

_____ Objectivity—Can you separate your ego from your work, or are you defensive?

_____ Ambition—Do you want a writing career? Do you love the business?

_____ Grace—Do people enjoy working with you? talking to you? meeting you?

_____ Other _____

IDENTIFYING PROSPECTS

The next step in your plan—once you have completed the above worksheets and the "positioning" worksheets that follow—is to begin your marketing research and networking. You will also begin to approach people you suspect might know someone in the industry.

Now, select your best prospects (producers, talent, directors, agents, and contacts). Generally, you will work with about eight people at a time. You will not contact any of them until you have done your homework (completed the worksheets).

Name _____ Title _____

Company _____

Buying (and/or other) history _____

_____

_____

Budget range (if applicable)_____

Current needs/wants _____

_____

How he/she prefers to be contacted_____

Name _____ Title _____

Company _____

Buying (and/or other) history _____

_____

Budget range (if applicable)_____

Current needs/wants _____

_____

How he/she prefers to be contacted_____

Name _____ Title _____

Company _____

Buying (and/or other) history _____

_____

Budget range (if applicable)_____

Current needs/wants _____

_____

How he/she prefers to be contacted_____

Name _____ Title _____

Company _____

Buying (and/or other) history _____

_____

Budget range (if applicable)_____

Current needs/wants _____

_____

How he/she prefers to be contacted_____

Name _____ Title _____

Company _____

Buying (and/or other) history _____

_____

Budget range (if applicable)_____

Current needs/wants _____

_____

How he/she prefers to be contacted_____

Name _____ Title _____

Company _____

Buying (and/or other) history _____

_____

Budget range (if applicable)_____

Current needs/wants _____

_____

How he/she prefers to be contacted_____

==

Name _____ Title _____

Company _____

Buying (and/or other) history _____

_____

Budget range (if applicable)_____

Current needs/wants _____

_____

How he/she prefers to be contacted_____

==

Name _____ Title _____

Company _____

Buying (and/or other) history _____

_____

Budget range (if applicable)_____

Current needs/wants _____

_____

How he/she prefers to be contacted_____

==

Weekly Action Plan

Main goal _____

Key milestones   1 _____

2 _____

3 _____

Time commitment _____

What specific actions will you take this week to achieve your milestones?

Marketing research _____

Meetings, pitches, groups, networking _____

_____

_____

Query letters _____

_____

Cold calls _____

_____

_____

Follow-ups by mail or fax _____

_____

Follow-ups by phone _____

_____

Contests _____

Other _____

Other _____

Other _____

Notes:

Correspondence Log
(Queries, Treatments & Scripts)

Date	Q/T/S	Script Title	Person/Company	Comments, response, follow-ups

Meetings, Telephone & E-mail Log

Date	Time	M/T/E	Person/Company	Comments, ideas discussed

Continued from page 277

As mentioned earlier, The *Hollywood Creative Directory* will be helpful, as will other directories and resources. Even the "Film and TV Production Charts" in the trades will be helpful. Keep in mind that sometimes a company grows weary of a particular genre and is ready for something different (but not *too* different).

Now look for potential *talent*. You may ask, *Why look for potential talent if producers are the buyers?* Because many actors and actresses have their own production companies and are looking for projects just for them. The interest of a bankable star can raise your script from obscurity.

Be sensible—you won't likely find Julia Roberts or Will Smith interested in a TV-movie about an insurance adjuster who must learn to cope with shingles. And keep in mind that a star's agent is usually a poor place to send a script. Unless you represent money, the agent may never get the script to the star. However, a hot query letter might get forwarded to the actor.

What *directors* might be appropriate for your project? If you're writing for television, this may not be applicable. A known TV director may not add that much to the project. But a film director or bankable star, even if they don't have a production company, can add value to a script if they express interest in it. Imagine saying to an agent or producer, "I have a script that Leonardo DiCaprio is interested in."

Finally, list the names of potential *agents*. First, get the Writers Guild list of approved agencies, then the Hollywood Creative Directory's *Hollywood Representation Directory*. Learn what you can about the agencies through your marketing research, but select individual literary agents to contact.

Making contacts

As Joan Rivers said, "It's not *who* you know, it's whom." This business is built on relationships, and it's a small town. Networking is how you find contacts. Contacts are your bread and butter. And even though Hollywood is the only town where you can die of encouragement (thank you, Dorothy Parker), you need connections. You must meet people and you must nurture the contacts you make.

As your agent circulates your script and as you contact people about your script, you will find many who will say no, but who respond favorably to your work. Write down their names along with the names of those who say yes (see pages 280-281). You will stay in touch with these people once or twice a year. In fact, you can ask them if you may e-mail them every so often. When you complete another script, they might be willing to read it, or refer you to someone it's right for. Don't underestimate the value of someone who has rejected you.

Very important! List anyone you know who might know someone in the business. (See the worksheet on pages 280-281.) That includes any friends, relatives, business colleagues, and acquaintances. Everyone knows someone who knows someone who works in Hollywood or at a local production company. Just pretend you are a new Amway distributor and list anyone and everyone. You may be shocked at all the contacts you have access to.

It's no secret that the number one way to break into Hollywood is by referral. Many producers and industry people will read a referred script that they would otherwise demand you submit through an agent.

My students are always surprised at the results of this powerful little exercise. Once they mention to friends, acquaintances, and relatives that they have written a screenplay, the windows of heaven often open before them, and blessings pour down on their heads.

You may discover that your Aunt Tilly once dated the head of Castle Rock Entertainment, or that your boss was a fraternity brother of Tom Hanks, or that your friend was a childhood playmate of the current president of ICM.

Take the time to ask around. This list of potential contacts could include producers, executives, actors, directors, script supervisors, assistants-to-whomever, agents, custodial engineers, gophers, gaffers, and grips. Yes, even gaffers and janitors are insiders. They may be closer to the action than you are.

Once you have a list of names, contact them by phone, fax, mail or e-mail. The first words out of your mouth or on the letter will be the name of the person who referred you. Then simply ask this contact to read your script. Tell him you'd love to get his opinion. I am always surprised at how generous people are in these situations. Because producers and agents often receive up to 100 scripts a week, it can be difficult getting your script to someone, and yet that same person may readily accept a referred script and place it at the top of their pile.

If your contact enjoys the read, he will know what to do with the script and to whom to give it. If your contact is a producer, she will refer you to an agent so that the script can be "officially" submitted. Sometimes the script will be referred to another Hollywood-type person. I've heard of assistants and mail boys just placing the script on someone's desk. Someone may even want to "discover" you.

One surprised student reported that she mentioned her script to a relative who happened to know a TV producer. This TV producer read the script and referred her to an agent. Now she is a working writer.

Don't think that the only possibilities lie in Hollywood. You might have opportunities in your own area. There are many regional production companies, and there are film people in every state and province.

As mentioned, you will also meet people in writers' groups, seminars, classes, screenwriting organizations, Internet chat rooms, blogs, expos, festivals, and conferences. You can even meet people through contests.

Contests

There must be 100 screenwriting contests available. Some are established and well-connected. Others are highly focused on specific genres or film areas. Some are not worth entering. When you evaluate any contest, ask yourself who's running it and why. Who's doing the judging? In Book VI, I list my favorite ten. There are others that might be excellent for your purposes. (Visit www.keepwriting.com for "Bible Updates.") There may be a few contests that are only available in your area. Contact your state film commissioner about opportunities for screenwriters.

Even if you don't win a contest, scripts are often judged by, or otherwise find their way to, industry professionals. You might make a contact, get a meeting, or even receive an offer. In fact, entering contests can be done concurrently with your other selling efforts.

In entering contests, be sure to read the rules carefully. Many contests have their own formatting requirements and some may be looking for specific types of scripts. Most will state their judging criteria. Make sure your script is polished before you submit it.

If you win a contest or place, you can insert this fact in the qualifications section of your query letter. You have more credibility now; plus you've achieved a milestone that can give you momentum and energy on your upward climb. Many students have "broken in" by winning or placing in contests, or making contacts with judges and readers.

Positioning Strategies

Positioning refers to how your product is placed in the mind of your prospect. The Positioning Strategies Worksheet (page 282) and accompanying checklist of questions (page 283) will help you create a viable positioning and marketing strategy.

Identifying prospects

Okay, you understand the nature of your project, you've targeted your market, and you have identified potential buyers and helpers. Now the fun begins. You match your project to these individuals whose names you have written down. Select at least eight people you think will be most helpful, regardless of their position in the industry, and fill in the worksheets on pages 284-286. You may do this for as many as 20 at a time.

List their name, title, and company. What is their buying history? If you don't know already, research it. Your marketing research efforts should continue throughout the selling process. What size projects are they looking for, budget-wise? What are their current needs and wants? And how do they prefer being contacted?

You may not be able to answer all the questions. Don't let that discourage you. Just do your best to learn about your prospects, using the marketing resources discussed. The more knowledge you gain, the more power and confidence you will have. Power? Confidence? Yes. Because these prospects are *real* prospects and *you* know you have something that *they* may want. At the very least, you are likely to find a good contact, a connection you can return to later in your career.

Don't be overly concerned with budget. Most producers want to produce something big. Budget becomes an important issue when your market is small independent producers and other programming where budgets are limited.

Don't rush the process. I've witnessed a lot of heartache from writers who became overanxious and approached the market prematurely, as described earlier.

Weekly Action Plan

You will want to make specific long-tem goals, in terms of both writing and selling. (I will share some thoughts on goal-setting at the end of this book in the "A Personal Challenge" section.)

The key to achieving your goals is consistent action. Persistence. To help you focus your energy and efforts, I recommend you take a moment at the beginning of each week to create a weekly action plan and make a specific time commitment (see page 287).

At the beginning of each week, plan your activities for that week and then commit whatever resources in time, money, and effort you'll need to accomplish those tasks. It may be twenty total hours, or four hours a day, or Tuesday and Thursday nights from 8:00-10:00 p.m. Whatever it is, make a goal each week in terms of time and specific actions. Some weeks, the only action will be to write. Other weeks, there may be several objectives.

What if you fail to achieve any of these goals? Don't kick yourself or quit. What's past is past. Make a new goal for this week. Your goals are motivators to freedom, not prison wardens. Onward!

Contact Logs

On pages 288 and 289, keep track of all your efforts for legal purposes, for tax purposes, and especially for marketing purposes. The correspondence log is really a submissions log. You keep track of your submissions of query letters (Q), treatments and synopses (T), and scripts (S).

With each contact you make, you will plan a *follow-up*. Schedule it. Maintain some kind of tickler to remind you of follow-ups, or just to touch base.

As you contact people, don't forget to apply the Purpose-Audience-Strategy Principle and other marketing principles we discussed earlier.

5. Implement your plan

Okay, you have protected your work, prepared your screenplay (product) for market, assembled ten selling tools, and created your strategic marketing plan. But your work is not done. Throughout the remainder of this book, we will explore specific techniques, strategies, and methods for implementing your plan.

How to find an agent

As you might guess, there are many advantages to acquiring an agent. Agents save you time. They know the territory and they know how to negotiate a deal. Because agents are expected by the industry to screen out crummy writers, the fact that you have one greatly multiplies your chances of finding work. Best of all, agents don't cost anything until they sell your script. Some large agencies, such as ICM and CAA, package scripts; that is, they add talent or a director to generate a studio deal. They are generally more difficult to break into than small agencies, but a small agency may be a better choice for the novice.

You may have heard how difficult it is to get read. First of all, it is true that agents will seldom read your script, but their assistants and readers may *if* agents are properly approached.

First, secure a list of approved agencies from the Writers Guild. Their list is coded so that you can select the agencies that are accepting submissions. Keep in mind that the Guild lists agencies, but not individual agents. For this, you may need to go to a directory. I recommend the *Hollywood Representation Directory* put out by Hollywood Creative Directories (listed in Book VI).

Study the various agency lists and directories you have acquired. Some directories list agents in order of seniority. When using those that do, select the agent farthest down the list in a given agency. If you admire an established writer, you may contact the WGA for the name of his or her agent. As a last resort, call specific agencies and ask, "Who is taking on new clients?" Do not tell an agent or agency that you are a new writer. You are a writer with a new script. And don't ever say that you are "seeking representation." Just ask, "Who's accepting new clients?" Or: "Who would I send a short query to?"

The point is to get the names of *individual* agents. You will *not* send them your script. You will instead fax or send a query letter to about five to ten agents at a time. Simultaneous submissions of queries and scripts are the norm in Hollywood. Don't e-mail a query unless an agency expressly states that they welcome e-mailed queries. Do not include a synopsis or treatment with your query. Mailing to five to ten agents at a time enables you to evaluate their responses and improve your query before you contact more agents. You will only contact one agent per agency.

WORKING WITH AN AGENT

Let's assume you have queried several agents (we'll discuss query letters in the next section), and one has requested your script. You mail your script to the agent with a cover letter. She loves your script and calls.

When an agent calls, she shows her interest by asking the magic question: "What else have you done?" Hopefully, you have written a second dynamite script, and have other ideas to pitch. Most likely this agent will want to meet you personally. There are a few issues that you and your agent will want to settle at this meeting.

One is the contract. The agent gets 10%. No reputable agent charges a reading fee. Be wary of requests for cash or for referrals to specific script consultants. However, an agent may legitimately ask you to cover the cost of photocopying your script.

In Writers Guild-signatory contracts, there is a 90-day clause: If the agent has not found you work in 90 days, you can terminate the contract. Before you do, however, remember that selling a script takes time. Many agents will not tender a contract until an offer is made by a producer for your script or services. If your agent is WGA-signatory, this is not a problem—the eventual contract will be WGA-approved.

Your agent will want to discuss your career. What do you want to write? Are any genres of particular interest to you? Do you want to write for television? Are you willing to travel to L.A. for necessary meetings? Are there certain things you are unwilling to write (such as stories that demean women)? Be careful not to sound too picky about what you'll write, but, at the same time, freely express your writing passion. While in Hollywood, choose your battles carefully. Many are not worth fighting; some are.

If you have several scripts, and an agent doesn't like one of them, ask for a release so you can go out and sell it yourself. If you feel uneasy about a particular agent, ask him to tell you about his current clients and recent sales. You'll get an idea of his ability. You may be able to research this in advance on the Internet.

Always remember, the agent's primary motivation is money, not helping writers with passion (although that can be a secondary motivation). The agent has 20 to 30 other clients, most of whom can bring in a higher commission than you. The agent represents you because he sees bigger sales down the road and believes you can write the material his contacts want, so don't say you want to write a screenplay every so often for extra money.

Instead, communicate to the agent your desire for a writing career, your willingness to work hard and to accept writing assignments and development deals. Keep in mind, though, that screenwriters rarely get assignments for adaptations and rewrites unless they've had a big sale, but these are not the only types of development deals available.

In addition to commitment, your agent wants to see in you an ability to perform as a writer and as a *pitcher*—how well you present yourself and your ideas.

Most agents work on a weekly cycle. Each Monday, they set out to sell one or two scripts by Friday. They're also hoping to secure writing assignments for their clients. In fact, they'll often meet with their producer contacts to match their writers to the producers' project ideas. If an agent loves your script and sees that it is similar to some producer's goal, they'll have it delivered to that producer. Often, that results in a meeting that you attend with the producer, which (the agent hopes) results in a development deal.

Although agents are not writing coaches, they will prepare you for meetings and advise you on the ebb and flow of market tides.

There are four kinds of situations that an agent can arrange:

1. The outright sale of your spec script. Your agent will suggest a strategy for selling your script. She will want to generate "heat," and solicit the interest of more than one buyer in your script. This can result in an auction. This is the stuff dreams are made of. You will be paid six figures or higher plus receive a bonus of a like amount or even greater amount *if* the screenplay is actually produced. There are also residuals on video cassettes and DVDs. It will all be spelled out in your lengthy contract.

2. A literary purchase and option agreement, commonly called an *option*. This is more likely to happen than an outright purchase. Here the buyer is not quite so enthusiastic or simply doesn't want to put a lot of money into the script immediately. In either case, the producer buys an option to the rights for a short period of time (six months to a year) for a small "down payment" of anywhere from zero (referred to as a *free option*) to $20,000. During that *option period*, the producer uses the script to attract talent and/or money. At the end of the option period, the producer will pay the purchase price, renew the option for another period of time by making another payment, or pass. In the case of a pass, you keep any option money originally given to you, plus the rights to the script revert to you.

3. A development deal. Here, the agent uses your script as a lure to arrange a meeting or pitching session with a producer where you pitch *your* ideas—this can result in a development deal or sale (if the story you pitch is already scripted).

4. An audition. The fourth and most likely scenario is that your showcase script secures you an audition meeting for an open writing assignment, such as a development deal to execute the producer's idea into a script. (We'll cover this in depth when we discuss "How to pitch without striking out.") In the case of episodic television, you will be paid to write a couple of episodes plus get residuals if the show goes into syndication.

Once the agent negotiates a deal and conditions are met, the check is sent to the agent, from which he pays you your 90%.

Some agents get you to work for them. You go out and make the contacts. When someone expresses interest in your script, you say, "I'll have my agent send you a copy." And then you will inform your agent. Even if you do all of the work, don't even think of attempting to cheat your agent out of the 10%.

Stay in touch with your agent. Get together on the phone periodically, or in person. During an active campaign, there should be contact at least once a month.

ENTERTAINMENT ATTORNEYS

An alternative to using an agent is an entertainment attorney. These lawyers are recognized by the industry as acting as agents, but they will charge you $150 to $600 an hour for their services, without any guarantee of a sale. This can get very expensive.

Perhaps a more appropriate situation in which to utilize the services of an entertainment attorney is when you have a legal question or need a contract negotiated or analyzed.

If an attorney misrepresents you, notify the State Bar. If you stop using an attorney, she must turn over her files to you.

MANAGERS

A few writers first find a manager, who then helps them find an agent or sells their script for them. A manager may charge 15%-25% of your writing income for their services, but they basically run your career for you. When meeting with a manger, ask her precisely what she does and what her commission is.

Whereas agents focus on sales, managers focus on developing you and your work. Managers are generally easier to query than agents, and managers usually have fewer clients so that they can spend more time with each. Sometimes, working with a manager in developing your talents is a good way to find an agent.

Some managers may want to attach themselves as producers of your project. This may or may not work for your project. Personally, I would hesitate unless "my gut" told me to go ahead. If you decide to go ahead with such a manager, make sure the "producer" label is appropriate for what he or she actually does. Managers are not WGA-affiliated.

One of the best ways to find an agent is through a producer, and although agents advise against this procedure, it is worth considering. I'll explain in "How to sell your work without an agent."

Crafting the query

One of the rules of the game is that you never, ever send a script to anyone unless they specifically request it. You get them to do that by sending a captivating query letter. Even when you respond to ads requesting scripts, always query *first*.

In this business, everything usually begins with a query letter. It's generally how you make your first contact with anyone. In cases where you call, the call will resemble the query letter in structure, tone, and content. I suppose you could call it a "query phone call." Many writers call or e-mail before they query to verify submission policy or if they are currently considering new material, or verify the spelling of a name (translated: to see if that person is still there).

One screenwriter/client wrote me with his tip of the day. He said that if you know already that a company does not accept unsolicited queries or screenplays, then tell them directly, "I have an unsolicited script. Who would I sent a short query to?" It's worth a try. What I like about it is the honesty. I've see too many examples of lying becoming fatal to people's careers.

If you want to approach a producer directly, with no agent or referral, and you have a great concept, you might try calling up the producer. You may have to pitch to an assistant first. But you may be able to get a meeting or at least the opportunity to pitch your idea over the phone. I hasten to add that pitching over the phone is less desirable than pitching in person.

The query letter is a written pitch. Its specific purpose is to get the recipient to request a copy of your script.

Query letters should be typed on 24-pound (or 20-pound) neutral-color paper (white, ivory, gray, etc.) using a conservative, easy-to-read 12-point font (Times Roman, Helvetica, Sabon, Arial, Palatino, Courier, etc.), and should look professional. You don't need a fancy printed letterhead, but be sure to include your name, address, phone number, fax number, and e-mail address (if you have one). Don't forget to put these on the letterhead itself.

Don't give yourself the title *screenwriter* or *writer*—it's a sign of an amateur. Graphics are not impressive; you are selling yourself as a writer, not as a graphic artist. Every written communication by you is a writing sample and will be seen as such. That's especially true with the query, so focus on the writing.

In terms of format, I recommend *standard block*, which means everything is brought to the left margin. Double-space between paragraphs and don't indent paragraphs. Other business formats are fine.

The letter should always be addressed to a specific individual and should never be longer than a page. The content of the letter should be concise, hard-hitting, and intriguing. As a general rule, shoot for three "brief" paragraphs. However, the letter needs to be long enough to convince the reader to call you, but short enough to lure someone into reading it. Big blocks of black ink won't do that.

Don't get chummy, and don't say, "I'm going to make you a billion bucks," or "Today is your lucky day," or "Renee Zellweger will want to play the lead." There's a big difference between confidence and conceit.

Your query letter should communicate five things, and these are not in any particular order:

1. The concept in a sentence or two
This is done with a premise statement (usually in the form of a "what if" question), a logline (the *TV Guide* version of the story), or story hook (e.g., "hard-boiled cop becomes kindergarten teacher"). This might be a good time to review the information on high concept in Book I.

2. The title and genre
The hook or story summary should imply the genre. If they don't, you may need to state the genre directly.

3. A brief pitch of the story
The pitch should be written in present tense, focusing on character, conflict, and action—beginning, middle, and end. The story is not about the mafia, it is about a

person in the mafia with a problem. Your story summary will be one or two paragraphs, with one being preferred to two. Show is better than tell. Don't say that your story is jam-packed with action and plenty of romance. Instead, write the query in such a way that the reader perceives as much. Give the reader a reason to believe.

Don't tease the agent with a statement like, "If you want to know how it ends, you'll have to read the script." That won't work. If your story is quite strong, but you have a weak concept, open with your story and forget the concept. The reverse is also true. But provide enough information that the agent or producer will ask for your script.

It's okay to use Hollywood buzzwords and phrases such as "hip with an edge"—just make sure they are in current usage, yet not overused. Reading industry publications will help you find that edge that makes you hip.

4. Your qualifications
There are many ways to qualify yourself.

- Referred by someone in the biz. In this case, open your letter with that person's name: "Robert Redford asked me to contact you."

- Any film-related experience.

- Any professional writing experience. "Professional" means you were paid. Be brief. Don't make a list of published magazine articles; just say you've been published in a number of national publications.

- Winner of a screenwriting contest (or placed).

- Endorsed by a professional. The best endorsements are from non-buyers-such as working writers and actors. Include their testimonial. Don't quote a producer because that begs the question, *If she liked your script so much, why didn't she buy it?*

- Expertise in the subject matter. If your character is a trial lawyer and that's your livelihood, consider mentioning it. I had a student who was a rock singer for ten years whose script was about a rock singer. I told her to mention her experience.

- A graduate degree from a recognized film school, such as UCLA, USC, NYU, Columbia, or AFI. It may help a little to mention other education or well-known writing courses you have taken, but it will not be as impressive as actual experience.

If you have no qualifications, omit this section. Never mention a negative. If you live out-of-state, don't worry about it. If you've written other scripts, mention that fact so the agent or producer won't think that the script you're pitching is your one and only. Don't mention that you've written a half-dozen or more screenplays *if* they have not had any action.

5. Request permission to forward your script
Most writers include an SASE (self-addressed, stamped envelope) or postcard to make it easy for the prospect to respond. On the back of the postcard, give the prospect a couple of options to check. (One will be, "Yes, send me a copy of your script LOVE FREIGHT" [or whatever the title of your script is].) Type his or her name at the bottom, so you'll know where it came from.

Should you fax, mail, or e-mail the query? Although many writers have had success by faxing, my recommendation is to mail a query letter the first time you're contacting someone. A few agents and producers may prefer e-mailed queries. Find out in advance what is preferred, even if that means placing a phone call.

If you mail your query, include a postcard or SASE, even though many recipients will not respond at all. Some writers recommend sending the letter without an SASE because it's so easy now to respond via e-mail or phone. Although I've always wavered on this issue, my advice is to include the SASE anyway.

Some writers believe the SASE or postcard is defeatist, so they add a line to the query that they'll follow up in a few days. If you fax your query, close with "I'll call in a day or two," since you cannot fax them an SASE. When you call, ask the agent's or producer's assistant for permission to send them your screenplay. Don't grovel.

In two to four weeks when you follow up by phone, if they can't find your original letter, offer to fax a duplicate right at that moment.

If someone tells you that they do not accept manuscripts from people not known to them, ask them for a referral to an agent or producer who does. You could also ask, "May I call back in a few months to see if anything has changed?" or otherwise use your persuasive powers to get them to just hear your concept. At the very least, you may make a contact that will pay off later.

Do not open your letter with long statements about seeking representation; they know you seek representation. And do not close it with long expressions of thanks for their consideration and time, or tell them how much you're looking forward to hearing from them. They know you are grateful and how much you want to hear from them. These expressions just take up space on the letter and don't help you get a positive response.

Do not send your script with a query. Do not send a treatment or synopsis to an agent unless requested. A producer, on the other hand, may request one. Remember, more Hollywood-types will be interested in your service (your ability to write) than in your product (your script).

If you know in advance how a particular producer or actor or agent likes to be queried, then those instructions supersede my own.

SAMPLE QUERY LETTERS

As mentioned, queries can be used to approach any industry professional. Always query before sending a script. Keep in mind that the purpose of the query is to obtain permission to forward the script. You accomplish that by getting the reader excited about your story. Here are a few sample queries.

Notice that the first letter does not open with any pleasantries, prologues, or small talk.

The Wizard of Oz

```
Dear Ms. Big:

A tornado throws a young farm girl into Oz, a magical land where
she must defeat vengeful witches and sinister flying monkeys to
find her way home. Dorothy befriends a cowardly lion, an airhead
scarecrow, and a sentimental, if rusty, tin woodsman. Each, like
Dorothy, feels outcast and misplaced.

They join forces to seek help from the Wizard of Oz, fighting off
the Wicked Witch of the North along the way; but when they finally
destroy the witch and meet the alleged wizard, they discover that
the blessing each traveler seeks has been with them all along.

My latest screenplay, THE WIZARD OF OZ, is a family-oriented
fantasy reminiscent of STAR WARS. Before writing it, I wrote and
produced a community-access cable program about tin woodsmen, and
I've had several short stories published in Munchkin Daily.

Please use the SASE or call me for a copy at 555/555-5555.

Sincerely,
```

The above letter was created by screenwriter Joni Sensel for her newsletter. She points out in her commentary that she would address the letter to an individual. In the first paragraph, she identifies the protagonist, her obstacles, and goal. I especially like the last sentence about feeling outcast and misplaced because it identifies an emotion.

The second paragraph tells the agent how Dorothy overcomes her obstacles. It identifies opponents and suggests the resolution. Note that the author told the story, but did not include the concept. The story itself, in this case, is sufficient. It includes character, conflict, action, emotion, and theme. The genre is implied.

The third paragraph refers to STAR WARS. This links the project to a proven success and signals to the agent that OZ could be big bucks. (It's usually best to refer to a *current* success, if at all.) Joni also indicates the genre and lists her qualifications.

The fourth and final paragraph succinctly tells the agent what to do without groveling or multiplying words of gratitude. The reference to the SASE is probably unnecessary—the SASE will be there for the agent to see. Including her phone number is a plus, even though it's already printed on the letterhead. This well-written letter flows smoothly and logically from point to point. If you use the phone to query, be just as succinct and self-assured.

Bed of Lies

This letter is provided by Kerry Cox, former editor of *Hollywood Scriptwriter*.

> Dear Ms. Agent:
>
> Thirteen years ago, J.T. Wheeler woke up at 5:30 a.m., showered, had a light breakfast, and savagely murdered his family of four. He then hopped into his Lexus and vanished from the face of the Earth.
>
> Or did he?
>
> It's a question Susan Morgan, wife of prominent attorney Lawrence Morgan, has to answer fast. The chilling fact is, the more she learns, the more she realizes that Wheeler's killing spree not only wasn't his first . . . it may very well not be his last.
>
> And she might be married to him.
>
> BED OF LIES is a psychological thriller and dark mystery with a strong female protagonist that builds to an ultimate shocker of an ending. It is also a story of trust, of betrayal, and the fine

```
line that divides the two when secrets are buried between husband
and wife.

I've written professionally for television, radio, and print,
including network TV credits and two published books. I've
also worked extensively as a crisis-intervention counselor for
Interact, a non-profit group specializing in teen and marital
crisis management.

Sincerely,

Kerry Cox
```

The first paragraph—with the punchline *Or did he?*—is the hook. The next section is the story, including the title, genre, and underlying theme about trust and secrets. Kerry's qualifications follow. Kerry's work as a crisis-intervention counselor qualifies him as an expert in the story's subject matter.

His writing style matches the mood of the story and uses detail effectively. If this query were for a comedy, he would probably have written the letter from a humorous slant.

Heart of Silence

What follows is a query letter that won a contest. Although the content of the letter is fine, the letter itself needs a shave and a trim. I eliminated words, phrases, and sentences that I felt were unnecessary.

In queries like this, many things are taken for granted. For example, the agent will realize that the writer has completed an original feature film script—why else would she be writing? The strength of this letter, I believe, lies in the intriguing concept hook: *A man* [is] *forced to confront his own divinity when his dead daughter rescues him from suicide.*

ORIGINAL

```
Dear Ms. Pikthis,

I have recently completed an original film script entitled HEART
OF SILENCE. It tells the story of a man forced to confront his
own divinity when his dead daughter rescues him from suicide. The
stage version of this story, entitled CRY OF SILENCE, won the 1989
Kumu Kahua Playwright's Award from the University of Hawaii. The
script is 104 pages.
```

HEART OF SILENCE has been reviewed by a professional reader, Kerry Cox, who commented: "An intelligently written script, professionally written and in proper format. Your characters, particularly the husband, were well-drawn and realistic." Dalene Young, a professional scriptwriter, said the material was "moving, believable, and dramatic."

I have also completed an original feature comedy entitled QUEEN KONG. It is a send-up of KING KONG, in which the hero is the love of the female beast. It runs 110 pages. Both scripts are available upon your request as a hard copy or on disk in WordPerfect 5.1 for IBM.

In addition to works of my own, I am also interested in working on rewrites and collaborations. I am able to travel to take meetings in Los Angeles.

Thank you for your consideration.

Aloha Pumehana,
Karen Mitura

REVISED

Dear Ms. Pikthis:

HEART OF SILENCE concerns the moving tale of a man forced to confront his own divinity when his dead daughter rescues him from suicide. My stage version of this story won the 1989 Kumu Kahua Playwright's Award from the University of Hawaii.

The screenplay has been reviewed by a professional reader, Kerry Cox, who commented: "An intelligently written script, professionally written . . . Your characters, particularly your husband, were well-drawn and realistic." Dalene Young, a professional screenwriter, said the material was "moving, believable, and dramatic."

Although I have many scripts and story ideas, I am also interested in assignments. I am able to travel to Los Angeles for meetings. I'll call your office soon to speak to you or your assistant.

Aloha Pumehana,
Karen Mitura

The first paragraph of the revised letter states the title, hints at the genre, pinpoints the concept hook, and affirms one of Karen's qualifications as a writer. In addition, I dress up the hook a bit to make it more attractive. After all, it is the only reference to the story in the entire query. Karen's thinking here is that the concept alone is strong enough to elicit a positive response.

The second paragraph continues with two professional endorsements.

In my revision, I omit the reference to QUEEN KONG, but inform the agent that Karen has written other scripts. As a general rule, I believe Karen's query should focus on one screenplay—her best shot—but could mention the fact that she has written other scripts.

The third paragraph also shows Karen's flexibility.

The third paragraph closes with the promise that she'll follow up by phone. If this letter is faxed, the final paragraph would begin, "I'll call your office later today [or tomorrow]." The reference to "assistant" shows that Karen understands the business.

Did you notice that I did not end with some pleasant expression or statement about wanting representation? The agent knows instinctively that the writer seeks representation, so why state the obvious? I concede that this is a debatable point. Most agents prefer letters that are short and sweet. The conciseness of Karen's revised letter is worth emulating.

A Cuban Cigar
How would you whittle down this query letter?

```
Keul Agent
Great American Agency
1234 Dreamland Parkway
Beverly Hills, CA 90210

Dear Ms. Agent:

Not unlike most people, baseball fan Jimmy Lansburger's life
didn't turn out the way he always dreamed it would. So when he
stumbles across a headline about the greatest Cuban baseball
player alive, Renaldo Rapido, he's more than willing to try
to become this man's agent and save his hide from bankruptcy.
However, Jimmy has two small problems: He doesn't have any money
and he doesn't speak Spanish. But he has plenty of gall. He talks
his sometimes-girlfriend, Selma, a straightlaced travel agent,
```

into helping him go to Cuba to smuggle Renaldo and any teammates
who will come out of Cuba to the land of opportunity.

The two are like fish out of water. Jimmy is a good guy who has
never been able to hold down a job for more than a couple of months
at a time. And Selma knows just enough Spanish to get her into
trouble. This results in a fanciful journey through Cuba, where one
crazy incident leads to another. And Renaldo the ballplayer, who
is known to love America, starts getting homesick for Cuba before
he even leaves. This story will touch your heart with romance and
excite you with action and keep you laughing all the way to the
happy end as Jimmy finds out what's important in life.

I'd like to submit ROMANCE IN CUBA for your consideration and
possible representation. I wrote ROMANCE IN CUBA with Meg Ryan and
Tom Hanks in mind. Who wouldn't love seeing these two together
again?

I've enclosed an SASE for your reply. Thanks very much for your
time and consideration. I'll be eternally grateful to you.

Sincerely,

Bill Bautista

Big blocks of black ink act like agent repellant. I doubt if the letter would even be read.
Here's my revision, which includes a title change.

Dear Ms. Agent:

Have you ever searched for that *one special person* who will turn
your life around?

Well, Jimmy Lansburger, certified baseball nut, thinks he's
found that *one special person* -- Renaldo Rapido, ace pitcher for
the Cuban Nationals. Jimmy's dream is to agent Renaldo and his
teammates into the American big leagues, and make a grotesque sum
of money.

But this lovable flake can't afford a plane ticket or even a
Spanish/English dictionary. So he hornswoggles his no-nonsense
travel-agent girlfriend, Selma, into helping him smuggle the
sentimental southpaw out of Cuba.

```
A CUBAN CIGAR is a misadventurous comedy romp where Jimmy finally
realizes that Selma, not Renaldo, is that one special person. May
I send you a copy of the script?

Sincerely yours,
```

The original query letter is authentic. As you can see, the revision is leaner and more focused. It uses stronger, more concrete words, and it avoids unnecessary repetition. It "shows" rather than "tells," focuses on concept and relationships, and it omits any references to current actors. It also opts for a humorous style since the screenplay is that style.

The phrase "one special person" is an attempt to bolster and unify the concept, characterize Jimmy, and create humor (since this is a comedy). The word "sentimental" is dropped in to raise the specter of conflict—it's not going to be easy to convince Renaldo to leave Cuba. (Besides, I like the alliteration.)

This letter might benefit from a stronger idea of what happens once they're in Cuba (but not having read the script, I don't know). Whether this letter grabs you or not, please note what changes were made and why they were made.

The writer had no experience or qualifications to mention in the letter—A CUBAN CIGAR was his first script. Thus, nothing was mentioned of qualifications. The writer's name, address, and phone number would appear in plain sight on the letterhead.

The Silk Maze

This final example by Jeff Warshaw capitalizes on Hollywood's penchant for sex. Although a one-paragraph story summary would be preferred to two, notice how Jeff's style creates suspense and intrigue. Jeff presented this in class to a standing ovation.

```
Dear Mr. Shmoe:

Jonathan Stark thought he knew all the angles. He thought he
knew what Lily, his beloved partner-in-crime, wanted from life.
He thought he knew how to please and manipulate Celia, the young
socialite who seemed to know too much about his sordid past. He
thought he could control the heart of Mazie, the one "client" who
cared for him. He was wrong.

Jonathan Stark knows next to nothing about the three equally
beautiful and treacherous women who rule his life. Trapped between
two women who love him for very different reasons, and one who
wants to destroy him no matter what it takes, Jonathan must walk
```

```
the tightrope between the true love he seeks and the easy, smarmy
sex life he's come to know. Will he make the right decision,
or is he riding for the biggest fall of his life? Caught in a
smooth, alluring web of intrigue, deception, and white-hot sexual
subterfuge, Jonathan Stark must stay one step ahead of the game if
he hopes to escape THE SILK MAZE.

THE SILK MAZE is a fast-paced, erotic thriller about a man so used
to lies that he can hardly see the truth before him, a man who
must learn to trust not only his instincts, but himself.

I wish to send you my third script, THE SILK MAZE. I am interested
in rewrites and adaptations. You may call me at (714) 555-5555 at
your convenience.

Very truly yours,

Jeffrey C. Warshaw
```

Jeff indicates his genre as a fast-paced, erotic thriller. He is wise to give his genre some pizzazz. Erotic thriller is better than thriller. Romantic action/adventure is better than action/adventure. My script KUMQUAT is not a romantic comedy; it is a *romantic comedy against a background of high adventure*. Don't overdo it, however, with something like sci-fi/action/drama/reality-based/environmental Western.

Jeff mentions rewrites and adaptations; he might consider the broader term "assignments." He concludes his letter with his phone number. Make sure that your address and phone number are somewhere on the letter. Don't expect someone to pick it up off your envelope.

The brief query
Query letters do not need to be long. In evaluating one client's script, I saw a clever angle to her story and wrote a query letter for her. The letter consisted of just one paragraph, and that paragraph was only five lines long. Even though she had no qualifications, she received 40 requests for her script.

Unfortunately, she had not followed my advice to polish her script before sending the query and to not mass-submit the query. This story, unfortunately, ended in heartbreak. Thus, she felt disinclined to share the letter with others.

The Secret Cave
Here's a letter of my own that pitches a project referred to frequently in these pages. My script was rejected at Disney, but I asked Barry Wise (name has been changed)

who he thought the story was right for. He gave me a referral. Since he used the word "perfect," I quoted him. The query was successful; that is, Ms. Miller (name changed) requested the script.

```
Dear Ms. Miller:

Barry Wise at Disney said the following screenplay was "perfect"
for you.

~ THE SECRET CAVE to a boy is what THE SECRET GARDEN is to a girl ~

THE SECRET CAVE is a tale of a long-forgotten cave, a "magic"
sword, and a family stranded without a TV set. It is the adventure
of a boy who discovers that the only "magic" he needs is already
inside him (his good heart). It is a laugh-out-loud family comedy
with a final surprise twist that will touch you deeply.

My experience includes several script sales, including a
successful DTV feature that I also produced (HERCULES RECYCLED),
a network MOW (A WINDOW IN TIME), and an award-winning family
comedy (THE PENNY PROMISE). In addition, I have published hundreds
of articles and stories, and I'm the author of The Screenwriter's
Bible, now in its fourth edition.

Request THE SECRET CAVE by calling (801-492-7898) or faxing
(801-756-5555) your release. Incidentally, I wrote this "hero's
journey" for kids aged 7-12 and their parents.
```

Kumquat

KUMQUAT is an unproduced screenplay that I sold for a nice chunk of change. Here's the entire pitch. Notice that this successful query focuses on two characters while communicating important story elements.

```
Philbert the philosopher -- melancholy, pensive, and playing it
safe -- is on the trail of the ancient Golden Kumquat of Tibet,
said to hold the meaning of life.

Cami the costume shop owner -- bubbly, resourceful, and chameleon-
like -- is on the lam and wanted for murder. She tricks Philbert
into helping her find the real killer.

Their riotous adventure teaches her to drop the façades and love,
and it teaches him how to take the risk to live. Together, they
partake of the KUMQUAT.
```

```
Wanna bite? Call me for KUMQUAT, a delicious romantic comedy
against a background of high adventure.
```

An old query format with a new twist
I'll let this client tell his own story:

> Dave, here's what I did. I queried three agents; three responded positively. I queried four production companies; two responded positively, and two are pending. Here's what I did differently. I centered my excellent title followed by the genre. I then double-spaced and centered the exact phrase I think their marketers would use on the movie poster. That was followed by a normal paragraph consisting of a two-sentence story summary. In my final paragraph, I listed my writing experience.

Another client had success using bullet points. In my letter above for THE SECRET CAVE, I centered a story hook and followed it with the logline and two story pluses.

Don't be afraid to be creative with your prose and formatting. On the other hand, don't outsmart yourself with something so "creative" that it's incomprehensible. The main thing is to loosen up when you write. If you are like other writers, you will feel some tension and pressure when you write the query. Find a way to get beyond that and relax.

WHAT NOT TO INCLUDE IN A QUERY LETTER

It can be tough finding the razor's edge between professionalism and creativity. And where does confidence and enthusiasm end and conceit and insolence begin? One rule of thumb is to ask yourself, *What does this agent or producer want to hear*? In other words, get the focus off you and what you want to say, and get into the head of the agent or producer you're writing to.

Here are excerpts from five would-be screenwriters who didn't figure that out. These were collected by screenwriter Joni Sensel.

```
A warm-hearted, romantic venture into the deepest of human
emotions, revolving around the love of one person for another
despite overwhelming odds, with a touch of comedy, proving yet
again that love conquers all. . . . And, of course, like all my
work, the story concludes with a stunning, unexpected ending.
```

This could describe a dozen stories. The problem here is the character is telling instead of showing, and is focusing more on theme than story. Write the story, including the ending, and we'll decide if it's heart-warming and stunning.

> I'm 22. I hope this will be my way over the "wall" and give me
> access to a struggling industry that could use the talents I
> possess to help it reach its potential. Cinema is my life and I
> hate to see it in the hands of incapable people.

Don't get cocky, kid.

> Your agency has been highly recommended to me by the Writers
> Guild. I have enclosed a short story that explains why I have
> chosen to be a screenwriter.

And we're all dying to read it. And please, no false flattery. Be aware of Linda Buzzell's two no-nos—"don't be dull or desperate" (from *How To Make It In Hollywood)*.

> Jesus Christ the man and I are both empaths. I'm this way because
> of Y. The symbol of God is a clock. I would like to meet the Pope
> someday.

Is this the story or your qualifications?

> . . . the constant epistemological question regarding the per-
> plexing attempt to explain the nature of being and reality and the
> origins and structure of the world . . . the metaphysical conflict
> between natural law (St. Augustine) and pragmatism (Kant-Dewey-
> James) and the question of the benefits of merging from . . .

Excuse me, please, but I just wanna make a movie.

ONCE THE QUERY IS SENT

The next step is to evaluate the responses to your query. Half or more may not respond at all. Most who do respond do so within four weeks, although responses have come as late as six months later. If you faxed your query letter, call in a couple of days. If you mailed your query, wait about two to four weeks before following up.

Usually a phone response is positive. Rejection generally comes through the mail. No response usually means no, although it is possible that the query was lost. So follow up with a phone call and offer to fax or e-mail the letter again. If the rejections pile up, then re-evaluate your query and your story. Make any necessary changes. Then go ahead and contact more prospects.

Once an agent or producer responds positively to your query, send your script with a cover letter that opens with a variation of, "As you requested, here is . . . " Remind the agent or producer of the contents of the original query, or attach the original query to your cover letter. The cover letter will be attached to the screenplay with a paper clip.

The script should be an excellent photocopy of a letter-quality original. Send it priority mail with the cover letter. Do not include return postage or an SASE. Scripts are seldom returned. It's okay to make a personal delivery, but you probably will not get a chance to meet the agent or producer.

It can take up to four months or more to hear back on a script submission. Wait at least four weeks before your first follow-up. Try once every couple of weeks or so after that. Be *pleasantly persistent*, not obnoxiously persistent. Generally, the best time to call is in the afternoon. A Thursday or Friday call will remind the agent to get the script read over the weekend.

When someone says, "We'll call you," or "We'll get back to you," your response will be, "Great! May I call in a week?" That makes it more difficult for them to summarily dismiss you.

If your script has not been read by your third or fourth call, then it's time to turn to another prospect, but before you do, try to get a referral to another agent or producer. Keep in mind that each agent has about 20 to 30 clients and is inundated with script submissions, and producers are similarly inundated. Things take time, so be patient.

If your script is rejected, don't be afraid to ask for honest feedback. (The rejection letter may not be honest.) Ask for a copy of the coverage. Remember, you are always building contacts; and some of your best future contacts will be today's contacts who rejected you.

Always treat the producer's or agent's assistant like a human being. Learn his name. Treat him with the same respect you'd accord the agent, and don't use the word "secretary." You may very well need to sell this person first. In fact, it's quite possible that the assistant will be the first and only person to read your script.

A former student and now-working writer tells the story of when she was just trying to break in. She met a lowly assistant to an independent producer. This writer later found an agent, and the assistant went on to become a studio executive. Together, the ex-wannabe writer and ex-assistant put together a feature deal that the studio bought.

No one in Hollywood is an assistant to be an assistant. Everyone is on their way up. So think of the assistant as your friend and accomplice. He can tell you how a particular agency or production company operates. You can ask, for example, "When should I expect to hear from so-and-so?" Or, "When can I call back?"

Remember that only a no is a no. If a prospect is too busy to read your work now, you can ask, "May I try back in a few months to see if anything has changed?"

Let me remind you that during this long period of searching for an agent and selling your script, you should not stop writing. Once you finish a script, take a week off and then start another one. Chances are you will finish it before the previous one has been sold.

How to pitch without striking out

What happens when an agent submits your script to a studio or a production company? First of all, what is a producer or an executive looking for? (Note: I use terms "producer" and "executive" synonymously in this book.)

To be honest, most have their own ideas to develop if they can just find the right writer. They may also be looking for a writer to work on a sequel, or even do an adaptation. Of course, they'll buy a spec script if they think it is an excellent marketing risk, but they're looking for writers. In fact, about 80% of the deals out there are development deals—producers hiring writers to execute their ideas. (The percentage varies.) The spec market tends to go in cycles. Some years can be excellent for spec scripts, other years not so good.

What will your agent do? Well, your agent will contact the highest-level executives and producers he knows. These will be producers with deals or executives at studios. Producers with deals are producers with contracts or other connections with studios or financial sources. The studios are usually the last to be contacted because their rejection closes the doors to outside producers wanting to bring the project to them.

Your agent will use the same or similar pitch or premise that you used in your query letter. If the executive or producer asks for your script, he will normally give it to a *story editor*, who will assign it to a *story analyst* or *reader*. The reader writes a *coverage* and makes a recommendation. If the recommendation is positive, the development executive will read at least a portion of your screenplay.

A development executive must love your script to champion it. Assuming he does love it, he will pitch it to other execs using the same or similar pitch or premise that your agent used with him. These other producers will then read your script, probably during the weekend. It will then be discussed at the Monday morning conference or some other meeting. The decision will be made to 1) buy it or 2) not buy it.

1. If they decide to buy it, you could be rolling in six figures. Or, they'll pay for an option (as explained earlier) and use your script to interest other parties (talent, director, other producers) and/or bring it to a studio. The script will likely be further developed by you and/or by other writers. Eventually, the project is either *greenlit* or not. A *green light* means it will go into production. Money and fame will soon be yours! If it is not greenlit, (and most scripts that get this far aren't), then the rights will either revert back to you (in the case of an option) or the project will go into *turnaround*; that is, offered for sale to another studio or entity that is will to cover the costs to date. There are many variations on this theme and many other pathways deals can take.

2. If they decide to pass on the script, *but* they like your writing, the executive will call your agent and ask to meet you. This means you're a semi-finalist in your bid to secure a development deal or other writing assignment. Your agent will arrange a meeting.

THE MEETING

The *meeting* is an opportunity for you to *position* yourself and your work in the minds of executives. From the executives' points of view, this meeting has one of two purposes.

One is to provide a forum in which you can pitch your own ideas. They will then choose one of your ideas and hire you to write the script—a development deal. More likely, however, they have a writing assignment that is open, and they want you to audition for it, based on your "sample script" that they just read. The meeting usually works out something like this:

You'll be seated on a couch or at a conference table facing two or more people. The meeting will last from 30 minutes to about an hour, but it could be much less. You'll know that when the meeting is set up. Some of the time is spent with getting-to-know-you conversation. At the beginning of the meeting, they will tell you how much they love your sample script. They're trying to make you feel relaxed. They will offer you a soda or water.

Some writers suggest that you dress above the executives in the room and sit in the chair that places you in a power position. There is merit to this, but I believe it is more important for you to feel comfortable. Dress comfortably, but don't come in rags. Many writers wear nice Levis, a T-shirt, and jacket. I recommend a collared shirt and slacks. For women, I recommend slacks or a casual dress. The important thing is to be comfortable. When you sit down, place your hind quarters hard against the back of the chair or couch—this helps you project your voice and maintain good posture. It's okay to bring a pen and notepad to take notes.

Be as conversational and natural as you can. At the same time, retain a level of professionalism. Don't try to get too chummy. First names are okay. Having a good sense of humor is a plus. Project positive energy—not Pollyanna, not God's gift to Hollywood—be upbeat and confident. Get the conversation going. Ask about something in the room—a trophy or painting.

If they are interested in hearing your ideas with an ear toward developing one of them, they will ask you to pitch them. If they are interested in the possibility of giving you a writing assignment, they will audition you by asking you what you've been working on. In other words, they're asking you to pitch a couple of ideas. They just want to get a feel for your work, your creativity, and your personality. After all, pitching is as much about making contacts and developing relationships as it is about swapping "stories."

In either case, have at least two to four pitches ready to go.

THE TWO-MINUTE PITCH

Brief pitches come in two stages—the story hook in 25 words or less, and a brief rendition of the storyline. In other words, the structure of this short pitch is quite similar to a query letter.

The hook must grab their attention and set a tone. The hook could come in the form of a premise, a logline, or a concept. If you haven't already, please review "The low-down on high concept" in Book I.

Here are some examples of hooks:

- HONEY, I SHRUNK THE KIDS. *Family comedy.* Here you've identified the title and genre. In this case, that's probably enough to grab the attention of the executives.

- *Family/sci-fi/thriller. An alien child accidentally left behind on Earth is befriended by some children who help him find his way home. We call it ET.* This is a logline.

- DANCES WITH WOLVES *goes to Japan.* This could have been the opener for THE LAST SAMURAI.

- *What if the president of the United States were kidnapped?* This is a premise statement.

- *Romance against a background of high adventure: When her sister is kidnapped, a lonely romance writer tries to save her, only to find true romance in the process.* This is a variation of the old pitching formula: When X happens (the Big Event), so-and-so tries to get Y, but ends up with Z.

- *Imagine you are driving down a dark road. Late at night. And someone is behind you. You turn; he turns. He is following you. You decide to get on a lighted street and suddenly find yourself at a stop light. Nowhere to go, and the car behind you gets closer and closer. Finally, he pulls up next to you and stops. You look over and he resembles you exactly. He is you!* This is a little long, but it's an example of a story concept.

When Gene Roddenberry pitched STAR TREK, he had problems. No one was interested in sci-fi. A popular TV show at the time was WAGON TRAIN. So Gene pitched STAR TREK like this: *WAGON TRAIN in space.* He hitched his "star" to a "wagon," and the rest is history. He combined the familiar with the unique—a new twist on a recently successful idea.

These days, you want to avoid the "cheap pitch." *DRIVING MISS DAISY meets the MEN IN BLACK.* Or: *NAPOLEAN DYNAMITE on the TITANIC.* Or: *GOOD WILL HUNTING falls in love with PREDATOR.* It's okay to refer to successful movies, but it should not be the core of your concept or pitch. Yes, ALIEN was pitched as JAWS in space, and TITANIC was ROMEO AND JULIET on a boat—that got their attention—but there was more to each story than just the concept. Use your common sense and don't misuse this tactic. There is some resistance to it now anyway. If you have a bona fide comparison that helps you present "the familiar with a twist," then use it as a hook.

In light of the above, it's both fun and instructive to watch the opening sequence of THE PLAYER and see all the established writers stumble through pitches. The tools of this book will help you minimize that stumbling.

Most often, development executives must sell your idea to higher-ups, and higher-ups will sometimes sell your idea to other producers or a studio. Even if they have a script, it's the script's story concept, logline, or hook that helps them do that. Likewise, distributors and exhibitors need a simple, easily understood idea to attract moviegoers to their movies.

However, if a producer's past work consists of literary films (such as EMMA or WINGS OF A DOVE), a blood-and-guts, special-effects, high-action pitch may not be appropriate; in fact, you may even be perceived as a hack. Be wise. Here's an example of a low-concept story hook:

- THE SECRET OF QUESTION MARK CAVE *is the story of a secret cave, a magic sword, and a family stranded without a TV set.* This hook implies the genre—a light, family comedy. Although low-concept, it might be high enough to someone looking for just this kind of story.

Once you have awed them with your hook, you will be favored with a nod or otherwise be encouraged to continue. You will then deliver your brief storyline. Present the entire story—beginning, middle, and end—building on what you've already told them. Your focus will be on two or three characters, conflict, emotion, and action. Don't forget the Big Event, the Crisis, and the Showdown.

If you're pitching several ideas, open with your best shot. Don't go into a pitching session with more than three or four pitches, unless your research tells you otherwise. Too many pitches make you look like a watch salesman in front of a hotel. Keep in mind that the main purpose of this Chamber of Horrors is to provide those you are pitching to with a means of evaluating you and your work. Do you have good ideas? Can they work with you?

If you're lucky, they might love one of your pitches enough to offer you a development deal. Congratulations. A development deal is an agreement in which they pay you to write a script for them. Or they might ask to see your script when it's completed. Congratulations, you've made a contact.

Most likely, they'll thank you for your ideas and begin talking about themselves. They have a reason for doing this. It's their turn to pitch you.

THE LONG PITCH

When your pitching is over, the producers may share an idea or two of their own. For example, a producer may say, "We're looking for a Faustian comedy for Tobey Maguire. What do you think?"

If you respond positively and intelligently, the executive may say, "Well, if you come up with a story for us, then let us know. We'd love to hear the pitch." Interpreted, this means: *Congratulations, you are now a finalist in your bid to secure a development deal. Have your agent call us when you have a 10- to 20-minute pitch ready.*

(Note: In some meetings and pitching situations, the allowed time for your pitch will be just five minutes. It all depends on the purpose of the meeting, the production company being pitched, and other factors. Your agent will give you guidance.)

Here's what's really happening: You and a dozen other finalists will create and pitch a Faustian comedy for Tobey Maguire. This way, the producer can develop her ideas without investing a dime of her own money. The producer will pick the pitch she likes best, and you will get the development deal to write the script.

Obviously, you will want to prepare for this major pitch—or for any pitch. Here's how.

Delivering your pitch

Do not read your pitch, but it's okay to have 3" x 5" cards or notes to prompt you. Be as clear and animated as your personality allows. You'll open with your hook followed by the storyline. You may also wish to introduce your key characters right at the beginning before you move into your story.

In the body of the pitch, focus on character, the goal, what's at stake, the emotional high points, theme, how the character will grow, the major dramatic twists, and, of course, how it ends. In some long pitches of complex stories, consider presenting the title, genre, and a brief introduction to your main characters. Two common traps to avoid in any pitch:

> First, don't try to cram your entire story and all the characters into your pitch. It shouldn't sound too complicated.

> Second, don't present a rundown of scenes: *This happens and then this happens and then this happens* . . . Your story will sink into the mud and you'll be dead in the water. Get to the heart. Talk them through the story. People can't follow all the details anyway, so hit the high points.

Here's the opening of a successful pitch I delivered for THE SECRET OF QUESTION MARK CAVE. I had just delivered the hook.

My story is about a boy, Seebee, who feels that his dad hates him. He does everything he can to please his dad, but Frankie berates him, criticizes him, hurts him. It's not that Frankie hates his son—he doesn't. He just wishes he knew how to show his affection.

Well, one night, Seebee sneaks into the attic against Frankie's orders and finds the old journal of his great, great grandfather. The journal tells the boy about a secret cave and a magic sword. Wow—with a sword like that, Seebee could solve all his problems! He vows to run away to the mountains, but then he hears a noise! Frankie is downstairs, and boy is he mad.

Of course, your pitch will continue all the way to the end of the story. Please note that in bringing you to the story Catalyst, I emphasized the *emotions* of the characters. The pitch needs to touch the executive's cold heart.

Don't refer to actors directly. Refer to them in a casual way, if at all. For example, you can say a Brad Pitt-kind-of-guy. And you will say it in a way that communicates that you are not assuming that Brad Pitt will be in your movie. You don't want to appear naive. Say, for example, "I guess this guy is kind of a Steve Martin-type."

Why do this? To make it easy for the listener to instantly visualize the character. You can use the same trick when selling your concept. Say something like, "in the vein of ETERNAL SUNSHINE OF THE SPOTLESS MIND," or "reminiscent of WAR OF THE WORLDS," or "in a way, it's a corporate version of PRIMARY COLORS."

Don't tell them what they are looking for. Don't say, "I know you'll like it because it has plenty of sex."

As I mentioned earlier, it's okay to bring notes to prompt you, but never read a pitch. It's also okay to take notes when you're listening, although I would ask permission: "Is it okay if I jot this down?"

Don't lie. Don't say that Ron Howard is looking at the project if he is not. The producer will simply call Ron Howard to find out. They follow up. Don't think they don't. Don't say that no one has seen the script if, in truth, dozens of executives already have a copy. On the other hand, if DreamWorks is interested in it, don't be afraid to say so.

In some pitches, you may be interrupted with questions, requests for clarifications, and suggestions. Go with the flow and be flexible, but do not allow the pitch to lose momentum. Be open to suggestions and be prepared to present a different angle on the story. Don't be afraid to express yourself. They want you to. If appropriate, let them contribute to the story, so they can own it, too.

Don't oversell. Once they say no, STOP. Once they say yes, STOP. Don't keep blabbing on.

When they are done with you, they will excuse you without telling you their decision. The truth is that they may not be the decision-makers. When a decision is made, that decision will be conveyed to your agent. Regardless of the outcome, send a note of thanks.

Personality

One thing's for sure: If these development executives hire you, they will be spending a lot of time with you developing the story. So almost as important as your ideas is your personality. Some meetings are arranged purely for interpersonal relations, and for developing contacts and relationships. In any case, they want to know what are you like to work with. On one worksheet of your Strategic Marketing Plan, you are asked to do a personal inventory.

There are four personality traits that are key to any situation when you're meeting Hollywood types: enthusiasm, objectivity, ambition, and grace.

Enthusiasm. Do you have the voice of conviction? Do you have a passion for your work? Do you communicate confidence? Do you believe in your ideas? I cannot over-emphasize the power of enthusiasm. By the same token, don't get so excited that you hyperventilate and pass out. They dock points for that.

Objectivity. Can you separate your ego from your work? Can you be objective about the pluses and minuses of your script? This does not diminish your passion. It means that you can adjust to what lies ahead: story development hell. (*Story development hell* refers to the process of working with the notes and other feedback you'll receive while developing the project.) You may be amazed at how these professionals view your script. Be open to criticism, but be diplomatic and firm where it matters. If you are defensive and rigid, then you're difficult to work with (from their point of view).

Ambition. Do you love the business? Do you want to be a full-time writer or do you want to just write an occasional script from your cabin in the woods?

Grace. Are you gracious? Do people enjoy meeting you and talking to you? Do you have any natural charm? Are you the opposite of dull and desperate?

Now don't present a façade personality, or disparage your weaknesses; just project your best self, focusing on your strengths.

Be prepared

Before the meeting, find out as much as you can about the company and the people you are meeting with. If you have an agent, he should be a big help here.

- Who are they and what are their titles?
- What is the purpose of the meeting from their points of view?
- What are their most recent credits?
- What genres are they most interested in? Who is *their* audience?
- What major talent has appeared in their most recent productions?
- Do they work with high or low budgets?
- What are they looking for now?

Bring anything you think they might want. If they haven't seen a sample script, bring one. If coverage has already been written on your script by a professional reader, and it's positive, bring it in.

Be prepared to answer questions. Be ready to continue your pitch after the initial two minutes have passed. Have a couple of other ideas or angles on the same idea—just in case. Also, prepare a little bio on yourself. This is not something you hand to them in printed form. You just want to be ready when they ask about you and what you have done.

Also, they may ask you who your ideal cast is. Be ready with ideas about casting. The reason they may ask this is that it helps them get a clearer picture of how you see your characters. It's seldom for casting purposes.

Finally, in driving to the meeting, allow adequate time to arrive and park. Take into account possible traffic jams. Be on time.

Creativity

In preparing for a long pitch, you might consider a creative touch. A minor innovation may make your pitch stand out from the dozens of hum-drum presentations that have dulled the producer's senses that week. One client used action figures to represent his characters. He introduced them one-by-one and spread them out on the table. The development executive was enthralled.

However, usually props are not a good idea, particularly in a short pitch. Don't try to act out your pitch and don't hire actors to perform your pitch for you. On the other hand, don't be afraid to use your voice for emphasis. Use your common sense and put your creativity into the content of your pitch.

Practice

The single best way to prepare for a pitch is to invite some friends and neighbors over and pitch to them. If the story appears clear and interesting to them, then feel encouraged. Practicing your pitch in front of real people (not the mirror) will help you immensely in preparing for the real thing. You might even role-play the entire meeting from beginning to end.

You may be wondering, *Why can't I just give producers a synopsis of the story in writing?* Why do I have to pitch it? Because they cannot "legally" ask for anything in writing without paying you for it. That's because they are signatory to the Writers Guild of America contracts. However, many writers leave a treatment or POP (one-page pitch on paper) on the table after their pitch.

If an executive asks for a treatment or outline, I think it's generally best if, instead, you offer to pitch the project for her to other producers. That's because you can convey more enthusiasm for your project than the development executive can. Keep in mind that if someone loves your idea, they will need to pitch it to higher-ups or to other production companies or to the studios. You want to be helpful to them.

If you're dealing with a producer who is not signatory to the Guild, then you can give him a synopsis or treatment directly and avoid pitching altogether. This is discussed in depth in the next chapter.

The happy ending
If your pitch does the trick, you will be offered a development deal. Your first development deal could be $50,000-$70,000. It will probably also be a step deal, which means that you can be cut out at any step in the writing process. You'll be paid a portion of the total purchase price at each step. Although there are many possibilities, it could work like this: 25% advance, 25% on treatment (first step), 25% on first draft (second step), 25% on polish (third step). If the film is eventually produced, expect another $50,000-$100,000 production bonus.

Throughout the writing process, you will receive notes from producers or executives-in-charge, and will experience firsthand what has come to be known as *story development hell.* At least you're being paid to suffer.

Summary
Do you see a pattern here? The dance proceeds as follows: You write two or three spec scripts. The spec script that best shows your talent becomes a sample script that finds you work. Sometimes you sell that spec script outright. Usually, you don't. Instead it becomes a divining rod that finds you an agent and/or gains you admittance to a meeting where you can sing for your supper.

Synopses, treatments, and outlines

A *synopsis* is a one- or two-page story summary, usually double-spaced, using a conservative 12-point font. Keep in mind that many people use the term *synopsis* to refer to any summary that is not used for marketing purposes and the term *treatment* to refer to any story summary used as a selling tool.

A *treatment* (actually *spec treatment*) used to market your script is not the long, 50-page document that you're sometimes paid to write in a development deal. A *spec treatment* is three to twelve pages in length—with most people preferring about three or four pages. Keep in mind that many people use the term *treatment* to refer to any story summary that is used for marketing purposes. Thus, it is possible that someone could request a one- or two-page treatment.

When a producer or agent asks for an *outline*, he or she is usually referring to a *spec treatment*. Although it is possible that she is asking for a simple *list of scenes*, it is highly unlikely that she is. Since the words synopsis, treatment, and outline are often used synonymously, ask the person making the request about how many pages they're expecting. Then you will have a better idea of the type of document to prepare.

Given what we have established above, I will use the term *treatment* throughout this chapter. In your discussions with professionals, you should use the term *treatment,* unless the other person uses one of the other terms.

A one- to two-page treatment will not usually need a title page, so be sure that your name and phone number are on it. You can do that with a header or simply by typing the contact information in the top left corner of the first page.

A one-page treatment or synopsis is sometimes called a *pitch on paper*. Because it is so short, it is similar to a query letter. It will begin with the logline, hook, or concept, and may be left behind at pitching meetings or handed off at gatherings.

The title page of a longer treatment (3-12 pages) should look like the script's title page. Both should be written in 12-point Courier or other conservative font such as Times New Roman. Do not bind with brads. Instead, send it loose or stapled.

A short treatment is usually double-spaced or one-and-a-half-spaced. Treatments that are about three or four pages or longer are often single-spaced. If you use that style, double-space between paragraphs and don't indent the paragraphs. That's the style I am using in this book.

Both a treatment and a synopsis can be registered with the Writers Guild. Follow the same process as registering a screenplay.

Think of the treatment as a written pitch—analogous to the long pitch discussed earlier. In fact, it may be voluntarily left behind after a pitch. It should be written in present-tense narrative (short story) form with no or little dialogue. It's not a scene-by-scene rundown, and you will only focus on about three to five characters. You cannot include all of the subplots. It emphasizes the crucial moments, the key events of the story, and the emotional highs and lows of your characters. In a script, you cannot describe what a character is feeling or thinking, but you can in a treatment.

A treatment not only tells the story, it sells the story. It is a marketing piece. You write it for producers, talent, and directors. You want them to love the story. You want them to say, "What a great story! Let me read the script!"

Some treatments begin with a description of the setting or "world" of the story. Others open with a story hook. A very few open with a brief description of the characters. Remember that the treatment is a selling document. Grab the reader's attention from the beginning in a manner that works best for your story.

I think it will be instructive to actually see the difference between a professional story synopsis and a treatment written for marketing purposes. Some time ago, I asked long-time Hollywood story analyst Leslie Paonessa (listed under "Script Consultants" in Book VI) to read my old script, THE SECRET OF QUESTION MARK CAVE, and write a coverage.

Her coverage consisted of her recommendations, an analysis, and a story synopsis. When she wrote her synopsis, her objective as a professional story analyst was not to pitch the story but to create a clear and complete summary of the story. As you will see, she did a superb job.

I suggest you read Leslie's synopsis on pages 338-340 right now, and then return to this page to read my treatment (below) of about the same length. (You'll note that I've been pitching this project throughout this book.)

• • • • •

The brief treatment that follows *treats* the same story as the story analyst's synopsis. Why is the writing style different? Because it is written for a different purpose. (Incidentally, this treatment and the associated screenplay led me to a development deal with Disney many years ago.)

My strategy for this synopsis was to apply the principles already stated in this chapter. The short length of the treatment forced me to focus on the essential story in terms of plot, character, and emotion.

I recommend that you write brief synopses or treatments when you're stuck, before a rewrite, and (of course) before a pitch. Because a treatment is a written pitch, consult the section about pitching (see page 315) for tips on writing a treatment. Although not necessary, I open this treatment with the story hook.

THE SECRET OF QUESTION MARK CAVE
by David Trottier

This is the story of a long-ago promised sword, a secret cave, and a family stranded without a TV set.

SEEBEE (nickname for Percival), age 11, fancies himself a knight, although he is kicked out of The Explorers Club for failing to perform a brave deed. Worse, his own dad (FRANKIE) calls him a "nothing kid." Actually, Frankie loves his son; he just doesn't know how to connect with him, and he's too busy watching TV to find out. Meanwhile, Seebee practices with his little wood sword.

One night, Seebee sneaks into the attic against his father's wishes and discovers several beautifully carved wood knights. He also finds the journal of his great-grandfather, Captain Cole. The journal tells the story of a "magic" sword (at least Seebee thinks it's magic) hidden in a secret cave deep in the mountains. Seebee vows to find the sword; he's sure it will solve his problems.

That day, Seebee and GLODINA witness a bank robbery through the window. When the RED HAT BANDIT races toward them, Seebee tells Glodina to hide in a car for safety, but the car she chooses is the robber's car. Seebee unsheathes his little wood sword to defend the car, but his fear paralyzes him -- he's no brave knight. The bandit drives away with Glodina still hidden inside his car. Seebee high-tails it home only to do something even worse -- he accidentally breaks his dad's TV set. So Frankie breaks Seebee's cherished sword in half, breaking his heart as well.

Seebee feels dejected and powerless; but that night, he dreams that his great, great grandfather, CAPTAIN COLE, gallops up on his horse and offers Seebee the sword mentioned in his journal. Cole says, "You have a power all your own," and Seebee awakens.

Emboldened, the boy tapes the pieces of his *wood* sword together. He runs away with his Explorers Club buddies to find the "magic" sword so he can use it to rescue Glodina. They overcome conflict and natural obstacles until they discover Question Mark Cave. Inside, they find Glodina (she is safe) -- the cave must be the bandit's hideout! A deeper search produces evidence of Captain Cole, but *not* the wondrous sword in his dream. Seebee is discouraged.

Just then, the Red Hat Bandit arrives. He's about to "rub out" the little band of four, but Seebee tricks the robber and the four children escape from the cave and race down the trail. But the robber is right behind, and boy is he mad!

Meanwhile, Frankie is fired. He feels dejected and powerless. Upstairs in his own secret cave (the attic), his precious wood carvings gather dust. He might carve more if his tools hadn't been stolen years ago. Enough of his troubles; he needs to find his runaway son.

Back on the trail, the bandit pursues Seebee and his friends until he catches them at a cliff that hangs over a canyon stream. There, Seebee unsheathes his taped wood sword and courageously holds the robber at bay while his friends get over the cliff to safety. When Seebee attempts to cross, the bandit catches him. In the struggle, Seebee defeats the bandit with his wood sword, and the famous Red Hat Bandit tumbles into the stream below, breaking his leg.

Seebee now realizes that he doesn't need a magic sword because he has *a power all his own*. His dream has come true! Plus, he has performed a brave deed to get back into the Explorers Club. In fact, he's president now! When Frankie arrives, Seebee offers his portion of the "Red Hat Bandit reward" to buy a new TV to replace the one he broke. But no, Frankie can use that money to buy new carving tools. Maybe now he's brave enough to do the work he loves. His "little knight" has healed his wound.

So Frankie takes Seebee into the attic (the secret cave) and removes Captain Cole's sword from a secret hiding place! Father, like son, had once wanted to be a knight, and had journeyed to Question Mark Cave years ago and had found the ancient sword. The sword becomes Frankie's connection with his son, the connection he has longed to find.

On the front lawn for all to see, he then knights his son "Sir Percival" and gives him the sword he deserves. Seebee then "knights" Glodina his "brave princess."

• • • • •

Don't expect to find work based on a treatment alone until you are established. You must have a finished script. If a producer loves your treatment—your story—but you have no script, he may buy the story for $1,000 or so and then hire a proven writer to write the script. Hollywood has plenty of ideas, but few great writers. Great ideas are not worth much without a script.

On the other hand, a great spec treatment can earn you a deal if you have contacts and some kind of track record that demonstrates your writing ability. Such treatments can be as long as 20 pages, but are usually much shorter.

The following is a treatment by David S. Freeman; the story is by David and a colleague. This story treatment was purchased by Paramount Pictures for $45,000. Not bad for five pages!

Readers might note some similarity between this story and the film SIMONE. It's worth noting that Paramount bought this story several years before that film came out.

Regarding treatment writing, David says, "Keep it short. Keep it colorful. You don't have time to get lost in the details or the subplots. The treatment should focus on giving us (1) the main beats of the story, (2) the principal characters—who they are, why they're unique, why we care about them, and how they change (if they do), and (3) the flavor of the story.

For those who don't know David, he has sold scripts to many studios, and, as this book goes to print, he has a pair of as-yet-unannounced fantasy epics shooting in the summer of 2005. He also teaches "Beyond Structure" (www.beyondstructure.com), which has grown to be one of the most popular screenwriting workshops in Los Angeles, New York, London, and elsewhere in the United States and around the world.

THE "IT" GIRL

LOS ANGELES.... ROD TRENTON has been a Junior Editor at a half-dozen trendy magazines. He's got wit, he's got sharp, offbeat insights into contemporary life ... and he's got a little too much cynicism and attitude. That's why he's never been promoted to Managing Editor. (It's also why he's single.) His latest haunts: *Centre* magazine, peeling back the onion skin of pop culture.

Media mogul DALTON QUINCE-TAYLOR, whom rebel Rod hates for his renowned anti-humanism, just bought *Centre*. Dalton gives his Managing Editor a mandate: Increase profits by downsizing staff. Rod learns he's next to go. He's desperate to save his job, for he's burned bridges everywhere else.

Rod decides to do a story on "The Most Irresistible Face In the World." Together with a computer-literate friend, he merges the faces of five beautiful women ... Rod gives this captivating, phantom woman a name: "CHRISTIANA SARINS."

Rod writes his story on "Christiana" (a.k.a. "The 'It' Girl"). Using some nefarious antics, Rod gets "Christiana" on the cover. The face captures the imagination of the public and the magazine sells like crazy. The Editor, who thinks that Christiana is a real woman, demands a follow-up "interview" of the young woman, and soon ENTERTAINMENT TONIGHT, OPRAH, DAVID LETTERMAN, and other shows demand Christiana.

But, since she's not to be found, people begin to suspect a hoax. The Editor gives Rod an ultimatum: produce Christiana or he's fired. Rod's desperate, for he's burned too many bridges to land an equally good job elsewhere.

Rod spends a frantic week crisscrossing the South and Midwest, locating any small-town beauty queen who might look like Christiana. No luck. Gloom overcomes Rod. Then he discovers TAMARA MILLS, a sincere wannabe actress from a white-trash neighborhood outside of Cincinnati. She looks close enough to the mythical Christiana that she could pass. While some might dismiss Tamara as unsophisticated, she more than compensates with her love of life, her quirky charm, and her corny but endearing sense of humor.

Rod spills his predicament to her. Will she pretend to be Christiana? She'll be thrust into fame. Tamara's reluctant ... this violates her ethics and her beliefs. But the idea of a short road to Hollywood is too tempting. She takes the deal.

In a MY FAIR LADY type of development, Rod becomes her mentor, giving her a crash course in civilization, Los Angeles-style. Making his job more difficult is the contempt he feels for her small-town ways. However, Tamara's great qualities soon win him over -- especially her guilelessness and her emotional responsiveness. She's very present and very genuine.

Rod's defenses can't hold out forever, and soon it's unclear who's recreating who. If he's turning her into an urban sophisticate, she's softening his rough edges and thinning out his protective coating. In truth, he's falling in love. They both are.

The one thing that Rod can't teach Tamara is how to be a Hollywood starlet. He calls on his actor friend JASON KAROW, who takes over Tamara's "education." Jason teaches her survival skills for the upwardly mobile actress in Tinsel Town, like how to walk into a room and capture every man's eye while pretending to be totally ingenuous; how to laugh so that everyone else wishes they could be as happy as they think she is; or how to use a Little Black Dress as a weapon.

The big evening arrives, although Rod is merely a spectator. Jason takes Tamara to a fancy movie premiere. "Christiana's" appearance causes a sensation. As the paparazzi's cameras snap away, Tamara handles the "audition" with splashy aplomb. She's a hit!

Rod's life is a dream. Things are going well at *Centre* and he's got a woman he loves. But the bloom is soon to fade from the rose ...

Tamara adjusts to the high life very quickly, and she adjusts to Jason Karow just as rapidly. Rod's bright, sure, but Jason can take her right into the middle of a world she's always dreamed of. Nothing compares to the fun and glamour of Hollywood.

What's happened is that, in a way, Rod and Tamara have changed places. He's learned to open up and become genuine; she's learned to how to bask in the superficial. Or at least that's how Rod sees things when she breaks off their budding relationship. She tries to let him down easily.

Rod is devastated. That short burst of warmth that Rod had bathed in disappears and is replaced by bitterness. As for Tamara, the world's her oyster as she becomes a hot item and signs on the dotted line with CAA. Next comes Leno and Letterman and magazine covers. She fails to notice the irony in how she occasionally acts superior to those around her, just the way others used to act superior to her before she was "remade."

Tamara is in such demand that her agent lands her a movie role in a film with a big male star. The rehearsals are very rough. Although Tamara studied acting in Cincinnati, although she has talent, and although she gets help from an acting coach and others on the set, she knows she's over her head. She needs time to bring her acting skills up to the level demanded of her.

Back at the magazine, Rod's writing has become more cynical than ever.

Tamara becomes increasingly ambivalent about being surrounded by people who just want her stardom to rub off on them. She tries in vain to find someone real she can talk to. Of course, there's Jason ... until she catches him having sex with another woman. And so ends another Hollywood romance.

Tamara has a crisis of the soul. Tired of living a lie, the next day on the set she spills the entire truth about her past and announces that she's leaving the picture. She wants the roles, the stardom, the whole works -- but when she's earned it, as herself, not pretending to be someone else. She's going to concentrate on her acting craft for a year. And then she'll return -- as Tamara Mills, not as Christiana Sarins.

The tabloids make humiliating fodder out of her story, although some admire her courage and honesty.

Tamara, having regained her integrity, wants to give it another go with Rod. She tracks him down in Aspen, where he's having discussions with Dalton Quince-Taylor, the hard-edged publisher of *Centre*. Dalton is about to fulfill Rod's dream by giving Rod his own magazine to helm. The magazine will bear the stamp of Rod's incisive, increasingly sarcastic wit.

When Tamara approaches Rod, he brushes her off. He tells her that he did love a woman once, a small-town girl with a radiant smile. But she turned into Christiana Sarins, who liked glamour over substance. He dismisses her and turns away.

Later, Dalton commends Rod for putting women in second place. Hearing this, Rod realizes that he's *turned into* Dalton, whom he has always despised. Rod's out of there in a flash. He abandons *Centre*; he even abandons this new magazine, which was going to be his own creation.

Rod flies to Cincinnati to pursue Tamara. When they connect, Rod is awkward. This time it's his turn to bare his soul. Tamara listens, torn. Tamara is hurt and reluctant ... but love will not be denied.

We see Rod pitching an idea for a new magazine. Cynicism is out, he argues; it's an occasional fun indulgence but no one wants it for a steady diet.

His new vision for a magazine is one that examines the scope of our lives, and all the seeming impossibilities of living. How do you find passion for life if you hate your work? How do you love your body if all the commercials and movies say that only young is beautiful? How do you stay honest when your political leaders tell lies? How do you stay genuine and still climb the ladder of success?

This is the focus that Rod pitches ... to a group of IMPRESSED INVESTORS. And so Rod's new magazine, *Scope*, is born. And love is rekindled, for Tamara, whose acting career has been revitalized, is at Rod's side when it happens.

How to sell your script without an agent

Much has changed during the last few years. Hollywood is inbreeding more. In other words, the system has become more closed to outsiders, and it's more difficult to break in. As with Jack in TITANIC, it's difficult gaining acceptance into the club.

Creating a marketing plan will help you penetrate the market at the same time you are searching for an agent.

Would you be surprised if I told you that many first scripts are sold without an agent? It's true. And although it's a distinct advantage to have an agent, it's possible for you to sell your script without one. In fact, one of the best ways to find an agent is through a producer who loves your script and then refers you to one or more agents. After all, as a general rule, producers are a little easier to connect with than agents.

If you are going to try to sell your script without an agent, make sure that you assemble your ten marketing tools (including your pitch elements, a pitchy query, treatment, and telephone script) and create a strategic marketing plan. I suggest you review Chapters 3 and 4 of this book before going on.

PENETRATING YOUR MARKET

Once you have your ten selling tools in your toolbox and a completed marketing plan, you can mastermind and implement your campaign.

Make sure that your screenplay is original, and don't market a script that will cost $100 million to produce if you are approaching independent production companies who make low-budget features in the $500,000 to $2 million range.

Don't be overly concerned with Hollywood trends. Keep in mind that your first script usually becomes a sample script that you use as a calling card. That's one reason my advice is to write what you have a passion for. You need that energy to get you through that first script. Even so, consider the advice of William Goldman, who said, "Don't write AMERCIAN BEAUTY because Alan Ball did." (*Hollywood Scriptwriter,* June 2000.) Don't write this year's hit. Don't imitate what others have written. Write your best original screenplay.

There are five groups of people you can approach to sell your script without an agent:

1. Writers Guild-signatory producers
2. Independent producers (the indies)
3. Actors and directors
4. Network television producers
5. Cable, independent television, regional markets, and the new technologies—Hollywood's back door

Before discussing each of these, let's look at the crucial role of the story analyst.

READERS

Story analysts, commonly called *readers*, read scripts for everyone in the industry. In fact, some people believe they're the only people in town who still read scripts. Just in case you don't know, you live or die with their opinion. If they say no to a script, it's no. The person paying them is not going to read it—ever.

Readers read five scripts or so over the weekend, *plus* what they read on weekdays. When a reader reads your script, she wants a correctly formatted narrative that flows like a river through her mind. She wants a "good read" [translation: an easy and riveting read]; and, if it isn't a good read, she gets even on the coverage.

The coverage is what she writes when she finishes reading your script. A coverage is a brief synopsis and analysis that *covers* the story. And it contains her recommendation to the agent or producer who hired her. A sample coverage follows:

SAMPLE COVERAGE

Here is an actual sample coverage by story analyst and script consultant Leslie Paonessa (listed under "Script Consultants" in Book VI).

STORY REPORT

TITLE:	THE SECRET OF QUESTION MARK CAVE	FORM: Screenplay
AUTHOR:	DAVID TROTTIER	PAGES: 100
CIRCA:	Present day	SUB. BY: Author
LOCALE:	The Rocky Mountains	SUB. TO: Leslie Paonessa DATE: 7/25/96
GENRE:	Family drama	ANALYST: Leslie Paonessa DATE: 7/30/96

LOGLINE: A boy and his friends go searching for a "magic" sword that belonged to his great, great grandfather, and in the process, they catch a bankrobber who has kidnapped another friend.

	EXCLNT	GOOD	FAIR	POOR
CHARACTERIZATION		X........X		
DIALOGUE	X.........X			
STRUCTURE	X			
UNIQUE STORY		X		
SETTING/PROD VALUE		X		

BUDGET: _____ HIGH _____ MED. __X__ LOW

RECOMMENDATION: __X__ YES _____ NO _____ MAYBE

THE SECRET OF QUESTION MARK CAVE
COMMENT

This is an unusual story that will attract a family audience, especially the youngsters. It has elements of fantasy, humor, and family values set against an entertaining and exciting adventure. It has a bit of dramatic tension, if somewhat simplistic, but it will certainly capture the imagination of kids as they get caught up in the story and identify with the characters.

SEEBEE, STINKY, RALPH, and GLODINA are the youngsters who live out the adventure. Seebee is our "hero" who comes from a very dysfunctional family. Father FRANKIE has been laid off from his job and does little but watch television. He is, in fact, a TV junkie, and it's not at all a positive image. We don't find out until near the end that he once was a creative artist, and it would strengthen his characterization if we could see his internal struggle more. We sense that he has some love inside when he nearly comes into Seebee's room to apologize but can't. Perhaps his relationship with Seebee's mother, FREDA, could help. She is caught up in all kinds of occult interests so that she rarely relates in a warm, motherly manner. Everyone in the story -- neighbors, Frankie, the cops -- thinks she's a nut. Though she provides good comic relief, there could be more poignant moments through her. It's only at the very end that we have any hope that Seebee can get love in this family.

Because the characters are broad, we assume that this story is for children, and to make it more of a crossover film, it would help if it weren't aimed at quite so young an audience. Teenagers will find this too juvenile. The RED HAT BANDIT never seems truly evil, and surely the writer was aware of not making him too frightening for young children.

Seebee as the lead character starts off as a victim, but then finds his own power. It's a very good transformation, and it's through the action that we see him gain strength. He has a mission and goes for it, gaining the admiration of his friends as he does so. Even his father has to admit that he's a hero, and their bonding together at the end is very satisfying. We also see Frankie regain his pride, but this could use some work in terms of making him a more complex character. Perhaps one instance of him watching television could be cut out.

The pacing of the story is strong, especially when we go out on the trail with Seebee and friends in the quest for the sword and Glodina. It's an exciting adventure, and it's written in a very visual manner. There could be more worry at the homefront with more intercutting to build the tension further.

This is a story that could be produced on a modest budget, possibly for an alternative to the huge summer releases.

It's an ensemble piece for young actors and could have wide family audience appeal.

THE SECRET OF QUESTION MARK CAVE
SYNOPSIS

SEEBEE LANCE, 11, and his two friends, STINKY MARANTZ and RALPH HARDY, play their favorite game as adventurers. Seebee's trademark is his wood sword, and he's even proficient in swordsmanship. Stinky uses a bow and rubber-tipped arrows. Ralph is a large boy dressed in camouflage. The game is interrupted when Seebee's mother, FREDA, calls him and his younger sister, VICKY, to come home.

Freda is a bit of a kook, often preoccupied by astrology, card-reading, and the occult. FRANKIE, husband and father, has just been laid off from his job and spends most of his time as a television junkie. At a family picnic in the park, Freda tells Seebee about his great, great grandpa, CAPTAIN PERCIVAL COLE, for whom Seebee is named. She also says that he had a sword with magical powers that may still be in the attic. Though Seebee is intrigued, Frankie forbids him from going into the attic.

GLODINA SANCHEZ, 11, tries to come up into the tree house used by the boys. All but Seebee object. They tell brave-deed stories, but Seebee is ostracized because he's afraid to jump off the high dive at the pool. Seebee and Glodina begin to grow closer.

Seebee makes a ladder and uses it to go up into the attic at night. He finds relics from Captain Cole, including a fascinating journal. Under the bedcovers later, Seebee continues reading the journal and fantasizes about Captain Cole and the sword. In the morning, Seebee tells Glodina the lore about his namesake, and that the sword is in a secret place called Question Mark Cave. He also sees how a loving family acts when Glodina's mother invites him for a morning hug. Later, in an effort to bond with his father about a TV show, Seebee accidentally thrusts his sword through the television screen. Frankie is furious, and Seebee leaves, hurt.

Seebee can't get the club to go with him to find the sword, because Stinky's the boss who makes the decisions. Seebee is left with Glodina, and he's depressed. They find Frankie's car on Main Street. He's in the bank, trying to get a loan, when the RED HAT BANDIT enters with a red ski mask, cap, and a gun! Seebee and Glodina are making believe they're truckers in Frankie's car. The Red Hat Bandit takes Frankie's car for his getaway. The Bandit tosses the bags of money into the car and tosses Seebee out, but he doesn't see Glodina in the back seat until he's on the road.

Seebee tells Ralph and Stinky what has happened, while Frankie returns home and tells Freda that his car was stolen. He takes out his anger on Seebee, saying that he stole Captain Cole's journal. He breaks Seebee's wooden sword and banishes him to his room. Though Frankie later feels a bit sorry about this, he is unable to do anything. Freda comes in to try to comfort Seebee, but she can only seem to resort to her kookie brand of spiritualism.

Alone in his room later, Seebee prays for Glodina and asks for a blessing on his sword so he can help her. That night, each member of the family has dreams. Seebee's makes him accept his own power and the need for him to save Goldina by going to Question Mark Cave -- guided by Captain Cole.

In the morning, Ralph comes in through Seebee's bedroom window, and hears the story of Seebee's dream and the journal. They go up into the attic to look for the sword, and they're almost caught when Frankie comes home. They meet later on the hill with Stinky, and the boys are dressed for the occasion as Explorers. Ralph even has a BB gun.

Glodina sits in a dark room inside a cave. The Red Hat Bandit has gone out to get snacks and brings back licorice for Glodina. He warns Glodina not to try to escape.

When the boys reach the canyon, Seebee consults the journal and finds the map to the cave. Stinky grabs it away, but Seebee sticks up for himself and retrieves it after a fight. Now he's the leader and takes the boys across the river cliff by hanging onto exposed tree roots, though Ralph is terrified. Back at home, the mothers find that their boys are gone. The POLICE arrive to talk to them.

Seebee spots the hidden opening of Question Mark Cave and is the first one to enter, feet-first. Then Stinky and Ralph go, using flashlights. They explore further and find the Red Hat Bandit's clothes in a second room! Then they find the money bags and hear Glodina's voice calling them. They find her with blankets, food and water, though she's a little dirty. Seebee is her hero.

Seebee asks her about Captain Cole's "magic" sword, but

Glodina hasn't seen it. He sees a crevice and enters another room, where he finds Captain Cole's skeleton but no sword. He falls back into Glodina's room and is dizzy but manages to bash The Red Hat Bandit in the face when he shows up. Seebee wishes he had the sword now as he and the other boys run toward the cave opening. Seebee realizes that they've left Glodina behind. When the Bandit's head pops out, the boys throw rocks at him. Now he's really mad. He pulls a gun on Stinky and Ralph, but Seebee is above on a ledge. He finally jumps -- like he was afraid to do at the pool -- and knocks the Bandit over! They overpower the Bandit and knock him out. Glodina is rescued, but the Bandit comes to and chases the kids down the trail.

Back at the house, Frankie goes into the attic and finds his precious wood carvings he was unable to sell when his old partner made him sign a paper forbidding it. OFFICER JONES is certain that he can now sell them, and Frankie seems to regain his pride. He also says he knows where Seebee is. The Police already have men at the canyon looking for the Red Hat Bandit. Frankie runs out. The kids stop to make a plan to ambush the Bandit. Ralph's BB gun and the others' primitive weapons slow the bandit down.

Then Seebee uses his swordsmanship and wood sword to force the Bandit into the raging river, where he breaks his leg. The kids meet up with Frankie, who is being pursued by a GOOFY COP who thinks he is the bandit. Seebee gives his father some of the stolen money to replace the television set he broke, but Frankie returns it as a matter of principle. The Bank President rewards all the kids.

When they get home, Frankie goes into the attic with Seebee and shows him where the sword is hidden. He gives it to him, and the family is reunited. The neighborhood watches as Frankie knights his son "Sir Percival."

WRITERS GUILD-SIGNATORY PRODUCERS

The studios and other large production companies are signatory to the Writers Guild. That means that they have agreed to use Writers Guild-approved contracts. Their names can be easily found in a variety of directories.

What are large producers looking for? Their perceived needs can change monthly, or even weekly. They're constantly assessing the markets. In general, they want something that can be easily pitched to other producers, studios, distributors, and moviegoers. So the concept or central idea must grab them immediately. They also want something written for an actor. They want a script that makes the difference between Bruce Willis doing the movie and George Hamilton doing it, or Julia Roberts as opposed to Shelly Long. The executive's contacts will want to know whom she can attach, who will direct, who will act.

Realize that Hallmark Entertainment is looking for a different script than Castle Rock, but all producers have their markets foremost in their minds. What do their moviegoers want to see, and who do they want to see? They probably don't want a film-noir sci-fi Western that they cannot sell to the moviegoing public. And who's the mainstream moviegoing public? Mostly high school boys, college men, and other male and female thrill-seekers between the ages of 15 and 32.

Realize that when a producer produces the script of a new writer, he's putting his job on the line. If the resulting movie fails, he could be canned for trying someone new. Whereas if a picture using a proven writer fails, it can be seen as a fluke. All producers have their lists of A, B, and C writers, actors, directors . . . and also their up-and-coming.

When a producer hires you, she's hoping you're up-and-coming.

These large producers have deals with studios, meaning that they have contractual arrangements to produce a certain number of pictures with a studio or production company, or a studio may have right of first refusal. This is another reason why it is better to let a producer take your project to a studio than to go directly to the studio yourself. These producers are big because they have access to the money needed to finance a picture.

Generally, large producers accept submissions only from agents.

However, if your query is strong enough, there are some WGA-signatory producers who may accept a script without an agent. In such cases, they will require a *submission agreement* or *release*. A submission agreement is a legal document that basically absolves the producer or executive of responsibility if your work is accidentally stolen. It sounds horrible, but you should consider signing the release to get your work sold and produced.

You will find a sample release on the next page.

Sample Release

TO _____

I, _____, acknowledge that the material

___(title and description)_____

_____

_____

_____ that I am submitting to you was created
and written by me without any suggestion or request from
you. I represent that I am the author of the material and
that the material is original with me; that I have the
exclusive rights to submit the material to you on the terms
and conditions set forth in this agreement; and that I have
the power and authority to grant to you all rights in this
material.

I realize that many ideas, programs, slogans, scripts,
plans, suggestions, and other literary and/or dramatic
and/or musical material (herein collectively referred to
as "material"), which are submitted to you, are similar to
material previously used, previously submitted by others, or
already under consideration by you. I further realize that
you must protect yourself against any unwarranted claims by
refusing to examine any material submitted to you unless you
are assured that you shall have the unqualified right to
finally determine whether such material or any part thereof
is in fact used by you or your successors, assignees or
licensees, and what compensation or other consideration, if
any, should be paid for such use.

I am submitting certain material to you herewith. In
order to induce you to consider this material, I hereby
irrevocably waive, release, and relinquish any and all
claims which I, or any person, firm, or corporation
claiming under or through me, may now or hereafter have
against you, your successors, assignees, and licensees,
and your and their respective officers, employees, and
representatives, for any alleged use, that you, or your
successors, assignees, or licensees may make of any such

material. I also expressly agree that your decisions as to whether you, or your successors, assignees, or licensees have used all or any part of such material and as to the compensation or other consideration, if any, which should be paid to me therefore, shall be conclusive and binding upon me and all persons, firms, and corporations claiming under or through me.

I agree that, should I bring any action against you for wrongful appropriation of the material, such action shall be limited to an action at law for damages and in no event shall I be entitled to an injunction or any other equitable relief. If I am unsuccessful in such action, I agree to pay you all the costs and expenses involved in defending such action.

I further understand and agree that you are not responsible for the return of any material submitted, and I acknowledge that I have retained a duplicate copy of such material in my possession.

I hereby acknowledge that I have read and understood this agreement and that no oral representations of any kind have been made.

Very truly yours,

Signature

Typed or printed name

Address

Telephone number

Why the release? Because these companies are afraid of lawsuits. Sometimes an executive hears a pitch or reads a script that resembles something already in development. When the writer sees the resulting movie, he sues the production company on the basis of that pitch or script.

Generally, these folks aren't interested in stealing your story. Theft occurs occasionally, but large producers are more interested in avoiding lawsuits than they are in theft. *Writer's paranoia* is the hallmark of an amateur. You've got to get your ideas out there. Perhaps your best protection is your writing ability, industry savvy, and completed script.

When querying these companies, considering asking them for their release form. That shows you understand the business and their needs, and it might make them a little more open-minded about your pitch.

Another angle is to pitch to producers on the phone rather than via a written query. Ask to speak to a specific development executive or producer, but realize you'll end up speaking to that person's assistant. Pitch to the assistant. You might conclude your oral pitch by giving the assistant a choice: "If you fax me your release, I can send you a synopsis or a script. Which would you prefer?" It just may be that the assistant will want to discover you and make points with the executive he works for.

When a producer receives a script from an agent or from you, it is handed to a story editor who checks to see if they already have a coverage written on it. If a coverage is already written, that means one of their readers has already read your script sometime in the past. That old coverage will then be attached to your script (even if this is a new, revised version) and returned to the development executive. That's why once any company *passes* on your script (that is, rejects it), you can't resubmit it for consideration.

Actually, there is a possible way around that. Revise the script and make sure the page count has changed. If the page count of your revised script differs from the page count listed on the coverage, the producer may assume that this truly is a revision and have another coverage written on it. Don't change the title, though, thinking you can fool them. That usually backfires.

If the development executive likes the coverage, then she will read a few pages, mostly dialogue, and sometimes the entire script. Development executives "read" 10 to 15 scripts a week. So yours had better capture their imagination. If it does, they'll have others in the company include it in their weekend read. If everyone feels comfortable with it, they will finance it themselves or, more likely, take it to another producer or to a studio.

If the production company you contacted is interested in your script, they will refer you to an agent or list of agents. This is perhaps the best way to find an agent. Ideally, agents want you to approach them first so that the marketplace is untouched, but they will not turn out an easy deal. If a producer refers you to more than one agent, interview each and try to determine which is most genuinely interested in your career as opposed to getting a quick sale. I've had a few clients who found agents in just this way.

The company will either buy your script outright or option it. The option is a smaller investment for them, and it gives them time to shop your script around before having to commit more money. We discussed this process earlier in the chapter "How to pitch without striking out."

The producer may actually be more interested in your writing ability than in your script. She might hire you to "develop" one of her ideas or a sequel or some other project. In other words, she will offer you a development deal. Please recall our earlier discussion in the "Working with an agent" section of the chapter "How to find an agent" and also in the chapter "How to pitch without striking out."

INTERNET SCRIPT BROKERS

There are many Internet writing-services companies that promise to get your story concept or synopsis seen by executives. Many advertise promising results. In evaluating these, I recommend caution but also an open mind.

Try to substantiate their claims. Scrutinize success stories. Ask yourself questions as you study the specifics of the deal. Is the site connected with industry professionals? (That might by a good sign.) Are they contacting potential buyers directly, or are they just hoping buyers will find their site? How are they contacting potential buyers? And so on.

As a general rule, I tend to be leery of a shotgun approach to marketing. However, if the results advertised by these companies seem bona fide, then they might be worth looking into. Since they are Internet services, you'll find them listed at my Internet site: www.keepwriting.com under "Hot Links."

THE INDIES

If you are taken to the cleaners, it will more likely be by an independent producer. Most of these are not signatory to the Guild, so there are fewer restraints keeping these guys off the paths of temptation. Also, they are relatively poor. You need to be aware of this because your first sale may be to an independent producer.

Be professional in contacting independent producers, beginning with a query letter, or with a query letter plus your synopsis (if your research suggest this), or with a phone call. They seldom require submissions through agents, but may ask you to sign a release.

The indies are notoriously cheap. It's not uncommon to have your pay deferred, or to be paid just a few thousand dollars. Seldom are you paid anything up front. In fact, they normally offer a *literary purchase and option agreement*, commonly called *option*. They will pay you a small amount of money, say $500, to tie up the rights to your script for a period of time, say six months. If the agreed-upon purchase price is $10,000, the producer must pay that amount before the six-month deadline. If he does, the producer owns the script. If he doesn't, the rights revert back to you, plus you keep the $500.

With an option, a producer can tie up the rights with just a few dollars. In fact, it is not unusual for an indie to ask for a "free" option—no money down. During the option period (usually six months), the producer uses your script to attract talent, a director, or another producer. Once he has a *package*, he goes to the money people and shops for a deal. If a deal is secured, he pays you for the script. If he doesn't secure a deal, you will have difficulty approaching people who have already seen your script.

Even if you're paid very little for your first assignment, a sale is a sale. You can begin building your career on such a sale. And credits, at this point, are worth more to your career than money. On the other hand, I had one student who sold his first script to an independent producer in New York for $110,000. So there is a wide variety of opportunities in these markets.

Don't be tempted to sign a deal that's bad for you. Don't write until you have a completed deal. And if you're not being paid as stipulated, then stop writing. And before you sign a deal with anyone, ask yourself these questions: Can this guy get the movie made? Can I work with this person? Such questions may not be easy to answer, but they are worth thinking through. Also, it's better to work with a jerk who loves your script and can get a deal than with a sweetheart that's going nowhere. If you have questions about a certain producer, contact the Producers Guild to see what information they might have.

If a producer asks you to rewrite your script for free before making any kind of deal, only do so if the script will be genuinely improved and you retain 100% ownership of the material, even if you use some of their ideas. Get an agreement to that effect.

If a contract is slow in coming, request a *deal memo*. A deal memo is a quickie contract that presages the larger edition later on. It can be used to clinch a deal, any kind of deal. The deal memo is simply a letter delineating the basic points of the deal. Sign the letter and return it. Sometime later, the actual contract will arrive.

A great number of independent producers are searching for scripts for very low-budget productions ($100,000 to $500,000 and up) with as few as one or two locations and just a handful of characters. This market should not be overlooked.

These indie projects can range from SEX, LIES, AND VIDEOTAPE to TEXAS CHAINSAW STEWARDESSES to BLAIR WITCH PROJECT to NAPOLEON DYNAMITE (which was made for $400,000). In fact, the producers of NAPOLEON DYNAMITE shot a ten-minute short-film version for $500 that they used to attract an executive producer to finance the feature film.

Don't overlook these smaller, independent market opportunities. They can be stepping-stones to more lucrative assignments down the road. The independent market, I believe, is broadening with Robert Redford's creation of the Sundance Channel along with the already successful Sundance Film Festival (held every January in Park City, Utah) and other independent markets and film festivals.

Every February, independent producers, foreign sales agents, and others gather for the American Film Market (AFM) at the Loew's Hotel in Santa Monica. A directory is printed by both the AFM and the *Hollywood Reporter*. This directory contains the identities of many independent companies that are players.

Canada

Since there is no major studio in Canada, the Canadian film business operates much like the independent film market operates in the United States, in terms of selling your work as a writer. Many American films are produced in Canada with Canadian talent and writers. That's because the government provides financial incentives for those who produce in Canada. There are also many Canadian productions for the Canadian market. One Canadian writing resource is the Writers Guild of Canada (www.wgc.ca).

APPROACHING TALENT

Don't approach actors (often referred to as *talent*) and directors through their agents, because their agents will not see you as potential money and will not pass the script along. Most big stars are more interested in offers than in scripts. One way to approach these people is to make a personal delivery. This is easier said than done. One writer found an actress in a public place and fell to his knees. With his script in hand, he gushed obsequiously, "I adore you. You have such range. Here, I wrote this for you and for you alone. Please, would you read it?" She did.

Many actors and directors have their own production companies, which are set up specifically to find projects equal to their talents. Most require script submissions through agents. Many will accept a script with a release. My personal experience has shown that they have a greater openness to queries than the large producers.

CREATIVE STRATEGIES

Sometimes you need a creative way to bring attention to your script. For example, one writer dressed up as a custodian after hours and dropped the script on someone's desk. That sounds too dangerous to me.

A friend of mine dressed up as a UPS man and delivered his script to Harrison Ford. Harrison Ford actually signed for it. Too bad the script was such a dog. Another writer sent his script in a pizza box.

THE TICKING MAN was sold by an agent who sent alarm clocks to about 20 producers. A note said, "The ticking man is coming." This resulted in a bidding war, and the script sold for $1 million. (Note: the agent did *not* wrap these up like bombs.)

Gimmicks like this work occasionally, but usually they backfire. Some time ago, I received a call from a writer who was at the Beverly Hills Police Department—he had become too clever for his own good. I told him that he should call his attorney, not me.

On the other hand, if you can find small, clever ways to differentiate yourself from the pack, then that's usually a plus, even if it's as simple as a clever format for a query. After graduating from my course, Robert Olague imprinted the logline for his screenplay THE COMING on the back of a jacket, and attended a writers' conference. The logline read, *In an attempt to take over the world, an alien imitates the coming of a messiah.* Robert made many key contacts that night.

Discrimination?

Don't let the rumors of ageism, sexism, and racism slow you down. You will not likely encounter such bias until you have broken in, and maybe not even then. When an agent or producer reads a great script, they don't care who wrote it. A client contacted me recently to refer me to an article in *Fade In* about her. She's a 49-year-old woman who lives outside the Los Angeles area who sold her script to a producer without the services of an agent.

There are almost as many ways to break into the business as there are writers. Look for your opportunities and find a way. Just remember, before you parachute into Tom Cruise's backyard, be sure you are carrying a great script. Don't leave home without it.

ACT AS A PRODUCER

Why not take the initiative yourself to put together the players to make a movie? When you interest talent in your script, you are "packaging an element"—a function of a producer. When you secure the rights to a true story and take the story to a producer, you are, in effect, co-producing. (I'll provide more on true stories in the next chapter.)

About half the movies made are from material adapted from another medium. Books, plays, and even short stories are converted into movies, usually because an audience already exists for the story. You cannot compete with the majors for the rights to "event" books, but there is material out there you can acquire.

Suppose you want to secure the rights to a novel. You will contact the subsidiary-rights department of the book publisher, or hire an entertainment attorney to do this for you. You will want to buy an option to the rights of the book. You do that by making a "down payment" of a small amount of money for the exclusive rights to the book for a period of time. That way, you only tie up a little money, but you must write the script and sell it before the deadline of the option agreement. If you buy the rights outright, obviously you are under no deadline because there is no option period.

Keep in mind *Trottier Rule #9*: Don't adapt it until you own it. You will only get hurt and waste time if you write a script on something you don't own. Don't write the sequel to anything unless you control the rights. Don't use a song as the basis of your screenplay unless you own the rights to the music.

When you buy rights or buy an option to the rights of anything, be sure your attorney reviews the contract and verifies copyright. She should also make sure there are no liens or encumbrances attached to the work.

Don Moriarty and Greg Alt played it smart. They got their start by buying the rights to the book *The Mark of Zorro*. Then they, with the assistance of yours truly, wrote a screenplay entitled ZORRO, THE COMEDY ADVENTURE, which evolved into ZORRO, THE GAY BLADE. They were able to attract a producer because they owned the rights to the book.

What about writing about famous people? First, consult an entertainment attorney. Second, don't assume anything. Third, don't write anything until you control the rights. As a general rule, if the person has exploited his life by granting interviews or running for office, etc., then he is "fair game"—probably. You don't want to run the risk of lawsuits or a libel charge. Truth is a defense of libel so long as there is an absence of malice. (Sounds like a movie I saw.)

History, of course, is in the public domain, but history books are not. For example, although the life of Charles Lindbergh is in the public domain, Steven Spielberg still paid a large sum of money for the rights to A. Scott Berg's biography about Lindbergh's life.

If you *base* your story on real people or a real incident, just make sure that your script is totally fictitious. If your script is based on a real person, and if that person's peers can deduce from the movie who the movie is about, then that could be *invasion of privacy*.

My advice is to avoid anything that could possibly get you into a legal entanglement. You should think twice even about buying an option to the rights to a book or someone's story. Make sure you want to make the financial investment.

If you decide that you want to be the producer from start to finish, then you need to do your homework. This is an area where you can lose your shirt if you are not careful. Read books and talk to other producers. Consider the Hollywood Film Institute's two-day course.

Television and Hollywood's back door

There are many opportunities in television. And television is where the money and power is for writers, but network television is hard to break into. Television is concept-driven, and most of it is staff-written. That's because they want to use proven talent. In most cases, you will need an agent to break into the networks. You may ask, *Well then, how do I break into television?*

TV MOVIES AND TRUE STORIES

The Movie-of-the-Week (MOW) market is difficult to break into at the network level, and fewer are being made these days. Disease-of-the-Week and period dramas are also tough for the newcomer to sell. Generally, network producers only use writers who are on the network-approved list. Furthermore, the networks, as a general rule, only accept scripts from agents, entertainment attorneys, and producers (sometimes called "approved suppliers").

Your job is to approach those producers who have deals with the networks. Where do you find them? In the weekly list of "Television Productions" found in *Variety* and *Hollywood Reporter*. Look for production companies working on MOWs. You can also find information in the *Hollywood Creative Directory*. Approach these producers as you would WGA-signatory producers. Some of these producers may respond to the right query.

Are you a Canadian? Since most MOWs are shot in Canada, Canadian writers have a slight advantage over American writers. That's because the Canadian government gives companies financial incentives to hire Canadians for their productions.

Traditionally, your MOW audience was composed primarily of middle-aged women. There's still truth to that. The main demographic for MOWs is women ages 18-45. As of this writing, ABC is looking more for material that appeals to both men and women, and NBC is targeting younger viewers. While ABC is a bit more focused on high-concept, CBS is staying with social and family themes that appeal to older audiences. Keep in mind that specific needs change rapidly, often due to a change in personnel. So the above network information may already be obsolete. Budgets can vary but usually come in close to $2.5 to $3 million.

• • • • •

The back door into this area is through non-network producers. More than half of all TV movies produced each year are developed and produced for cable. And each of those markets is clearly defined: Lifetime (the women's channel), TNT (the men's channel, with some historical projects), USA (usually features strong female protagonists; likes high-concept and occasional thrillers), the Sci-Fi Channel (owned by USA, now produces sci-fi projects, including *Mystery Science Theater 3000*), the E! channel, and so on. These cable outlets are involved in productions every week.

There is much more programming in these areas than in the feature film area, and there are fewer people trying to supply them.

Don't overlook pay-TV networks that are not advertiser-supported, such as Showtime (usually issue-oriented and contemporary, and "event" pictures), the Disney Channel (family; likes films for kids), and HBO (who see themselves as any other theatrical production company).

The above cable markets are often forgotten in the rush to make it big with network television or features. Remember, programming needs change. When you investigate them, determine their *current specific needs* before contacting them and the producers who work with them. Some of the producers who have deals with these companies accept scripts without agents.

Perhaps the best way to break into Movies-of-the-Week and other markets is by finding a true story and acquiring the rights to that story. Do not look for front-page stories that are well-known—those rights are tied up before the ink dries on the newspaper article. And no one wants to know how your Uncle Bob went mad.

Look for personal stories of individuals battling against impossible odds and other marketable stories. If you find such a story, consider consulting an entertainment attorney. You will probably be advised to buy an option to the rights.

During the option period, you will write the script and then approach MOW producers. You can hook a producer more easily simply because you own the rights to a true story, but have a script ready first. If you already have a couple of excellent sample scripts, you may only need a treatment plus the rights in order to land a development deal to write the screenplay. When the producer buys your script, he will also pay for the rights to the story (exercise the option).

PILOTS

If you have never sold a script and want to develop a pilot or miniseries, you might as well try parting the Red Sea. Generally, you need a track record as a TV writer before you're granted entrance into this arena. Your best strategy is to write your TV pilot as a movie script. Then in the selling process, as people express interest, you can say, "You know, it'd make a great TV show."

EPISODIC TV AND REALITY TV

TV executives look for network-approved writers, although once their show is established, they'll try new writers for one or two scripts. You must have an agent to approach them. Cable shows are more open and pay less.

To break into episodic television, and situation comedy in particular, you write a feature-length script plus one or two TV scripts similar to the show you want to write for. These are submitted as work samples. The feature script proves that you can write a complete story. Generally, if you want to write for WILL AND GRACE, you don't submit a WILL AND GRACE script. The errors in your script will be very obvious to the story editor of that series. They tend to look at scripts for their own shows with a jaundiced eye. Besides, they rarely purchase spec scripts outright. Instead, submit a script for a similar sitcom show. Keep in mind that policies differ from show to show, so you will want to do some research if you wish to write for a particular show.

Before you write a TV episodic script, ask the producer for the show's bible. The bible is a printed guide that sets forth the rules of the show, including character sketches, and information on what's forbidden and what they're looking for. The STAR TREK bible even delineates what can and cannot be done on the ship, and includes detailed drawings. Some producers may not send you a bible except through an agent.

Now write a couple of scripts and submit one or more to the TV producer of your choice. The WGA journal *Written By* lists TV markets that are open. If the producer or executive likes your work sample, then a meeting will be arranged. This meeting is a forum set up for you specifically to pitch story ideas for episodes. Have a dozen ready to go. If you've reached this milestone, it means that you are being considered to write one or more episodes.

In pitching, use the same guidelines presented earlier. The opening headline for your EVERYBODY LOVES RAYMOND script could be, "Ray buys a snowmobile without his wife's permission." Keep in mind that producers often make up their minds in the first 30 seconds of the pitch.

If you have a series idea for a new sitcom, you face huge obstacles in marketing it. Generally, you need to be somewhat established in the television industry to have a chance. At the very least, you will need an agent or some creative inroad.

Reality TV is surprising similar to other TV shows in terms of how scripts are written and shows are produced. Business practices are quite similar. Many current writers for reality TV started as production assistants. That's an entry-level position. See "Alternative Tactics" at the end of this chapter.

Reality TV uses writers, but often gives them different titles, such as producer-type titles. They often perform functions in addition to their writing contributions. Reality TV shows generally follow the same basic rules of storytelling that we discussed in Book I. The difference is that they use "real people" rather than actors. Often, the ending is determined before the show is shot, although that is not true for elimination-type shows such as SURVIVOR.

THE BACK DOOR

Perhaps the best way to break into the writing business is through Hollywood's back door. It's not as closely guarded and fewer writers are trying this entrance. There is a huge market in public, independent, pay, and cable television, as mentioned above. Think of all the stations and networks that must provide programming 24 hours a day: HBO, Showtime, Turner Broadcasting, the super stations, and the dozens of other cable networks, stations, and channels.

The PBS network includes such stalwarts as KCET in Los Angeles, WNET in New York, WGBH in Boston, and ETV in South Carolina. Approach these stations individually or PBS directly. Don't overlook the American Playhouse and Wonderworks consortia.

One evening after presenting a seminar on the East Coast, I received a call from a very young 18-year-old who had never written so much as a page. He told me that he had called a PBS station and presented a series idea over the phone. The producer loved it, but since the kid did not have a sample script, the producer suggested that he connect with a professional writer. Imagine! If this kid had had a decent sample script (or had been willing to write one), he likely would have been hired.

The Direct-to-DVD market (formally referred to as the Direct-To-Video market) provides opportunities for many writers. These are low-budget ($1 to $1.5 million, but often in the $50,000 to $250,000 range) features made specifically for DVD sales. The most common genres are horror, action/adventure, and thrillers, and they are not released theatrically. Approach independent producers. To find the names of these producers, simply look for the credits on recent Direct-to-DVD releases.

Related to this area is the information/instructive video market. Videos such as BUNS OF STEEL and HOW TO REMODEL YOUR HOME are examples. Keep in mind that regardless of the market, the basic approach is similar in each.

Already mentioned are the non-network TV movie markets and the many low-budget producers looking for scripts that can be produced for less than a half-million, $1 to $2 million, and so on. Also note the regional markets. There may be production companies in your state or province. If you live south of the border or overseas, realize that the film business is increasingly global.

Don't ignore the many magazine shows, educational shows, soap operas, children's shows, game shows, infomercials (Direct Response Television), and reality programming. Because scripts for animated feature-length movies earn about half as much as regular features, this becomes an area of less competition and perhaps more opportunity for beginning writers (see below). And keep an eye on how the coming *electronic film distribution system* alters the marketplace.

ANIMATION

Thanks to the information age and the development of computer software, animated productions continue to increase, but historically animation has gone through many ups and downs. Feature animation projects (such as SHREK, THE INCREDIBLES, and FINDING NEMO) are developed much like feature films are, since they feature top-talent voicing the characters.

Animated TV shows don't have 22-episode seasons or 13-episode seasons like television shows do. Although most shows do not have staff writers, they use a pool of writers to write scripts. There are two kinds of animated series: weekly and daily. Because of the greater number of episodes produced by daily shows, they might be better targets for new writers.

For your information, animated scripts *include* camera directions and angles. (That's because they're being written for a storyboard artist rather than a director.)

You will probably need only one imaginative and fanciful sample script to break in, and animated shows generally are open to queries from writers without agents. If your sample script gets you noticed, you can pitch with treatments, synopses, and premises.

The pay for animated TV scripts and feature Direct-to-DVD and direct-to-video projects is about half of the basic rate for projects featuring human characters (rather than toons). Generally, you earn no residuals, no ancillary rights, and no royalties on toys based on your characters.

NEW TECHNOLOGY AND THE INTERNET

Videogames, videos based on videogames, virtual reality, 3DO, interactive programming, multimedia, Internet movies, and CD-ROM represent markets on the rise. I believe this broad area will become a huge growth industry with increasing opportunities for writers. In fact, production has increased markedly in recent years, and agents have materialized to handle multimedia material.

At the moment, producers in this area are open to ideas. Surprisingly, it is better to approach these people with a treatment than with a completed script—at least for now. Also include game concepts and flow charts if applicable. Your final script may earn you $25,000 to $50,000. For information on writing or designing videogames, I recommend *Creating Emotion in Games* by David Freeman (www.freemangames.com).

You can learn a great deal about writing for, or producing for, Internet movie companies by searching the web. Be sure to visit the site of Atom Films. Internet movie companies are monitored by feature producers. You may get noticed with an Internet production. Many companies have Internet connections or are web-driven. One example is the Oxygen channel.

Keep in mind that this market is growing rapidly, and the parameters may change rapidly as well. There are many interactive companies now. Most studios and many special-effects companies have formed interactive divisions. Contact them directly or have your agent call.

DVDS AND VIDEOS FOR BUSINESS AND EDUCATION

More money is spent in non-broadcast audio-visual than in the U.S. motion-picture and television industry. Kodak sells more raw stock to Detroit than to Hollywood. Writing video and DVD scripts for business and education can be both profitable and fun.

You will contact video producers (see the yellow pages) for possible assignments, or call video production managers at corporations. Present yourself as a freelance writer and have a sample 12-page script handy. In some instances, your other writing experience may be sufficient.

Pay is about $150 per finished minute of the eventual video, or 10% of the budget. That comes to about $1,500 a week for your time.

You can earn up to $10,000 writing an infomercial show. Infomercials are written by writers, so why not you? Find producers by searching the Internet or reading direct-response magazines such as *Response Magazine*. Visit www.retailing.org.

KNOCK AND THE DOOR SHALL OPEN

The truth is, writing opportunities are springing up everywhere. Overall, the pay is generally lower at the back door, but the experience is good, and entrance is easier. Use these markets as a platform to greater success.

ALTERNATIVE TACTICS

Many writers break in to the business by becoming readers. Why not become one yourself? You will meet people and will learn quickly what makes a salable script. The pay is low, from zero to $80 a script, and you'll need to live near your employer's office—they often want scripts read overnight. You get hired by presenting a sample coverage and any credentials to agencies and production companies in your area. Offer to write a free coverage for one of their scripts.

Likewise, some writers take advantage of internships offered by some production companies and studios. Others get hired as production assistants (gophers for the production crew), producer's assistants, agent assistants, manager assistants, script coordinators, transcribers, mail-room clerks, etc., to get their start. The central idea here is to get involved in the film business. These inroads are worth considering, especially if you are young and without children. You'll quickly learn the business.

Some screenwriters keep body and soul together writing for other markets—business writing, magazine writing, copywriting, column writing, and so on. In my book *The Freelance Writer's Bible*, I explain 17 different ways to make a living as a writer and show you how to succeed as a writer. For information, visit www.keepwriting.com.

How to break into Hollywood when you live in Peoria

Living outside of the Los Angeles area is not a problem when you are selling your first script. You can sell it from anywhere. It is seldom a problem even after you've sold your first script. In fact, one's domicile is becoming less and less of an issue in our technology-laden society.

Most Hollywood producers are more concerned about your writing ability than your current address. If you write well and know what you're talking about, their fears will be allayed. However, an L.A.-based agent will want to know if you are willing to visit Los Angeles on occasion to attend meetings with producers and executives.

The idea of relocating after your first big sale may be raised. Obviously, if the deal is sweet enough and the situation warrants it, you will relocate. But you likely will not have to. And even if you do, it won't be forever. Once you have established your name, you can buy a farm in Vermont and write there.

On the other hand, you may want to move to the Los Angeles area, just to have more opportunities to meet people. Living in L.A. does have its advantages.

If you want to write for episodic television, you must live near production headquarters, but don't move until you get the assignment.

You'll be pleased to know that more regional opportunities are opening up all the time. There are three reasons for this. Union shoots in Southern California have become very expensive. California is generally unfriendly to business. And the Information Age has created a huge demand for programming.

Many new opportunities exist in areas outside of Hollywood. Production companies are sprouting up all over the map. Some of these can be found in industry periodicals, directories, or literary references guides. Call around. Your state film commissioner should have up-to-date information concerning the film industry in your state.

Although there are agencies in every part of this country, you may not need an agent to sell to the many independent, regional markets. Look for opportunities in your own backyard; you may be surprised at the acres of diamonds you find there.

In summary, don't let your current residence deter you from pursuing a screenwriting career. Concentrate on your writing first and your geographical problems second.

A personal challenge

Now just a few words concerning your writing career. Take it seriously. You are a screenwriter.

Create a vision for your career. Pretend that 20 years have passed and that the PBS program AMERICAN MASTERS is going to present a tribute to you and your career. Or, if you prefer, ENTERTAINMENT TONIGHT is spotlighting your work. How do you want to be remembered? What kind of work will you do during the next 20 years? Where is your career going to be in 20 years? (Or 10 years, if you prefer.) Write this down.

What would you like to accomplish this year (or within the next 18 months)? What excites you the most? Is it to sell your spec script to a company like Imagine? Is it to be a story editor for a reality TV show like EXTREME MAKEOVER: HOME EDITION? Set this milestone goal. Spend some time with this; you need this motivating energy.

Think of the script you're working on now. When do you plan on finishing the first draft? How about the final draft? Or, if you're beginning the selling process, by what date do you want to sell your script?

Remember, goals are specific and measurable. They help you work faster and with more focus. Use them as motivators, not guilt-inducers. If you fail to achieve a goal, learn from the experience and set new goals.

Have a writing schedule. Four hours a day is ideal, but if that is unfeasible, try to set aside whatever time you can. That's your time to write. Your loved ones need to understand that.

Keep logs of contacts, power lunches, phone calls, script submissions, queries, and anything that would affect the "business" of your career. You need this information for follow-ups. This business is built on contacts and relationships. Even when your script is rejected, if anything positive takes place between you and the contact, nurture that contact with occasional notes (once or twice a year), e-mails, or calls. In doing this, do not impose on their time. And hold on to your screenplay—it may be the perfect vehicle 10 years hence.

Keep track of your expenses. I'm afraid the IRS will insist on it. You will use the Schedule C to report income and business expenses. You must make a profit in three of the first five years that you declare yourself to be a writer. IRS Booklet 334 would be helpful if it were easier to understand.

If you have a writing partner, make a written agreement before you write.

Keep a writer's notebook of thoughts, ideas, clippings, bits of dialogue, etc. Some writers carry small microcassette recorders. Treat your writing career with respect.

Continue your education, but don't stop writing while you learn.

Learn how to take criticism. Be able to stand apart from your work and look at it objectively. Don't rush into rewrites; let advice sink in. Consider what others suggest, but remember that you are the screenwriter and the script is yours until it is sold.

Most of all, enjoy writing for the sake of writing, whether you sell anything or not. Creating something new and original is its own reward. Writing is a fundamentally worthwhile way to spend your time. It's good therapy, too. If you write because you want to, then the financial rewards are more likely to follow.

Writers write.

Now, finally, I'd like to take a moment to salute you. You have not chosen an easy road. You will need to draw upon your inner resources and believe in yourself. When you get up in the morning, face the person in the mirror and say, "I am the next great screenwriter." Then perhaps one morning, you may awaken to find that you are the next great screenwriter. Don't be surprised. Just keep writing.

RESOURCES

AND

INDEX

BOOK VI

Resources

What follows are several lists that I believe will be helpful to you, the next great screenwriter. Each list contains carefully selected entries. Of course, none of the lists is complete. I have purposely chosen resources I am familiar with that I think you will find most useful, including some respected competitors that I believe provide worthwhile services and products. Naturally, I cannot guarantee any entity or person's services or products.

UPDATES TO *THE SCREENWRITER'S BIBLE*

To be totally up-to-date, visit www.keepwriting.com and click on "Bible Updates" for all updates and changes to this work.

INTERNET SITES

For a list of helpful screenwriting and film sites, visit www.keepwriting.com and click on "Hot Links." These links include Internet script brokers, writing resources, marketing aids, and script sources. For more information on Internet script brokers, see page 345 in Book V.

INDUSTRY ORGANIZATIONS AND GUILDS

Academy of Motion Picture Arts and Sciences (www.oscars.org), 8949 Wilshire Blvd., Beverly Hills, CA 90211, (310) 247-3000. Script library and *Academy Players Directory*. Sponsors the Nicholl Fellowship (listed under "Contests").

Academy of Television Arts and Sciences (www.emmys.org), 5220 Lankershim Blvd., North Hollywood, CA 91601, (818) 754-2800. Script library.

American Screenwriters Association (www.asascreenwriters.com), 269 S. Beverly Dr., Suite 2600, Beverly Hills, CA 90212-3807, (866) 265-9091. Non-profit organization that sponsors the annual Selling to Hollywood Conference.

Copyright Office (www.copyright.gov), 101 Independence Ave. S.E., Washington, DC 20559-6000, (202) 707-3000.

Dircctors Guild of America (www.dga.org), 7920 Sunset Blvd., Los Angeles, CA 90046. (310) 289-2000, (800) 421-4173. In New York: 110 W. 57th St., New York, NY 10019, (212) 581-0370. In Chicago: 400 N. Michigan Ave., Suite 307, Chicago, IL 60611, (312) 644-5050. Sells a directory of members.

Producers Guild of America (www.producersguild.com), 8530 Wilshire Blvd., Suite 450, Beverly Hills, CA 90211, (310) 358-9020. In New York: 100 Avenue of the Americas, 11th Floor, New York, NY 11013, (212) 894-4016.

Screen Actors Guild (www.sag.org), 5757 Wilshire Blvd., Los Angeles, CA 90036, (323) 954-1600. In New York: 360 Madison Ave., 12th Floor, New York, NY 10017, (212) 944-1030. Contact for the phone number of a specific actor's agency or point-of-contact.

Writers Guild of America, east, Inc. (www.wgaeast.org), 555 W. 57th St., New York, NY 10019, (212) 767-7800. Registration number: (212) 757-4360. Registration Service is $22; Agency List is available. Sells a directory of agents and members. Services available to non-members.

Writers Guild of America, west, Inc. (www.wga.org), 7000 W. 3rd St., Los Angeles, CA 90048-4329, (323) 951-4000; registration office (323) 782-4500. Agency list is available. Script library. Registration Service: $20.00. Services available to non-members.

Writers Guild of Canada (www.writersguildofcanada.com), 366 Adelaide St. W., Suite 401, Toronto, Ontario M5V 1R9, (800) 567-7907, (416) 979-7907.

WRITER'S ORGANIZATIONS

American Screenwriters Association (www.asascreenwriters.com), 269 S. Beverly Dr., Suite 2600, Beverly Hills, CA 90212-3807, (866) 265-9091. Non-profit organization that sponsors the annual Selling to Hollywood Conference.

Black Filmmaker Foundation (www.dvRepublic.org), 11 W. 42nd St., 9th Floor, New York, NY 10036, (212) 253-1690.

Chicago Screenwriters Network (www.chicagoscreenwriters.org).

CineStory (www.cinestory.com), P.O. Box 3736, Idyllwild, CA 92549, (909) 659-1180. National screenwriting organization.

Independent Feature Project (www.ifp.org). Centers in Los Angeles, New York, Chicago, Miami, Minneapolis-St. Paul, and Seattle. For independent filmmakers. Writers are welcome.

Minnesota Screenwriters' Workshop (www.mm.com/user/mnsww), 528 Hennepin Ave., Suite 507, Minneapolis, MN 55403, (612) 659-8292, mnsww@mac.com.

National Writers Association (www.nationalwriters.com), 10940 S. Parker Bd. #508, Parker, CO 80134, (303) 841-0246. Provides reports, editing help, local chapters, and other services.

Northwest Screenwriters Guild (www.nwsg.org), (206) 264-5454.

Organization of Black Screenwriters, Inc., P.O. Box 70160, Los Angeles, CA 90070-0160, (323) 882-4166. For African-American writers.

Scriptwriters Network (www.scriptwritersnetwork.com), 11684 Ventura Blvd. #508, Studio City, CA 91604, (323) 848-9477. Professional organization. Must submit a completed script to gain full membership.

Wisconsin Screenwriter's Forum (www.wiscreenwritersforum.org). Writers organization, newsletter, and contest.

Women in Film (www.wif.org), 8857 W. Olympic Blvd., Suite 201, Beverly Hills, CA 90211, (310) 657-5144. Provides a variety of services and programs to foster professional growth. To join, you must have at least one year of professional or academic experience.

SCRIPT CONSULTANTS AND TEACHERS

Flaxman, Robert (www.deepfeedback.com), P.O. Box 15528, Beverly Hills, CA 90209, (310) 278-9578, (213) 896-1692. Line-by-line, page-by-page analysis.

Freeman, David (www2.beyondstructure.com), (310) 394-6556, (866) 239-2600. Conducts popular, technique-based workshops and script consults.

Hauge, Michael (www.screenplaymastery.com), Screenplay Mastery, P.O. Box 55728, Sherman Oaks, CA 91413, (818) 995-8118, (800) 477-1947. Script analysis and seminars.

Marks, Dara (www.daramarks.com), P.O. Box 103, 323 E. Matilija St. #110, Ojai, CA 93023, (805) 640-1307.

McKee, Robert (www.mckeestory.com), P.O. Box 452930, Los Angeles, CA 90045, (888) 676-2533. Seminars, script analysis.

Nelson, Donie A., (310) 204-6808. Career strategies for writers.

Pace, William R. (www.scripteach.com), (212) 749-8628. Script consultant.

Paonessa, Leslie (www.lpscripts.net), 2231 Montana Ave. #3, Santa Monica, CA 90403, (310) 395-3648. Coverage and script analysis.

Rainey, John (www.mythmakerjohn.com), (800) 304-6557.

Seger, Dr. Linda (www.lindaseger.com), 4705 Hagerman Ave., Cascade, CO 80809, (719) 684-0405, lsseger@aol.com. Script doctor and script consultant.

Smart Girls Productions (www.smartgirlsprod.com), P.O. Box 1896, Hollywood, CA 90078, (323) 850-5778. Query-letter mailings, script consulting.

Suppa, Ron, (818) 879-1383. Career coaching and screenplay consultation.

Trottier, Dave (www.keepwriting.com), (800) 264-4900. Script consulting, query-letter analysis, and synopsis analysis.

Truby, John (www.truby.com), Truby's Writers Studio, 664 Brooktree Rd., Santa Monica, CA 90402, (310) 575-9630, (800) 338-7829. Seminars, script consulting, audio tapes.

Walter, Richard, Leslie Kallen Seminars, 15760 Ventura Blvd. #700, Encino, CA 91436, (800) 755-2785. Seminars.

Yoneda, Kathie Fong (www.kathiefongyoneda.com), (626) 440-9023. Script consultant.

Young, Paul (www.scriptzone.com), Literary & Screenplay Consultants, 22647 Ventura Blvd., Suite 524, Woodland Hills, CA 91364, (818) 887-6554.

SCHOOLS

American Film Institute (www.afi.com), 2021 N. Western Ave., Los Angeles, CA 90027, (323) 856-7600, (800) 999-4AFI. Seminars and courses.

Columbia University, School of the Arts, Film Division, 513 Dodge Hall, 2960 Broadway, New York, NY 10027, (212) 854-2875.

Flash Forward Institute (www.flashforwardinstitute.com), (323) 850-7392. Classes for career advancement.

Hollywood Film Institute (Dov S-S Simens) (www.hollywoodu.com), 1223 Olympic Blvd., P.O. Box 481252, Santa Monica, CA 90048, (800) 366-3456, (323) 933-FILM. Two-day film-school crash course. Producing, writing, directing, and financing classes.

Hollywood Scriptwriting Institute (www.moviewriting.com), 1605 N. Cahuenga Blvd., Suite 216, Hollywood, CA 90028, (323) 461-8333, (800) 727-4787. Home study and on-site.

New York Film Academy (www.nyfa.com), 100 E. 17th St., New York, NY 10003, (212) 674-4300. In Los Angeles: (818) 733-2600. In London: 020-7848-1523. Total-immersion, eight-week workshops where each individual writes, directs, shoots, and edits his of her own film.

New York University, Tisch School of the Arts, 721 Broadway, New York, NY 10003, (212) 998-1820.

Screenwriting Center (www.keepwiting.com), (800) 264-4900, (801) 492-7898. Dave Trottier conducts online courses, workshops, and correspondence courses. Script evaluation, query evaluation, books, software, information.

Sherwood Oaks Experimental College (www.sherwoodoakscollege.com), 7095 Hollywood Blvd. #876, Los Angeles, CA 90028, (323) 851-1769.

UCLA, Dept. of Film and Television, 405 Hilgard Ave., Los Angeles, CA 90024.

USC, School of Cinema-Television, University Park, Los Angeles, CA 90089.

Writers University (www.writersuniversity.com), (866) 229-7483.

Note: Most universities and colleges have continuing-education departments that sponsor writing seminars, workshops, and non-credit courses.

SOFTWARE

Collaborator (www.collaborator.com) — Story and character development.

Dr. Format Screenwriting Software (www.keepwriting.com) — Formatting. (800) 264-4900.

Dramatica Pro — Story development. (800) 84-STORY, (818) 843-6557.

Final Draft (www.finaldraft.com) — Formatting. (800) 231-4055, (818) 995-8995.

How to Make Your Movie: An Interactive Film School (www.interactivefilmschool.com).

IdeaFisher (www.ideafisher.com, www.ideacenter.com) — Idea creation and development.

Movie Magic Screenwriter (www.screenplay.com) — Formatting. (800) 84-STORY.

My Screenwriting Project™ (www.myscreenwriting.com) — Story development software based on the principles and techniques of *The Screenwriter's Bible*. Nominal fee.

Power Structure (www.write-brain.com/power_structure_main.htm) — Story development. (800) 450-9450.

Script Assist (www.scriptassist.com) — Formatting and story/character development.

Script Wizard (www.warrenassoc.com) — Formatting "add-on" for Microsoft Word. Also produces *ProsePro* for novelists.

ScriptWright (www.indelibleink.com/swright.html) — Formatting "add-on" for Micosoft Word. (212) 255-1956.

Scriptware (www.scriptware.com) — Formatting. (303) 786-7899.

Sophocles (www.sophocles.net) — Formatting and more.

Storybase (www.ashleywilde.com) — Story-creation software. (310) 456-1277.

Storycraft (www.writerspage.com) — Fiction writing software. (800) 97-STORY.

StoryView (www.screenplay.com) — Brainstorming/story development. (800) 84-STORY.

Truby's Blockbuster (www.truby.com/software.html) — Story planner. (800) 338-7829, (310) 573-9630.

WritePro (www.writepro.com) — Sol Stein's fiction-writing program. (800) 755-1124.

Writer's Blocks (www.writersblocks.com) — Organizes story ideas. (800) 229-6737.

DIRECTORIES

Academy Players Directory, Academy of Motion Picture Arts and Sciences, 8949 Wilshire Blvd., Beverly Hills, CA 90211, (310) 247-3000.

Annual Agency Guide (www.fadeinonline.com), TWN, Inc., 287 S. Robertson Blvd. #407, Beverly Hills, CA 90211, (310) 275-0287, (800) 646-3896.

Complete Directory to Primetime Network TV Shows by Brooks and Marsh. Published by Ballantine Books.

Creative Directory—See *Hollywood Creative Directory*.

Hollywood Creative Directory (www.hcdonline.com), 5055 Wilshire Blvd., Los Angeles, CA 90036, (323) 525-2369, (800) 815-0503. Publishes excellent directories of agents, producers, etc. These directories can also be purchased at Samuel French Bookshops (see "Bookstores"). HCD is now owned by *The Hollywood Reporter*.

Spec Screenplay Sales Directory by Howard Meibach (www.hollywoodlitsales.com). This directory lists the sales of spec scripts.

Writer Guide to Hollywood Producers (www.fadeinonline.com), TWN, Inc., 287 S. Robertson Blvd. #407, Beverly Hills, CA 90211, (310) 275-0287, (800) 646-3896.

PERIODICALS

Canadian Screenwriter, quarterly magazine available from Writers Guild of Canada (www.writersguildofcanada.com), 366 Adelaide St. W., Suite 401, Toronto, Ontario M5V 1R9, (800) 567-7907, (416) 979-7907.

Creative Screenwriting (www.creativescreenwriting.com), 6404 Hollywood Blvd., Suite 415, Los Angeles, CA 90028, (323) 957-1405, (800) 727-6978. Screenwriting magazine.

Daily Variety (www.variety.com), 5700 Wilshire Blvd., Suite 120, Los Angeles, CA 90036, (323) 857-6600. The most-read trade publication. There is also a weekly version, *Weekly Variety*, at the same address. In New York: 360 Park Ave. South, New York, NY 10010.

Fade In: (www.fadeinmag.com), 287 S. Robertson Blvd. #467, Beverly Hills, CA 90211, (800) 646-3896.

Hollywood Reporter (www.hollywoodreporter.com), 5055 Wilshire Blvd., Los Angeles, CA 90036, (323) 525-2000. Daily trade publication. They also publish a directory of participants of the American Film Market in February.

Hollywood Scriptwriter (www.hollywoodscriptwriter.com), P.O. Box 11163, Carson, CA 90746, (310) 530-0000. Established trade publication.

Screenwriter Magazine (www.nyscrccnwritcr.com), P.O. Box 170086, Brooklyn, NY 11217-0086, (800) 418-5637, (718) 398-7197.

Premiere, (800) 289-2489. Film magazine available at any newsstand.

Scr(i)pt, 5638 Sweet Air Rd., Baldwin, MD 21013, (410) 592-3466. Timely and useful information on writing and selling scripts of every kind: features, TV, cable, MOW, interactive, documentary, and DTV. Highly recommended.

Variety—See *Daily Variety*.

Writer's Digest (www.writersdigest.com), published by F&W Publications Inc., 1507 Dana Ave., Cincinnati, OH 45207. Monthly for writers in every medium. Available on any newsstand.

Written By, Writer's Guild of America, west, Inc. (www.wga.org), 7000 W. 3rd St., Los Angeles, CA 90048-4329, (323) 782-4522.

BOOKSTORES

Biz Books, 302 W. Cordova St., Vancouver, BC, Canada V6B 1E8, (604) 669-6431.

Drama Book Shop, 723 7th Ave., 2nd Floor, New York, NY 10019, (212) 944-0595. New York's top film and drama bookstore.

Larry Edmunds Bookshop, 6644 Hollywood Blvd., Hollywood, CA 90028, (323) 463-3273. Industry books of every kind.

Limelight Bookstore, 1803 Market St., San Francisco, CA 94103, (415) 864-2265.

Samuel French Bookshop, 7623 Sunset Blvd., Hollywood, CA 90046, (323) 876-0570. Books and directories. They also have a location in the Valley: 11963 Ventura Blvd., Studio City, CA 91604, (818) 762-0535, (800) 8-ACT NOW, FAX (323) 876-6822, samuelfrench@earthlink.net. They carry everything for screenwriters, playwrights, and filmmakers.

Screenwriter's Store (www.thescreenwritersstore.com), Suite 2, 8th Floor (East Wing), Friars House, 157 Blackfriars Road, London, England SE1 8EZ, 44 207 261 1908.

Theatrebooks (www.theatrebooks.com), 11 St. Thomas St., Toronto, Ontario, Canada M5S 2B7, (416) 922-7175.

Writers Store™ (www.writersstore.com), 2040 Westwood Blvd., Los Angeles, CA 90025, (310) 441-5151, (800) 272-8927. Your complete source for software, books, and tapes. Writers University online courses (www.writersuniversity.com).

Note: Scripts may also be found in college libraries, the WGA offices, the Academy of Motion Picture Arts & Sciences, the American Film Institute, and the New York Public Library for the Performing Arts (40 Lincoln Center Plaza, New York, NY 10023).

BOOKS FOR SREENWRITERS AND TV WRITERS

See my suggestions for ten books to read now. Visit www.keepwriting.com/store.htm.

CONTESTS

Note: What follows is a "short list" of contests that are worth considering, but there are many other major and minor contests. Contests are listed in most screenwriting publications and on the Internet. Here are three sources of contest information:

> *www.moviebytes.com/directory.cfm*
> *www.filmmakers.com/contests/directory.htm*
> *www.screenwritersutopia.com (Click on "Screenwriting Contests.")*

There are also many small contests sponsored by colleges, universities, film schools, and writing groups. These may be advertised in the trades and other film and writing publications. Contact your state film commission for information on local contests.

When reviewing, contest information, keep in mind that contest sponsors may change deadline dates, procedures, and other parameters. *Contact each for up-to-date information. Parameters change often.*

20/20 Screenwriting Contest (www.lets-do-lunch.com), 3639 Malibu Vista Dr., Malibu, CA 90265.

AFI/Maui Writers Conference International Screenwriting Competition (www.mauiwriters.com), (808) 879-0061. Award: $2500. Entry Fee: $50.

American Accolades Screenwriting Competition (www.AmericanAccolades.com), 2118 Wilshire Blvd., Suite 160, Santa Monica, CA 90403.

American Screenwriters Association/Gotham Writer's Workshop (www.goasa.com), 1841 Broadway, Suite 809, New York, NY 10023, (877) 974-8377.

Austin Film Festival Screenplay Competition (www.austinfilmfestival.com), 1604 Nueces, Austin, TX 78701, (512) 478-4795.

Chesterfield Writer's Film Project (www.chesterfield-co.com), 1158 26th St., P.O. Box 544, Santa Monica, CA 90403, (213) 683-3977.

CineStory Screenplay Competition (www.cinestory.com). Award: $2,000 plus expenses to CineStory Writers' Retreat. Entry fee: $50.

Great American Pitchfest (www.pitchfest.com).

Hollywood Scriptwriting Contest (www.moviewriting.com), 1605 Cahuenga Blvd., Suite 213, Hollywood, CA 90028, (800)-SCRIPT.

Nicholl Fellowships in Screenwriting (www.oscars.org), Academy of Motion Picture Arts and Sciences, 8949 Wilshire Blvd., Beverly Hills, CA 90211-1972, (310) 247-3059. This is probably the most prestigious screenwriting competition. Entrant cannot have earned more than $5,000 as a screenwriter. Award: $25,000. Fee: $30. Deadline: May 1. Winning scripts can be read at the Academy's Margaret Herrick Library on 333 S. LaCienega, Beverly Hills, CA 90210.

PAGE International Screenwriting Awards, 7510 Sunset Blvd., Suite 610, Hollywood, CA 90046, (323) 969-0993. Awards given in nine different genres, including TV. Award: $25,000 in cash and prizes. Places material in the hands of Hollywood professionals.

Project Greenlight (www.projectgreenlight.com).

Red Inkworks Screenwriter's Competition (www.redinkworks.com), 312-125 W. 18th St., N. Vancouver, BC, Canada V7M 1W5, (604) 562-5678.

Scr(i)pt Magazine Open Door Contest (www.scriptmag.com), sponsored by Kaplan/Perrone Entertainment.

Scriptapalooza Screenwriting Competition (www.scriptapalooza.com), 7775 Sunset Blvd., #200, Hollywood, CA 90046, (323) 654-5809. Also sponsors a TV writing competition.

Slamdance Screenplay Competition (www.slamdance.com), 5634 Melrose Ave., Los Angeles, CA 90038, (323) 466-1786. Entry fee: $75 (for coverage); $40 (no coverage).

Sundance Institute (www.sundance.org), 8857 W. Olympic Blvd., Beverly Hills, CA 90211, (310) 360-1981. Conducts script development workshops in Utah each summer and winter. Possibility of production. Run by Robert Redford. Fee: $30.

Telluride IndieFest (www.tellurideindiefest.com), Box 860, Telluride, CO 81435, (970) 728-2629.

Texas Film Institute Screenplay Competition (www.texasfilminstitute.com), P.O. Box 260, Boerne, TX 78006, (830) 249-6870. Free analysis to semifinalists. Cash prizes.

Walt Disney Studios/ABC Writers Fellowship, 500 S. Buena Vista St., Burbank, CA 91521, (818) 560-6894. Award: $50,000 plus year-long internship at Disney. Program is open to all writers in motion picture and television (except WGA members), but gives preference to women and minorities. No entry fee.

Warner Brothers Writers Workshop (www.warnerbros.com/writers workshop), 300 Television Plaza, Burbank, CA 91505, (818) 954-7906.

WriteMovies (www.writemovies.com), 1384½ S. Robertson Blvd., Los Angeles, CA 90035, (310) 276-5160.

The Writers Place (the writersplace.org), P.O. Box 11426, Pensacola, FL 32524-1426. Provides feedback. Winning and placing scripts are submitted to managers, agents, or producers. Fee: $55 Features; $35 Shorts.

SCRIPT CONSULTING

Dave Trottier combines the best of three disciplines to evaluate your script. He is a successful screenwriter, writing coach, and script consultant. With more than a decade of experience in all three areas, he is uniquely qualified to render a thorough and useful evaluation of your script.

Your script's commercial potential
Dave does not provide a quick "form letter" analysis, but tailors his comments to your individual script. His evaluation will help you strengthen the structure, bring your characters to life, improve your dialogue, correct your formatting, and enhance your commercial prospects.

A free story conference with Dave
Most writers love the two-for-one aspect of Dave's evaluation. Once you digest his thoughtful and incisive analysis (usually 8-14 typed pages), then you may call him for a story conference to discuss the evaluation, the script, or just brainstorm new ideas—whatever you need.

Screenwriter's agree
Dave's clients and students include two Nicholl winners, a National Play Award winner, and dozens of working writers. Write for a brochure, or visit www.keepwriting.com.

QUERY LETTER EVALUATION

You should spend as much time on your query letter as you do on a key scene. Your query letter is one of your prime break-in tools. Now you can get Dave's evaluation of your query, his assessment of its marketing potential, and recommendations for its revision. Send for info.

General Index